HANDBOOK
OF GREEK PHILOSOPHY

FROM THALES TO THE STOICS

ANALYSIS AND FRAGMENTS

Substantial and Complete Essay
on Ancient Greek Philosophy
with Fragments Included

Nikolaos Bakalis

The true is found and known for ever
And joins all noble minds together
The Ancient truth perceive and hold!

- Goethe (Testament 7-9)

To Doris and my sons Ioannis and Stamatis

ACKNOWLEDGEMENTS

I would like to express my gratitude to the persons who have provided inspiration, patience, ideas and technical assistance for this work. In particular I would like to thank:

My partner in life Doris Schaefer for her inspiration, her loving patience with the editing work, and her extraordinary painting offered for the cover of this book.

Thomas Schaefer for his ideas and technical assistance concerning the cover and the lay-out of this book.

David Schaefer for his technical assistance with regard to the computing work of this essay.

Nikolaos Bakalis

CONTENTS

I.   INTRODUCTION

Why even today Ancient Greek philosophy? Justifiable query in the era of globalisation, of the computer, of the concourse of views and opinions, of the absolutely specialized knowledge. Why philosophy and why especially Ancient Greek? How useful could be such a knowledge, when there is a specialized scientific knowledge with regard to each sector of human activity?

These questions we will try to answer in the present essay, as we are going to investigate the development of a man's thought and reasoning, which started in Ancient Greece and signified the beginning of a new era for the mankind. We refer to the era of the philosophical and scientific thought.

Our modern life runs away with us since we run from one activity to the other in order to satisfy our "needs", while searching for joy and in the hope of achieving our happiness. Therefore, we run after our supposed "needs" somehow instinctively, and without having reflected on their significance. However, we soon realize that our happiness is not an easy object. Then we leave behind the supposed means that could make for happiness and search for new ones. During this searching we confront with a crisis of moral values, which leads us to revaluate them and find out new and modern ones. Throughout this inquiry we realize that we must search for real and true moral values, which could help us to break our deadlock, and guide us to the achievement of happiness. When we proceed further to this inquiry, we meet with the matter of human nature itself and questions just like: "what really fits to this nature and what is incompatible with it?". "Which values could really help our nature and raise it to the real human level?".

In order to give an answer to these questions, - to what human nature is and what is in accordance with it - we meet with philosophy, the principles and ethics of different philosophical schools. As we go on, we soon realize that the

4

main philosophical systems are based upon the main principles of Ancient Greek philosophy.

Therefore in our opinion, it would be helpful to each one, who is searching for real moral values and for deeper meaning in his life, to know the main principles of Ancient Greek philosophy. As one goes through with this chronological review of the main principles, he realizes that all these questions have been examined closely by the Ancient Greek philosophers, who tried to give an answer.

However, anyone who wants to know about Ancient Greek philosophy is all at sea in thousands of writings. Considering this difficulty, we tried to present its main concepts gradually, so as to enable the reader to be initiated little by little into the main principles. Due to chronological presentation, one begins to know first the simple philosophical terms and concepts, and then proceeds to the more complex ones. In this way, we believe that one can go deeper into the reasoning of the great Greek thinkers.

The original fragments of the Ancient Greek philosophers have been carefully selected and thoroughly analyzed, so as to enable the reader to understand their principles with regard to their Gnoseology (epistemology), Ontology and Ethics. Due to the included original fragments, we aspire to help the reader to comprehend the way of thinking and reasoning of the great philosophers.

With this essay we hope that we may shed light on the question of human nature with regard to happiness, a matter which all the thinkers of today deal with. Or at least, that this inquiry may spark off further reflection on these matters.

4

II. ANCIENT GREEK PHILOSOPHERS

We begin our presentation and investigation of the Ancient Greek philosophy in chronological order, starting with the first philosophers, namely the Presocratics. Then we will proceed to Socrates and Plato, afterwards to Aristotle, Epicurus and in the end to the Stoics. In this way, in our opinion, one can understand better the development of the philosophical thought and be initiated progressively into the philosophical terms and doctrines, proceeding from the simple to the most complex ones. Throughout this presentation, we hold that the reader will be able to know the main principles of the great Greek philosophers, their Gnoseology and Ontology, as well as their Ethics, which is based upon them. We believe that this knowledge can help all of us to go deep into the problems of human nature, and with this motto to discover real values, which might help each one of us personally or even the mankind as a whole, to break its deadlock and lead a dignified and happy life.

A. Presocratic philosophers

With this term are defined the philosophers who lived and taught before Socrates' death. However some of them were contemporary with Socrates or even Plato. Therefore, strictly speaking, the term "**Presocratics**" refers to the philosophers, whose teaching was not connected to the philosophy of Socrates. Since their philosophy was connected to the study of nature, they were also called **natural philosophers** (*φυσικοί φιλόσοφοι*: physikoi philosophoi).

1. Thales (635 – 545 BC)

Thales of Miletus (Asia Minor) was one of the seven wise men of the Greek Antiquity and founder of the **Ionian** school of philosophy.

Thales was the first one who tried to explain rationally the natural phenomena, as he went beyond the religious beliefs with regard to cosmology. With Thales begins to make an appearance the first scientific philosophical thought, when a man is not content with mythology, and tries to discover the laws and the principles, which govern the universe.

" Thales is traditionally the first to have revealed the investigation of nature to the Greeks." (Fr.1 Simplicius n Phys. p. 23, 29 Diels).

He was the first one who searched for the **principle** (αρχή: arche) in the form of matter of all things, and which is beyond all the material forms. He concluded that this "principle" is the **water** (ύδωρ: hydor) and that the rest of the elements arise from that.

" Most of the first philosophers thought that principles in the form of matter were the only principles of all things; for the original source of all existing things, that from which a thing first comes into being and into which it is finally destroyed, the substance persisting but changing its qualities, this they declare is the element and first principle of existing things... Thales the founder of this type of philosophy, says that it is water (and therefore declared that the earth is on water), perhaps taking this supposition from seeing the nurture of all things to be moist, and the warm itself coming-to-be from this and living by this (that from which they come-to-be being the principle of all things) – taking the supposition both from this and from the seeds of all things having a moist nature, water being the natural principle of moist things." (Aristotle, Metaphysics A 3, 983 b 6).

The rest then of the four elements come into being from water through solidification, mingling etc. Apart from Aristotle's interpretation we could say that perhaps Thales, from seeing that water is the life-force and the essential constituent of the world, drew this conclusion. On the basis of this conclusion, he tried to explain the earthquakes, since the earth, according to him, rides like a ship on the water and therefore it is moving in accordance with the water's movement.

" For he (Thales) said that the world is held up by water and rides like a ship, and when it said to 'quake' it is actually rocking because of the water's movement." (Seneca Qu. Nat. III, 14).

Thales studied the movement of planets, and through this study on Astronomy he discovered the cause of eclipses, the nature of sun, the solstices etc.

With regard to the **soul,** he held the view that the soul is mixed with matter and is the prime mover of the perpetual change, just like the Magnesian stone (magnet), which moves the iron. As all things in sum are pervaded by this life-principle with its kinetic power, therefore he said that all things are full of gods.

" Thales too to judge what is recorded about him seem to have held soul to be a motive force, since he said that the magnet has soul in it because it moves the iron." (Aristotle On the Soul 405 a 19).

" Certain thinkers say that soul is intermingled in the whole universe, and it is perhaps for that reason that Thales came to the opinion that all things are full of gods." (Aristotle On the Soul 411 a 7).

Very significant are considered to be his sayings, which are known even nowadays, just as: "**know thyself**" (*γνώθι σαυτόν*: gnothi sauton), as well as "**all things in moderation**" (*μηδέν άγαν*: meden agan). These two notions had influenced the subsequent philosophers, particularly the first one we find mainly in Socrates' philosophy, while the second one in Aristotle's state of the "mean", as we are going to see.

We quote some fragments of Thales' wisdom, which are regarded as well timed even nowadays:

" To Thales are attributed the following sayings: <the most old being is god, for he is ungenerated. The most beautiful thing is the world, for it is god's work. The quickest is the intellect, for it can run through all things. The most powerful is the necessity, for it governs all things. The wisest is the time, for it reveals all things.>.

When he was asked what is most difficult thing, he responded <to know yourself>, what is the easiest? <to give an advice>. What is the most divine? <what has no beginning and end>. How can we live well and rightly? <by not doing what we reprove>. Who is the happiest man? <The one who has healthy body, rich soul and cultivated character.>". (Fr. 1 Diogenes Laertius I, 35, 36).

2. Anaximander (610 – 546 BC)

Anaximander was a kinsman and pupil of Thales, and was the first philosopher who introduced the philosophical term **"principle"** (αρχή: arche), referring to the originative substance, which causes the coming to be and the destruction in the universe.

" **Of those who say that it is one moving and infinite, Anaximander, son of Praxiades, a Milesian, the successor and pupil of Thales said that the principle and element of existing things was the _apeiron_ (infinite) being the first to introduce this name of the material principle.**" (Fr. 9. Simplicius, In Phys. 24, 13).

As Anaximander tried to examine closely the matter of coming to be and passing away of all things in the universe by reasoning, he concluded that the first principle (primary substance) of all existing things is the **infinite** (άπειρον: apeiron). The coming to be and the passing away is eternal, since the motion is for an infinite time. First time in philosophy Anaximander introduces the concept "infinite" or else "indefinite", as infinite time, infinite worlds, eternal motion etc.

" **For those who supposed the worlds to be infinite in number like the associates of Anaximander and Leucippus and Democritus and afterwards those of Epicurus, supposed them to be coming-to-be and passing away for an infinite time, with some of them always coming-to-be and others passing away; and they said that motion was eternal.**" (Simplicius, In Phys. 1121, 5).

This "infinite" is considered to be a matter (according to some interpreters of Anaximander), or an immaterial "primary principle", while the matter is considered to be the subject receptive to this principle (immortal cause), according to Aristotle's interpretation of Anaximander.

" In the four-fold scheme of causes, it is plain that the infinite is a cause in the sense of matter, and that its essence is privation, the subject as such being continuous and sensible." (Aristotle, Physics 3, 207 b, 35).

" Further they identify this (infinite) with the divine, for it is deathless and imperishable as Anaximander says.." (Aristotle, Physics 3, 203 b, 13).

The "infinite" through the eternal cyclical transformations of the elements and the recycling of the worlds, causes the eternal coming to be and passing away, since its whole nature remains indestructible.

" Anaximander who was the companion of Thales said that the apeiron contained the whole cause of the coming-to-be and destruction of the world, from which he says the heavens are separated off, and in general all the worlds, being apeirous (innumerable). He declared that destruction and much earlier coming-to-be happen from infinite ages, since they are all occurring in cycle." (Fr. 10 Plutarch Strom. 2).

In his fragment Anaximander describes the coming to be and passing away in rather poetical terms, as follows:

".. Some other indefinite (ἄπειρον) nature, from which come into being all the heavens and the worlds in them. And the source of coming-to-be for existing things, is that into which destruction, too, happens, according to necessity; for they pay penalty and retribution to each other for their injustice, according to the assessment of time."(Fr. 1 Simplicius In Phys. 24, 17).

We could try to interpret the above fragment and say that: the coming to be and passing away of all things takes place due to the **necessity** (κατά τό χρεών: kata to chreon), namely in order that the universe is preserved eternally, and it is repeated **periodically** (assessment of time: κατά τήν τού *χρόνου τάξιν*: kata tin tou chronou taxin) for an infinite time. Anaximander with this saying introduces first time in the philosophical thought **'the sufficient reason'** in the form of necessity. The continuous strife of the "**opposites**" sometimes leads to the **balance** (**justice**: *δίκην*: diken, after retribution) - and in this case starts the creation and the coming to be - and sometimes leads to the **domination** (**injustice**: *αδικία*) of one opposite principal over the other, and in this case starts the passing away and dissociation (**penalty**). The same term "strife of the opposites" we find later in Heraclitus philosophy as well.

The "opposites" are the "**contrarieties**", according to Anaximander, namely the "hot" the "cold", the "moist" and the "dry". These contrarieties are separated out of the infinite and with a substratum of matter, produce the coming to be through the changing of the four elements into each other, according to necessity, in a certain time, and this cyclical alteration is repeated eternally.

" **It is clear that he (Anaximander), seeing the changing of the four elements into each other, thought it right not to make none of these the substratum, but something else beside these; and he produces coming-to-be not through the alteration of the element but by the separation off of the opposites through the eternal motion. Anaximander says that the opposites are contained in the infinite being and emerge from it by separation off. Opposites are hot, cold, moist and dry.**" (Fr. 9 Simplicius In Phys. 24, 21, 150, 22).

Very significant for his times are considered to be Anaximander's views about the balance of the earth in the void, the cylindrical shape of the earth, as well as his "Darwinian" view that the man originated from fish.

" **The earth is on high, held up by nothing, but remaining on account of its similar distance from all things.**"

" **Its shape is curved, round similar to the drum of the column; for its flat surface we walk on one, and the other is on the opposite side.**"

" Living creatures came into being from moisture evaporated from the sun. Man originated from another creature to which was similar, that is to fish." (Hippolytus, Ref. I, 6, 3, I, 6, 6).

3. Anaximenes (585 – 526 BC)

After Anaximander, Anaximenes continued his thought with regard to the principle from which all things come into being, however he defined this principle as a material one, and he said that this is the infinite **air** (*αήρ*).

" **Anaximenes son of Eurystratus of Miletus, a companion of Anaximander, also says, like him, that the underlying nature is one and infinite, but not undefined as Anaximander said but definite, for he identifies it as air; and it differs in its substantial nature by rarity and density. Being made finer becomes wind, then cloud, then (when thickened still more) water, then earth, then stones; and the rest come into being from these. He, too, makes motion eternal, and says that change, also comes about through it." (Theophrastus ap. Simplicium in Phys. 24, 26).**

As we can realize, he defines the perpetual motion and change as an innate quality of the matter, and through that all things come into being and pass away. Since the first material principle is the air, all the existing things are its products and even the very gods arise from that principle.

" **Anaximenes ... said that infinite air was the principle, from which the things that are becoming, and that are, and that shall be, and gods and things divine, all come into being, and the rest from its products..."** (Hippolytus Ref. I, 7, 1).

On the basis of this view he tried to explain all the natural and meteorological phenomena, just as the wind, clouds, rain, hail, snow, lighting, earthquake, rainbow, day, night etc.

" **Anaximenes said that clouds occur when the air is further thickened, when it is compressed further, rain is squeezed out, and hail occurs when the descending water** coalesces, snow when some windy portion is included together with the moisture." (Aetius III, 4, 1).

" The rainbow is due to the reflexion of different sun-beams by air." (Hippolytus Ref, I, 7, 7-8).

" Anaximenes said that the earth, through being drenched and dried off, breaks asunder, and is shaken by the peaks that are thus broken off and fall in" (Aristotle Meteor. B 7, 365 b 6).

As we have seen, Anaximenes tried to find out the causes of natural phenomena absolutely through the reason, so to say that he was a kind of a natural scientist of his times.

With regard to the **soul**, Anaximenes holds that it is air, and by drawing a parallel between the originative substance of the universe (air) and the air (or breath) of the soul, he concludes that as our soul holds our body together and controls it, so the originative substance (which is also air) holds the world together and controls it.

" **As our soul, he says (Anaximenes), being air** (αήρ) **holds us together and controls us, so does wind** (πνεύμα: pneuma, breath, spirit) **and air encloses the whole world.**" (Aetius I, 3, 4).

*From what has been already said about the Milesians, it is evident that with them began the first rational attempt to understand the nature of the world, and to find out the principles, which govern it. Therefore, we could say that the Ionian school signifies for man, the first attempt to get away from his **animism** and develop the first scientific and philosophical thought.*

4. Pythagoras (580 – 500 BC)

He was the founder of the well-known School of the Pythagoreans, which combined **mysticism** with **numerology**, **mathematics** and **philosophy**. He was born on the island of Samos and at a very young age was taught philosophy by

Pherecydes of Syros and then by Ermodamas the Milesian. After **Miletus** he went to **Phoenicia,** where he was initiated into the secret books of Phoenicians. Then he went to **Egypt,** where he studied mathematics, geometry, astronomy and Egyptian philosophy, and there he was initiated into the mysteries of death and resurrection by the Egyptian priests.

After Egypt he was transferred as a prisoner of war to **Babylon,** where he was taught by the Persian Magi and Chaldean wisemen the Zoroastrian religion and the science of numbers and music. In a trip to **India** he met the Brahmans and as it is said, he also met Buddha himself.

After having acquired a great deal of knowledge Pythagoras returned to **Samos,** where he started teaching his own philosophy. From there he also contacted the Orphics of Thrace and was initiated into their mysteries by Aglaophamus. After his deportation from Samos by its tyrant Polycrates he finally settled down in **Croton** on the southern coast of Italy, where he remained until his death and founded **Omakoeion** the well-known religious and philosophical brotherhood of Pythagoreans.

Numerology – Geometry – Music

The main characteristic of the Pythagoreans was their study of numbers and mathematics, since they believed that the substance of the beings were the numbers. Since the numbers cannot be perceived through the senses but can only be grasped through the intellect, therefore the essence and the first principles of the universe must be intelligible and abstract. The study then of the numbers can lead one to the knowledge and understanding the first principles and laws of the universe.

" **The Pythagoreans, as they are called, devoted themselves to mathematics; they were the first to advance this study, and having brought up in it, they thought its principles were the principles of all things." (Aristotle Metaphysics I 985 b, 25).**

Apart from the study of mathematics, due to which they discovered many theorems, the Pythagoreans developed the metaphysical numerology according to which each number expresses a certain cosmic principle or ethical symbol. We quote epigrammatically some of the symbols of the numbers.

The unit (1) symbolizes energy, aither, **intellect** (*νούς*: nous), the universal generative force (unlimited spirit). The number two (2) is the symbol of matter, fertility, woman, **knowledge** (*επιστήμη*: episteme). Number three (3) symbolizes time, **opinion** (*δόξα*: doxa), plane. Number four (4) is the symbol of cosmic order, space, **senses**. Number five (5) symbolizes the five elements (earth, water, air, fire and aither), the pentahedron from which the universe has been created, as we are going to see in Plato's *Timaeus*, as well as justice, marriage etc. Number six (6) is the symbol of the living beings and resurrection. Number seven (7) symbolizes the seven planets, evolution and the harmony of the universe. Number eight (8) the eight notes of the music scale, number nine (9) the nine cosmic spaces and number ten (10) the universe. Significant is also the table of ten pairs of opposites, which the Pythagoreans regarded as the principles of all things. These are: **Limit and unlimited, odd and even, one and plurality, right and left, male and female, resting and moving, straight and curved, light and darkness, good and bad, square and oblong.**

Apart from the numbers there were eleven Pythagorean tetrads, the first one of these is the well-known **Tetractys** (*τετρακτύς*), on which the Pythagoreans used to swear. It consists of the sum of the first four numbers: **1+2+3+4 = 10,** which is considered to be the number of the universe and the harmony of Sirens who rotate the universe. Other significant tetrads are: The one of the four elements (earth, water, air, fire), of the four polyhedrons (tetrahedron, octahedron, icosahedron and cube), as we are going to see also in Plato's *Timaeus*. Apart from these, is the tetrad of knowledge: 1: intellect, 2: knowledge, 3: opinion, 4: sense, the tetrad of the parts of the soul: 1: rational part, 2: spirited part (emotional), 3: appetitive part (desires), 4: body as a dwelling place of the soul, and the one of the human age: 1: childhood, 2: puberty, 3: manhood, 4: old age.

Furthermore, the Pythagoreans represented geometrically all the numbers by the use of **gnomon** (*γνώμων*), namely the right angle, and they also believed that each number is expressed through a geometrical symbol, for example: one (1) is referring to point, two (2) to straight line, three (3) to flat and four (4) to volume. They invented many theorems, just as that the sum of the angles of a triangle is equal to two right angles, the well-known Pythagorean theorem, the similarity of geometrical patterns, the hyperbola, parabola, ellipse, the even and odd numbers.

Concerning the geometrical patterns, each one of them had a certain symbol, for example: a straight line symbolizes the knowledge since it can be intersected and extended to the infinite, a circle symbolizes the reflecting being, an equilateral triangle the pure soul, a square the deity, an obtuse angle the excess, an acute angle the deficiency and the right angle the virtue.

Since they invented the arithmetical and geometrical proportions, as well as the harmonies, they applied this knowledge to the theory of music. Specially the following proportion: α / [($\alpha+\beta$)/2] = [$2\alpha\beta/(\alpha+\beta)$] / β, which represents the arithmetical middle term, it was used by them to define the frequencies of the eight musical notes and the seven spaces of the musical scale. The syllables which were used for the eight notes were : **te** (*τη*: **do, C**), **ta** (*τα*: **re, D**), **tae** (*τε*: **mi, E**), **to** (*τω*: **fa, F**), **te** (*τη*: **sol, G**), **ta** (*τα*: **la, A**), **to** (*τω*: **si, B**), **te** (*τη*: **do, C**).

The doctrine of the "**harmony of the spheres**", in which the Pythagoreans believed, was referring to the sounds that the heavenly spheres produce while rotating, which are proportional to their distance, and also proportional to the spaces of musical scale. These sounds compose an excellent harmony, which Plato mentions also in the ***Republic*** as a **harmony of Sirens**. Men cannot hear it, since they hear it from the first moment of their birth, just as they cannot perceive the air that they breathe.

" **And up above on each of the rims of the circle stood a Siren, who accompanied its revolution, uttering a single**

16

sound, one single note. And the concord of the eight notes produced a single harmony. And there were other beings sitting at equal distances from one another, each on a throne. These were the Fates, the daughters of Necessity: Lachesis, Clotho and Atropos. They were dressed in white with garlands on their head, and they sang to the <u>harmony of Sirens</u>." (Plato, Republic 617 b).

Cosmogony – Soul

The centre of universe according to the Pythagoreans was the **fire** (πύρ: pyr), which they called "**hearth of the world**" (εστίαν τού παντός: hestian tou pantos), from where started the expansion of the universe through its "breath".

" **Philolaus (Pythagorean) places fire around the centre of the universe, and calls it the <hearth of the world>, the <house of Zeus>, <mother of the gods>, <altar, bond and measure of the nature>**" (Aetius II, 7, 7).

As "respiration" of the universe is considered to be the mixture of the universal generative force (unlimited spirit) with the void, which results in its expansion and the separation and distinguishing of the things and the beings. The expansion of the universe as we know, is accepted also by the modern physics. They conceived the existence of the void, from the void that distinguishes the numbers.

" **The Pythagoreans too, held that void exists, and that it enters the heaven from the unlimited spirit – it so to speak breathes in void also. The void distinguishes the nature of the things, since it is the thing that separates and distinguishes the successive terms in a series. This happens in the first instance in the numbers; for the void distinguishes their nature.**" (Aristotle, Physics, 213 b 22).

This Pythagorean belief that fire is in the centre of the universe, led Copernicus to discover the heliocentric system, since Pythagoras believed that the earth turns around itself and the sun.

The world is divided into the visible and intelligible one, the latter is immortal and therefore the soul belongs to this world, since it is a spark of the universal fire, namely of the universal and divine soul, and it is imprisoned in the human body. It possesses the faculty of self-motion and after the death of the body passes into another body.

However, the soul which has lived pure and virtuous life goes to the intelligible world and joins the universal deity. On the other hand, the soul which is not pure reincarnates many times in order to have the possibility to be purified. Otherwise is led to the Tartara to be punished and purified. Everything is determined by the Divine Law, which works according to the necessity and reward, the so-called **hemarmene** (*ειμαρμένη*), namely fate or destiny. Man cannot change this law, therefore he must bear it with patience, for this can help him to develop himself, possess the virtues and resemble god.

In order one to possess virtues it requires daily practice and training, therefore one had to be initiated into the Pythagorean teaching. On this basis have been created all the Pythagorean Schools, having as a pattern the School of Pythagoras in Croton (*omakoeion*), and were all characterized by their mystic nature.

Pythagorean mysticism

The prospective disciple of Pythagoreanism, according to the regulation of the School, had to be tested for his courage (e.g. he had to stay all night long in a cave, where there were rumors that lived evil spirits). Afterwards, he was received as an **external disciple** without belonging to the brotherhood. This stage lasted five years, and the pupil had to attend lectures without being able to see the face of his master, and he was bound to secrecy.

After that stage, he could become an **intimate disciple** and member of the brotherhood, which was called **hetaireia** (*εταιρεία*). The form of the brotherhood was twofold. One group were called the "**Mathematicians**" (*μαθηματικοί*) and the other one the "**Acousmatics**" (*ακουσματικοί*). The "Acousmatics" dealt with the moral and religious part of Pythagoras' teaching (regulation, rituals and interpretation of his sayings), the "Mathematicians" learnt the elaborated knowledge and made a scientific research.

18

There were strict regulations in the Pythagorean brotherhood, which included gymnastics, certain nutrition and diet, collective prayer and personal retrospective account of the disciple's deeds. The latter was referring to the duty that each intimate disciple had every evening before going to bed, so tom say to pass in review all the day, therefore he had to recall retrospectively all the events of the day, in order to find out "**wherein had he done amiss, what had he done, what he had neglected**". This practice was essential for the disciple, since it helped him to improve himself and possess gradually the virtues of **moderation, prudence, courage** and **justice,** which were considered to be the main virtues of a man, according to the Pythagoreans. Because of the above mentioned regulations as we can realize the "**Pythagorean life**" (*πυθαγόρειος βίος:* **pythagoreios bios**) was a byword for pure, frugal and austere way of life.

The first Pythagorean brotherhood, which was founded by Pythagoras in Croton as we said, was called "**omakoeion**" (*ομακοείον*) from the Greek words "**omou**" (*ομού*: together) and "**acouo**" (*ακούω*: hear), since the teaching that all the disciples used to hear, as they were gathered all together, was mainly verbal. For Pythagoras loyal to his mysticism never left any writings but only under a pseudonym. We quote some of the symbols and "**acousmata**" (*ακούσματα*: things heard), which were parts of Pythagorean teaching: "**What are the isles of the blessed? Sun and moon**", "**What is the oracle at Delphi? The tetractys, which is the harmony in which the Sirens sing**", "**What is the most just thing? To sacrifice**", "**What is the wisest? Number**", "**What is the most powerful? Knowledge**", "**What is the best? Happiness**" etc. (Iamblichus, Life of Pythagoras 82).

The members of Pythagorean brotherhood were bound together with intimate friendship and solidarity, loyal to Pythagoras' saying: "*φιλότης – ισότης*" (**philotes – isotes:** friendship – equality). **Justice**, the most significant virtue of the Pythagoreans, according to which all their communities functioned, was based upon **equality** of their members, therefore each member had to deposit all his wealth in the treasury of the brotherhood, since according to Pythagoras **"what belongs to friends is a common property"** (*κοινά τά τών φίλων*: koina ta ton philon).

The members of the brotherhood were bound to secrecy and used to swear on the name of **Tetractys.** As a sign of mutual recognition they used the **pentagram,** a five-pointed star (*πεντάγραμμον*: pentagrammon).

Ethics – Golden Verses

The whole philosophical and ethical teaching of the Pythagoreans is included in a poem of 71 verses which is called **"Golden Verses",** and was written probably by Pythagoreans in the 4th century BC, since some parts of the poem we also find in Chrysippus' writings of the Stoics.

The poem begins with reference to **piety,** namely the writer exhorts the disciple to worship first the gods and then to honour the heroes, the daimons (individual souls or spirits of dead), the parents and the close relatives.

Afterwards, he is referring to **friendship,** which is considered to be very significant virtue, by exhorting the disciple to make friendship on the basis of virtue, which Aristotle also regards as a perfect friendship, as we are going to see. Therefore, he exhorts the disciple to make his friend the one who distinguishes himself by his virtue, and to be tolerant of his friend's faults, since the necessity of maintenance the friendship can give him the power of forgiveness.

> **" Of all the rest of mankind make him your friend**
> **who distinguishes himself by his virtue.**
> **Always give ear to his mild exhortations,**
> **and take example from his virtuous and useful**
> **actions.**
> **Avoid as much as possible hating your friend for a**
> **slight fault,**
> **for power is near neighbour to necessity."**
> **(Golden Verses 5 – 8).**

As the poem goes on, the writer is referring to the main virtues of the Pythagoreans, starting with **moderation** which consists in self-control and abstinence from bodily pleasures (food, drink, sex), and also continence with regard to anger and sleepiness. **Temperance** is connected with feeling of ashamed of oneself and self-respect, and as a result respect for the others. This sense of **respect for oneself** we also find in Democritus' philosophy at the same time when the poem was written.

> " **Know that all these things are as I have told you ;**
> **and accustom yourself to overcome and vanquish**
> **the following:**
> **First gluttony, sleepiness, lasciviousness and anger.**
> **Do nothing evil, neither in the presence of others nor**
> **privately;**
> **But above all things respect yourself."**
> (**Golden Verses 9 – 12**).

The next part of the poem is referring to **justice** in words and deeds, which is related to the universal law and destiny. In other words, the man who realizes that some day will perish, just like all the people, does not concern himself with acquiring wealth, just as he was going to live forever. Furthermore, according to the universal law of justice one can make or lose fortune, therefore it is in vain to pursue the acquiring of wealth. On the other hand, the man who has this aim, becomes greedy and imprudent, and as a result violates the law and takes no account of the universal justice.

> " **In the next place, observe justice in your actions and**
> **in your words.**
> **And accustom not yourself to behave in anything**
> **without reason,**
> **but always make this reflection, that is ordained by**
> **destiny**
> **that all men shall die. And that the goods of fortune**
> **are uncertain;**
> **and as they may be acquired, so may they likewise be**
> **lost."**
> (**Golden Verses 13-16**).

The next part is referring to the **courage** that one should have to suffer the buffets of fate. The writer suggests the disciple to bear the misfortunes with patience, without feeling despair or indignation, and also to try to remedy what he can and not to remain passive and to become fatalist. As we can realize, the virtue of bravery has a wider sense for the Pythagoreans, which means courage and patience in the face of misfortunes without feelings of panic, despair, helplessness and anger. Apart from that, the Pythagoreans believed that the divine Providence does not send many misfortunes to virtuous men.

> " Concerning all the calamities that men suffer by divine fortune,
> support with patience your lot, be it what it may,
> and never repine at it, but endeavour what you can to remedy it.
> And consider that fate does not send the greatest portion
> of these misfortune to good men."
> (Golden Verses 17 – 20).

Furthermore, the writer examines closely the virtue of **prudence**, which consists, on the one hand, in knowledge and on the other hand, in foresight before each action. He exhorts the disciple neither to admire nor to reject easily every reasoning and speech, but to judge by reason everything, and if he finds falsehood in these, he should face it with calmness. Apart from that, whatever he wants to do he should reflect before the action and decide by himself, taking into account the consequences of his action. Unbiased judgement, foresight, and harmony of actions with principles in relation to continence, all these contribute to prudence, as we can see.

> " There are among men many sorts of reasonings, good and bad;
> Admire them not too easily nor reject them,
> but if falsehoods be advanced, hear them with mildness,
> and arm yourself with patience.
> Observe well on every occasion, what I am going to tell you:
> Let no man either by his words or by his deeds, ever

22

seduce you.
Nor entice you to say or to do what is not profitable
for yourself.
Consult and deliberate before you act, that you may
not commit foolish actions, for it is the part of a
miserable man
to speak and act without reflection, but do that
which will not
afflict you afterwards, nor oblige you to repentance.
Never do anything which you do not understand,
but learn
all what you ought to know, and by that means
you will lead a very pleasant life."
                    (**Golden Verses 21 – 31**).

Afterwards, the writer returns to the matter of **moderation** with regard to food, drink and gymnastics, by exhorting the disciple to lead a pure, frugal and healthy life, and have his motto in life the **due measure** which is **excellent** (*μέτρον δ' επί πάσιν άριστον*: metron the epi pasen ariston). Furthermore, the disciple must avoid whatever causes envy, prodigality and avarice and in general whatever could have serious consequences.

In the last part of the exhortations we find the personal practice of retrospective recall and self-analysis that we have already mentioned, which the disciple had to do in the end of the day in order to discover his mistakes and weaknesses. After that, he could either praise himself for the good deeds or rebuke himself for what he had done amiss or neglected with regard to moral duty. And if the disciple follows all these advises with continuous self-criticism and discipline, he will be able to know and possess the divine virtue. In the end the writer invokes the oath of the Pythagoreans in order to certify his promise.

    " **Never suffer sleep to close your eyelids before**
going to bed,
till you have examined by reason three times all the
actions of the day.
<u>**Wherein have I done amiss? What have I done?**</u>

What have I omitted that I ought to have done?
If in this examination you find that you have done
amiss,
Reprimand yourself severely for it,
and if you have done any good rejoice.
Practice thoroughly all these things, meditate on
them well;
You ought to love them with all your heart,
for these they will put you in the way of divine
virtue,
  < I swear it by him, who has transmitted into our
   souls
the Sacred Tetractys, the source of nature whose
cause is eternal>."
                (Golden Verses 40 – 48).

The last two verses constitute the oath of Pythagoreans by which the promise of the writer is corroborated. The man who transmitted the **Tetractys** (the harmony of Sirens, who possess the secret knowledge of the universe, **p**. 14,15) is probably Pythagoras himself, who was considered to be demigod by his disciples.

As the writer goes on, he promises that the disciple he can possess the knowledge of the constitution of all things, namely the substance which pervades all things in the universe. According to the Pythagoreans, the immortal soul is a common substance of all things and each individual soul is a part of the universal constitution, which has once grasped the knowledge of the universal constitution in the intelligible world, as we are going to see also in Plato's philosophy. Therefore, the disciple through further initiation and personal enquiry he could discover within himself this knowledge of the constitution.

  " But never begin to set your hand to any work,
  before you have first prayed to gods to accomplish
  what you are going to begin. When you have made
  this habit
  familiar to you, you will know the constitution of the
  Immortal Gods

24

and of men. Even how far the different things extend,
and what contains and binds them together. You shall likewise know
that according to law, the nature of the universe is in all things alike.
So that you shall not hope what you ought not to hope;
and nothing in this world shall be hidden from you."
(Golden Verses 48 – 53).

Afterwards, the writer is referring to the misfortunes of men, who since they go astray in matters good and evil, they are led by the nose from the external events, and react mechanically and imprudently, just like cylinders which roll here and there. Therefore, they bring about their own ruin, since they are guided by their passions without having reflected upon the consequences of their actions. According to the Pythagoreans the "strife" is innate in the human soul and prompts the people to pursue their personal interest and dissociate themselves from the universal and divine constitution, which binds together all the beings. For this reason one must avoid this impulse and not to provoke it. The same principle "**strife**" (*ἔρις*: eris) we also find in Heraclitus' philosophy as a cosmic force of dissociation and destruction (**war**: *πόλεμος*, polemos), as well as in Empedocles' philosophy as *νείκος* (neikos).

" You will likewise know, that men draw upon themselves
their own misfortunes voluntarily, and of their own free choice.
Unhappy that they are! They neither see nor understand that
their good is near them. Few know how to deliver themselves
out of their misfortunes. Such is the fate that blinds mankind,
and takes away his senses. Like huge cylinders they roll to and fro,

and always oppressed with ills innumerable. For
fatal strife, innate,
pursues them everywhere, tossing them up and
down;
nor do they perceive it. Instead of provoking and
stirring it up,
they ought by yielding to avoid it."
(Golden Verses 53 – 60).

As the writer goes on, he consoles the disciple and tells him
not to lose his hope on his way for knowledge, since man is of
noble and divine origin, and therefore he has the potentiality
to know the secrets of the universal constitution. For the
universal constitution, although is of a mystic nature, reveals
its secrets to the virtuous and the initiates. The man who
possesses the knowledge of himself, namely of his personal
soul (**personal daimon, δαίμονι**), possesses the knowledge of
the **universal constitution** (*φύσις:* physis, nature) and of the
destiny, since the same principle governs all things. That
mystic nature of the constitution we also find in Heraclitus'
philosophy " nature is accustomed to hide itself".

" Oh ! Jupiter our Father ! If You had delivered
men from all the evils that oppress them,
show them of what daimon they make use.
But take courage; the race of men is divine,
sacred nature reveals to them the most hidden
secrets."
(Golden Verses 61 – 64).

The writer concludes with reference to immortality, since
the immortal personal soul which has possessed virtues and
become conscious of itself, when abandons the body - which
is considered to be the grave of the soul according to the
Pythagoreans - will go to the pure aither, where live the
immortal gods. In order to achieve this immortality the
disciple must follow all the previous mentioned advises. Apart
from that, he must abstain from the forbidden food, mentioned
in the "Purifications" and the "Deliverance of the soul", which
are probably texts of Orphics, concerning the forbidden food.
The rule that the disciple should go by, must be the **supreme**

26

good, which means through prudence he must always judge everything by reason and in accordance with his aim, which is the knowledge of the supreme good (divine constitution). Until he will have grasped this knowledge, he must follow the "**best opinion**" (*γνώμην αρίστην*: gnomen aristen), namely the teaching of Pythagoras. In this way he can remedy his soul from the ignorance caused by the "strife", as we have seen.

> " If she imparts to you her secrets, you will easily perform
> all the things which I have ordained to you. And by the healing
> of your soul you will deliver it from all evils, from all afflictions.
> But abstain from food which we have forbidden in the
> <Purifications> and in the <Deliverance of the soul>.
> Make a just distinction of them and examine all things well,
> leaving yourself always to be guided and directed by the best opinion which comes from above,
> and that ought to hold the reins.
> And when, after having divested yourself
> of your mortal body, you will arrive at the most pure Aither.
> You shall be a god, immortal, incorruptible, and death
> shall have no more dominion over you."
> (Golden Verses 65 – 71).

5. Heraclitus (544 – 484 BC)

The philosopher from Ephesus, who is known from his saying "**all things are in flux**" (*τά πάντα ρεί*: ta panta rei). He is considered to be the pioneer of many posterior philosophical schools, contrasted one with the other, as well as the founder of **rational relativism**. Perhaps, the most

HANDBOOK OF GREEK PHILOSOPHY

controversial personality of Ancient Greek philosophy, therefore he was called " **the obscure**" or "**the dark**" (σκοτεινός: skoteinos). The laconic and enigmatic expressions were typical of him, as we are going to see through his original fragments of his teachings, as well as his poetical approach to philosophy.

Bipolarity – Opposites

The basic principle of his philosophy is that, everything comprises within a pair of "**opposites**" (ενάντια: enantia), which are in a state of potential balance. These evident opposite tensions form an essential and indivisible unity. Day and night, born and unborn, young and old, mortal and immortal, joy and sorrow, etc., although they apparently look different, essentially are united and compose the whole, since each one will be transformed into its opposite. What today is young, it is going to be old later on, what today is unborn, will come into being after some time. All the terms then are relative, since there is a continuous "**change**" and "**coming to be**" (γίγνεσθαι: gignesthai). When we examine the terms, the determining factor is the moment that we refer to (time), and the position on which we stand (space). The same person that now is young, after some years will be old. What is standing above us, when we change our position, it will be below us.

" **Heraclitus claims that the whole is divisible and undivisible, born and unborn, mortal and immortal, logos and time, father and son, god and justice. <Listening not to me but to the Logos, it is wise to agree that all things are one> ." (Fr. 50 Hippolytus Ref. IX, 9, 1).**

" **They do not apprehend how being at variance it agrees with itself; there is a back-stretched connexion, as in the bow and the lyre." (Fr. 51 Hippolytus Ref. IX, 9, 1).**

" **God is day night, winter summer, war peace, satiety hunger (all the opposites, this is the meaning)..." (Fr. 67 Hippolytus Ref. IX, 10, 8).**

" **And as the same thing there exists in us, living and dead, the walking and the sleeping, and young and old; for these things having changed round are those, and those** having changed round are these." (Fr. 88, ps.—Plutarch Cons. Ad Apoll. 10, 106 E).

" The path up and down is one and the same." (Fr. 60 Hippolytus Ref. IX, 10, 4).

Therefore nothing is stable, and each thing can be transformed into its opposite, since the complete opposites are the two aspects of the same thing, the 'two different sides of one and the same coin'. Therefore, it is absurd to desire or adhere only to the one opposite, excluding the other, since both opposites co-exist within everything. Good – evil, love – hatred, etc. co-exist within us, as they are the two aspects of the same impulse, and they are in a state of potential balance.

Balance requires the existence of two opposite tensions, which when they are associated one with the other, a great harmony is composed just like in nature, music, painting etc. Due to the total balance and harmony, the whole appears to be as a single, coherent and still, as a 'unity' (*éva*: ena, one), and as a result we cannot realize the existence of the two "opposites".

" Contrariety is expedient. The best harmony arises from things differing." (Fr. 8 Aristotle, Nicomachean Ethics VIII, 1155 b 4-5).

" It may perhaps be that nature has a liking for contraries and evolves harmony out of them and not out of similarities (just as she joins the male and female together and not members of the same sex), and has devised the original harmony by means of contraries and not similarities. The arts too imitate nature in this respect. The art of painting, by mingling in the picture the elements of white and black, yellow and red, achieves representations, which correspond to the original object. Music, too, mingling together notes, high and low, short and prolonged, attains to a single harmony amid different voices; while writing, mingling vowels and consonants, composes of them all its art. The saying of Heraclitus <the obscure> was to the same effect. < Things taken together, wholes and not wholes, what is being brought together and brought apart, what is in tune and out of tune; from all the one (*ἕνα*: ena) **and from one all (*πάντα*: panta).>" (Fr. 10 Aristotle, On The Universe 5, 396 b, 7-24).**

When the balance is overthrown, then starts a new change, until a new balance is restored, which is also changeable till to the next alteration and so on. This perpetual motion is the '**eternal change**' (*γίγνεσθαι*) and takes place everywhere in the Universe. The cause of this 'change' is, when creation takes place the "**privation**" (*χρησμοσύνη*: chrismosini, **lack**), and when destruction takes place the "**satiety**" or else "**saturation**" (*κόρος*: koros). Both procedures are accomplished through the "**consumption by fire**" (*ἐκπύρωσις*: ekpyrosis). The means by which this change is carried out is the continuous "**strife**" or the "**war**" (*πόλεμος*: polemos) between the two "**opposites**". In other words, lack pushes to creation, and satiety pushes to destruction. Even the very "justice" is a continuous strife between the 'opposites', which get to balance temporarily, till the next strife.

" **It is necessary to know that war is common and justice is strife, and that all things happen by strife and necessity." (Fr. 80 Origen c. Celsum VI, 42).**

" **War is the father of all and king of all, and some he shows as gods, others as men; some he makes slaves, others free." (Fr. 53 Hippolytus Ref. IX, 9, 4).**

" **This world-order (the same of all) did none of gods or men make, but it always was, and is, and shall be: an ever living fire, kindling in measures and going out in measures." (Fr. 30 Clement Strom. V, 104, 1).**

" **Fire's turnings: first sea, and the half of sea is earth, the half 'burning' (lighting or fire), <earth> is dispersed as sea, and is measured so as to form the same proportion as existed before it became earth." (Fr. 31 Clement Strom. V, 104, 3).**

" **<Thunderbolt steers all things>, by calling thunderbolt the eternal fire. He (Heraclitus) claims that fire possess prudence, and is the cause of management of universe"**

" He calls fire <u>lack</u> and <u>satiety</u>. Lack, according to him, is the creation of the universe, and consumption by fire (εκπύρωσις) is satiety." (Fr. 64, 65 Hippolytus Ref. IX, 10).

As we can see, in the transformation between the elements, the determining factor is the element of "**fire**" (πύρ: pyr). Whilst all the other elements are temporary forms, since the one can be changed into the other, the element of fire is everlasting, which means eternal, and determines all the other changes. At this point, we could liken the 'fire' to the transformation of mass into energy and to the contrary. Since all the transformations in the universe are taking place with absorption or emission of energy, the 'fire' of those times, is what we nowadays call 'energy'. This eternal fire follows a periodical, circular and perpetual motion (fr. 30), by creating and destroying on its way the different physical forms.

" **All things are an equal exchange for fire and fire for all things, as goods are for gold and gold for goods.**" (Fr. 90 Plutarch de E. 8, 388 D).

From all the above mentioned "principles" of Heraclitus' thought - so to say, creation (**privation**), destruction (**satiety**), eternal and perpetual change due to the strife between the opposites (**war**) that constitute the everlasting and continuous change (γίγνεσθαι), - it is understood that nothing remains still, everything changes, without beginning and end.

" **Heraclitus says, <that everything gives way and nothing stays still (τά πάντα χωρεί καί ουδέν μένει)>, and resembling the things that are to the flowing of a river, he says that < you cannot step into the same river twice>.**" (Plato, Cratylus 402 a).

" **The sun ... is new each day.**" (Fr. 6, Aristotle Meteor. B 2, 355 a 13).

Logos

All these laws of continuous and eternal change comprise a universal constitution, which determines everything, and Heraclitus calls it "**Logos**" (Λόγος: reason). Logos governs all things in the universe, it is common, pervades everything and is eternal.

" Of Logos, which is as I describe it, men always prove to be uncomprehending, both before they have heard it and when once they have heard it. For although all things happen according to this Logos, men are like people of no experience, even when they experience such words and deeds, as I explain, when I distinguish each thing according to its constitution and declare how it is; but the rest of men fail to notice what they do after they wake up, just as they forget what they do when asleep.

Therefore, it is necessary to follow the common; but although the Logos is common, the many live as though they had a private understanding." (Fr. 1, Fr. 2, Sextus adv. Math. VII, 132-133).

" The many are in opposition to the Logos, with which they are always in intimate contact, and which governs all things, and what they meet every day, appears to be alien to them." (Fr. 72 Marcus Aurelius IV 46).

As we can see in the previous fragments, according to Heraclitus, the majority of the people (**the many**), are not aware of their mechanical actions, and although are in daily contact with the Logos, they cannot realize this universal law which determines all things. Therefore, he likens them to **"sleepers"** (*κοιμώμενοι*: koimomenoi), as we are going to see.

The 'sleepers' due to their automatically and unconscious actions take part in the events of life (good and bad ones), therefore they are accomplices, since they have private and subjective understanding about good and evil, and they only act as prompted by personal motives, without having comprehension of this law. Therefore, their opinions about life and death are subjective, and they demand from life to go by in accordance with their desires, since they are unaware of the law of the eternal change. So, the sleepers are afraid of death, they desire the pleasant, dislike the unpleasant, and they pursue the secure, stable, permanent etc., by ignoring the strife between the opposites. In this way, they throw themselves into the pursuit of pleasure and passing fancies, which means into

32

death of their consciousness (rest), due to their lack of self-knowledge, and the ignorance of the universal law.

On the other hand, the **awake** are aware of the Logos, they think and act in accordance with this law, and as a matter of fact, they form objective (common) opinions and not personal ones (private). They understand the necessity of death and eternal change, as well as the coexistence of pleasure and pain in life, and therefore they do not pursue the ephemerals, since they know, that all the ephemeral things will abandon them as time goes round.

" Sleepers (Heraclitus calls them) are workers and accomplices of what is happening to the world." (Fr. 75 Marcus Aurelius VI 42).

" Those who cannot understand (the Logos), when they hear it, look like the deafs. For those gives evidence the saying <being presents, they are absents>." (fr. 34 Clement Strom. V 116).

" Those things (which the Logos reveals) the many cannot understand, neither those who happen to meet those things, nor when they are taught them, however they believe that they have understood them." (Fr. 17 Clement Strom. II 8).

" They, after being born, decide to live and suffer death, or rather to rest, and leave children behind, to become also food for death." (Fr. 20 Clement Strom. III 21).

" For the awake, the world is one and common, but each one of the sleepers takes refuge in his own world." (Fr. 89 Plutarch On Des. 3, 166 c).

" Human beliefs are toys of children." (Fr. 70 Stobaeus Anth. II, 1, 16).

Gnoseology – Virtues

All men, according to Heraclitus, can acquire **prudence** (φρόνησις: phronesis), which means they are able to think rightly and consciously. However, this requires knowledge of oneself, so as not to think and act mechanically, without knowing one's hidden impulses, in other words not to be a 'sleeper'. Therefore, the first step for us to stop being 'sleepers' is to search out and know ourselves. Through this slow process of self-knowledge we can gradually acquire prudence. Heraclitus particularly points out that the knowledge he acquired, started with the search of himself.

" **Prudence is at every one's disposal.**" (Fr. 113 Stobaeus Anth. I, 179).

" **All human beings have the capacity of knowing themselves and acquiring prudence.**" (Fr. 116 Stobaeus Anth. V, 6).

" **I searched out myself.**" (Fr. 101 Plutarch adv. Colotem 20, 1118 c).

After having acquired prudence, which is a real virtue, one can achieve **wisdom** (σοφία: sofia) that is distinguished from all the other virtues, since the wise man is no longer 'sleeper', he has a knowledge of his nature, of the universal constitution, possesses the comprehension of the Logos, and acts in accordance with it. For wisdom is the understanding of the principles that determine all the changes, which are taking place in the Universe, as well as within the human being. This comprehension enables the wise man to get away from his personal weaknesses and to be raised to the divine level, since his judgements and actions rely on the universal law.

" **The wise is one thing, to be acquainted with true judgement, how all things are steered through all.**" (Fr. 41 Diogenes Laertius IX, 1).

" **None of those I have heard their teachings goes to the length of knowing that the wise is distinguished from all the rest.**"(Fr. 108 Stobaeus Anth. III, 1, 174).

" **To be prudent is a great virtue, and wisdom is one to say the truth and act in accordance with nature, after having understood it.**" (Fr. 112 Stobaeus Anth. I, 178).

" **Those who speak with sense must rely on what is common to all, as a city must rely on its law, and with much greater reliance. For all the laws of men are nourished by one law, the divine law; for it has as much power it wishes and is sufficient for all and is still left over.**" (Fr. 114 Stobaeus Anth. III, 1, 179).

The way to achieve self-knowledge, prudence and wisdom is long, difficult and boundless, since the self-consciousness and knowledge are not static, but gradual and progressive. Because, after having realized something, this understanding allows us to wonder and think about something else, that we were not able to think before. Each understanding brings a new question about, and the latter another personal discovery. For **knowledge** is a continuous and endless process, an eternal **"coming to be"** (*γίγνεσθαι*).

" **You will not find out the boundaries of soul, even by travelling along every path; so deep a measure does it have." (Fr. 45 Diogenes Laertius IX, 7).**

The unfulfilled desires are the motivations, which help the people to start thinking and reflecting on the causes of their impulses. In this way starts the path to self-knowledge, due to the "**privation**" (*χρησμοσύνη*) of satisfaction, which is as we have seen the cause of each change and creation.

Just like, when we fall ill, we mobilize to recover and regain our health – which only then, we estimate and enjoy it more than before – in the same way, when our desires are not fulfilled, we mobilize to search and find out the cause of our desires' failure. This continuous search can lead us to understand gradually all our hidden impulses, and achieve self-consciousness, in other words, to know ourselves.

The same as, when we feel hungry we mobilize to satisfy our hunger, when we are tired, to rest etc. This "lack" of satisfaction (the same with privation as a cause of creation) is the driving force that mobilizes us to get to know the causes of the natural events, as well as of our impulses and desires (**self-knowledge**).

" **It is not the best for men, their desires to be fulfilled." (Fr. 110 Stobaeus Anth. I, 176).**

" **Disease makes health pleasant and good, hunger satiety, weariness rest." (Fr. 111 Stobaeus Anth. III, 1, 177).**

" **They would not have known the name of justice, if those (abuses) there were not." (Fr. 23 Clement, Strom. IV, 10).**

In this last fragment we can see, that Heraclitus regards each ideal term (e.g. justice) not as static and unchangeable, but as something that is also part of the "eternal change" (*γίγνεσθαι*), and is always changing in connection with its opposite, during the continuous "strife between the opposites". By becoming aware of the injustice, we change every time our conception of justice, and adapt it to the new circumstances, and always by the criterion of "privation". So, the concepts are relative in themselves and always changeable. This **relativity** we find in the next fragment, where we can realize that what is good for one species, it is bad for the other one.

" **Sea is the most pure and most polluted water; for fishes it is drinkable and salutary, but for men it is undrinkable and deleterious.**" (Fr. 61 Hippolytus Ref. IX, 10, 5).

Parallel to the self-knowledge, the friend (*φίλος* : philos) of wisdom (*σοφία*: sophia), the **philosopher** (*φιλόσοφος*: philosophos), must know the different philosophical doctrines (polymathy), which will enable him to broaden his views, but solely this is not sufficient to achieve wisdom. For memorizing and rehashing of teachings (polymathy) does not lead to the deep comprehension of nature.

" **Friends of wisdom (philosophers) must be enquirers into many things.**" (Fr. 35 Clement Strom. V 141).

" **The learning of many things (polymathy) does not teach understanding; if it did, it would have taught Hesiod and Pythagoras, and again Xenophanes and Hecataeus.**" (Fr. 40 Diogenes Laertius IX, 1).

"**Teacher of many people was Hesiod. They believe that he knew a lot, he who did not know what is day and night, for they are one.**" (Fr. 57 Hippolytus Fr. IX, 10).

The deep knowledge is based upon the personal experience and understanding of what is happening within us and also in nature, by putting the philosophical principles to test either in ourselves or in the nature, in order to confirm empirically these theoretical principles. Simple rehash of learnings or beliefs do not lead us to this understanding. For as we have seen (fr. 41), if a philosophical principle is considered to be wise, must be able to explain how all things in universe are steered, and also to be confirmed after being examined by trial.

" **The things of which there is a seeing, and hearing and perception, these do I prefer.**" (Fr. 55 Hippolytus Ref. IX, 9, 5).

" **Eyes are more precise witnesses than ears.**" (Fr. 101 a, Polybius XII, 27).

" **I searched out myself.**" (Fr. 101 Plutarch, adv. Colotem 20, 1118 c).

So, deep knowledge can neither be based upon beliefs nor upon rumors (ears), but its truth has to be verified through trial and error, therefore it proceeds gradually. The comprehension of the nature and our mechanical impulses is growing steadily as we are heading for knowledge.

" **There is a reason (logos) within the soul which grows by itself.**" (Fr. 115 Stobaeus Anth. I, 180 a).

To have a clear conception of the laws that determine ourselves, we first have to understand our desires and fight with them. This is very difficult, since all our desires in order to be fulfilled demand a part of our soul and diminish it.

" **It is hard to fight with desire** (θυμῶι, thymoe: anger, desire)**; for what it wants it buys at the price of soul.**" (Fr. 85 Plutarch Coriol. 22).

Soul – Happiness

The **soul** (ψυχή: psyche) as a faculty of perception, self-consciousness and thinking, according to Heraclitus, when is under the influence of desire, enjoys the pleasure (τέρψις: terpsis), and therefore, it falls into oblivion and becomes "**moist**" (υγρήν: ygrin). In other words, the soul in this state loses the faculty of perception and self-awareness, just like when one is drunk does not know where he goes and is not at all aware of his motions. For the soul, under the influence of desire, is intoxicated with joy and pleasure and as a result loses its "**fiery**" faculties of "Logos", which can only lead it to knowledge and wisdom (dry soul).

" For the souls it is pleasure or death to become <u>moist</u>." (Fr. 77 Noumenius Thedinga Porph. 10).

" A man when is drunk is led by unfledged boy, stumbling and not knowing where he goes, having his soul moist." (Fr. 117 Stobaeus Anth. III, 5, 7).

" A <u>dry</u> (ξηρή: xeri) <u>soul</u> is wisest and best." (Fr. 118 Stobaeus Anth. III, 5, 8).

Through the sensational pleasures we cannot achieve "**happiness**" (ευδαιμονία : eudaimonia), for the human nature is not animal like, so as to be content with satisfying only its bodily needs, therefore it does not suit the human nature to wallow in the "mud". Understanding the human nature means to realize, that since a man is not simply an animal, but has in addition the faculty of prudence and wisdom, he cannot achieve happiness through the sensational pleasures. For all the species are happy, when they live in accordance with their nature, just like the ox is happy when it finds to eat sweet peas, and the pig when it wallows in the mud. Therefore a man can achieve happiness, only when he acquires **prudence** and **wisdom**, which are in accordance with his true nature. The orgiastic rites to Dionysus help the people to relax their animal instincts but not to acquire prudence and wisdom, since they are distinguished from the sensational pleasures.

" If happiness was found in bodily pleasures, then we should have called happy the oxen, when they find sweet peas to feed on." (Fr. 4 Albertus Magnus Veget. VI 104).

" Man should not find pleasure in mud."

" Pigs find pleasure rather in mud than in clear water." (Fr. 13 Clement Strom. I, 1, 2).

" For if it were not to Dionysus that they made the procession and sung the hymn to the shameful parts (αιδοίοισιν : aidoioisin), the deed would be most shameless; but Hades (Αίδης : aides) and Dionysus for whom they rave and celebrate Lenaean rites are the same." (Fr.15 Clement Protrepticus 34).

" The <u>best</u> choose one thing in place of all else, everlasting glory among mortals; but the <u>many</u> are glutted like cattle." (Fr. 29 Clement Strom. V, 59, 5).

As we can see in this last fragment, Heraclitus distinguishes the "**best**" (*άριστοι* : aristoi) from the "**many**" (*πολλοί* : polloi). The "many" are the "sleepers", who as they have not self-consciousness, they are lead by the nose from their desires for sensational pleasures. On the other hand, the "best" have only one desire, which is beyond the sensational pleasures. They only desire the knowledge of the eternal "Logos", and the happiness and glory which arise from this understanding and wisdom.

The achievement of this knowledge requires strenuous efforts and continuous enquiry, and although the outcome compared with the efforts is minimal, the wisdom that we can achieve is precious like a **gold**. It also requires to hope against hope, so as to be able to carry on searching, even though we have no instant success in our efforts. The rehash of teachings (**hay**) panders to those who are content with the accumulation of learnings – which rather leads them to arrogance and self-assertion – but not to the "best".

" **Those who search for gold, dig up a lot of earth and find out a little.**" (Fr. 22 Clement Strom. IV, 4).

" **If one does not expect the unexpected one, will not find it out, since it is not be searched out and is difficult to compass.**" (Fr. 18 Clement Strom. II, 17, 4).

" **An ass would sooner have hay than gold.**" (Fr. 9 Aristotle Nicomachean Ethics 1176 a, 7).

A significant problem for the friend of wisdom can be the **arrogant pride** (*ύβρις* : hubris), since when one has a great deal of knowledge, feels superior to the others and these feelings of haughtiness and self-contained can stop him from further searching out. Therefore, self-knowledge and moderation are significant as opposed to polymathy.

" **Hubris is more to be extinguished than conflagration.**" (Fr. 43 Diogenes Laertius IX, 2).

The assumptions of the matters concerning life and natural laws should be based upon sense-data, and not upon simple beliefs in supernatural. For as we have seen according to Heraclitus, the process of knowledge is continuous and gradual, and the truth of our views must be always confirmed by trial.

" **Let us not make unfounded assumptions about the great issues.**" (**Fr. 47 Diogenes Laertius IX, 73**).

One should not make the same mistakes of the past and forget his aim, for which he started his way of searching. Therefore, the paths of thought that one has followed, he should not forget where they got him at, and repeat the same mistakes.

" **Let us remember the one who forgets where does the road lead.**" (**Fr. 71 Marcus Aurelius IV, 46**).

One should look with a critical eye on the impressions of the environment, and not react mechanically and unconsciously to them, like a 'sleeper', but with full self-awareness.

" **We should not act and speak like those who are asleep.**" (**Fr. 73 Marcus Aurelius IV, 46**).

The views that we adopted in our childhood during our upbringing have solidified within us, and through them we analyze and judge all the everyday events. These points of view prompt us to react mechanically, in other words to speak and act like been asleep. Therefore, we must get rid of these traditional views, which it is true that they serve the "many's" needs of survival, but they do not lead us to the wisdom of the "best".

" **We should not speak and act like children of our parents, or in detail, according to what has been down to us.**" (**Fr. 74 Marcus Aurelius IV, 46**).

Therefore the way to knowledge and wisdom, requires doubting of conventional and traditional values and searching out new ones closer to "Logos", since the word "**going near to**" (*αγχιβασίη*: agchivasie) and "**doubting**" (*αμφισβατείν*: amfisvatein) have the same meaning according to Heraclitus. In this way one can come closer to "Logos".

" *αγχιβασίη*, **Heraclitus.**" (**Fr. 122 Suda Lex.**).

Deep thought and analysis come up against our feeling of insecurity and fear, which do not allow us to examine closely our desires and wrong beliefs about the natural constitution.

40

" The fool loses his courage in every reasoning." (Fr. 87 Plutarch De aud. 41 a).

" The most of the divine matters we cannot realize, due to our mistrust." (Fr. 86 Plutarch Koriol. 38).

This fear of unbiased judgement and independent reasoning arises from our adherence to the common sense, public opinion and whatever flatters the "crowd". This fear forces one to disbelieve even his own personal revelations, since they do not comply with the public opinion, and as a result he is not sure about them. Therefore, for the fear of becoming outsider, one does not dare to conflict with the public opinion. For the deep and unbiased thought leads us inevitably to conflict with the mentality of the herd, therefore courage is necessary. The mentality "what the many desire" is false, since the "many" are "sleepers" but the "best" are only "a few", therefore we should not follow the "many" with their absurdity.

"What reason and mind do they have? They follow the folk singers and have as their master the crowd, without knowing that <the many are bad (κακοί : kakoi) and only the few are good (αγαθοί : agathoi)>." (Fr. 104 Proclus in Alc. I, S 117).

Another obstacle on the way to achieve wisdom is our habits, with which we have to conflict. Our habits arise from the desires, which after continuous repetition become a part of ourselves, become our character, therefore we are dominated by them, and so it is very difficult for us to change them. However, when we succeed in getting out of a habit, due to that change, the part of the soul that was enslaved by the desire (Fr. 85) it is liberated. In this way, when the disturbance of mind stops, then springs up the clarity of perception and thought, free from desire and refreshed, and only afterwards one can be in a position to perceive the unity of Logos.

" It is very tiring to labour at the same things and be dominated by them."

" After having changed it takes a rest." (Fr. 84 b, 84 a, Plotinus Enn. IV 8, 1).

After having overcome these obstacles, the philosopher can achieve the knowledge and understanding of the universal Logos and become wise and "**best**" (*άριστος*). Therefore his worth is equivalent to ten thousands of people (*μύριοι*: myrioi).

" **One man is as ten thousand for me, if he is best."** (Fr. 49 Theodor Prodromus Ep. 1).

The "many", as we have seen **(fr. 17),** cannot realize the law that steers all things (Logos), since they cannot interpret correctly the sense-perceptions through the intellect, therefore they are misled by superficial appearances. For this reason, they interpret everything according to their own disposition, e.g. the corrupt sees everywhere the corruption, the sensual the sensation, the resentful the hatred and so on.

" **Evil witnesses are eyes and ears for men, if they have barbarian (*βαρβάρους*) souls."** (Fr. 107 Sextus adv. Math. VII, 126).

Their attitude towards the wise men is completely hostile, since they cannot understand them, they (the many) throw mud at them, for they judge the wise men's teachings with their own "barbarian souls". Since what the wise men teach, awakens to them the fear of independent thought, they react violently and just like dogs that bark at strangers, they "bark" at them, for of what the wise men teach they are completely ignorant.

" **They do not know how to hear and how to speak to the others."** (Fr. 19 Clement Strom. II, 24).

" **One should better hide his ignorance than to bring it out into the open."** (Fr. 95 Stobaeus Anth. I, 175).

" **Dogs bark at those they do not know."** (Fr. 97 Plutarch An seni resp. 787 c).

The man who possesses knowledge and wisdom understands the motives of the human behaviour, and has a clear perception of the universal law of the eternal change (Logos), therefore he raises to the "divine" level and his actions are in harmony with Logos, namely are "divine". Just as the adult calls the baby "**foolish**" (*νήπιος*: nepios), since it is ignorant and a prey to its desires, in the same way god calls the unconscious and "asleep" people "foolish".

" **Human disposition does not have true judgement, but divine disposition does.**" (Fr. 78 Origen c. Celsum VI, 12).

" **God calls the adult baby** (νήπιος), **just as the adult calls the child.**" (Fr. 79 Origen c. Celsum VI, 12).

Just like monkeys that imitate a man's behaviour, without being able to think, in the same way the wisdom of a man - which is without true judgement and universal knowledge - is simply an imitation of the Logos, the same as art is an imitation of nature.

" **The finest of monkeys is foul put together with a human being.**" (Fr. 82 Plato Greater Hippias 289 a).

" **The wisest of men is seen to be monkey compared to god in wisdom and beauty and everything else.**" (Fr. 83 Plato Greater Hippias 289 b).

The wise man who possesses the knowledge of the Logos, understands its necessity, relies on this law and as a result he gets out of his weakness, and acts in accordance with this constitution, just as the citizen of a state who understands the necessity of the state's law and complies with it. This divine law is much more powerful than the state's laws, since it is sufficient for all the changes that are taking place always all over the universe, for it is eternal. Universal Logos works under certain and strict laws (**Justice**: δίκη, diki) and even the very sun must comply with it. It acts always from expediency, since it serves the purpose of eternal motion and existence of the universe. However, common men cannot understand this, therefore they consider some things in the world to be unjust and some others just.

" **Those who speak with sense must rely on what is common to all, as a city must rely on its law, and with much greater reliance. For all the laws of men are nourished by one law, the divine law; for it has as much power it wishes and is sufficient for all and is still left over.**" (Fr. 114 Stobaeus Anth. III, 1, 179).

" Sun will not overstep his measures; otherwise the Erinyes, ministers of <u>Justice</u>, will find him out." (Fr. 94 Plutarch de exil II, 604 a).

" To god all things are beautiful and good and just, but men have supposed some things to be unjust, others just." (Fr. 102 Porphyrius in Iliadem IV, 4).

" Sea is the most pure and most polluted water; for fish it is drinkable and salutary, but for men it is undrinkable and deleterious." (Fr. 61 Hippolytus Ref. IX, 10, 5).

The wise man realizes the necessity of the Logos, as well as the simple fact that the same thing can be good or evil, in accordance with its use or the species that is referring to. He understands the real meaning of altruism and sacrifice, which must serve higher purpose and be accomplished without personal advantage or self-interest.

" I distinguish two kinds of sacrifice. Those that the completely pure men make, and such seldom one makes, as Heraclitus says, or only a few that can be counted on the fingers. The other sacrifices are material or bodily etc." (Fr. 69 Iamblichus Myst. V 15).

The "awake" is aware of the fact that life and death are interdependent, since death of one species gives life to another, and one sort of energy is transformed into another in this perpetual circle of eternal change.

" Death is what we see when we are awake and sleep what we see when we are asleep." (Fr. 21 Clement Strom. III, 21).

" The name of bow is <life> (βίος: bios) but its work is <death>." (Fr. 48 Etym. Gen. βίος).

" Common is the beginning and the end on the circumference of a circle." (Fr.103 Porphyrius ad Hom. Il. Ξ 200).

" The path up and down is one and the same." (Fr. 60 Hippolytus Ref. IX, 10, 4).

" Upon those that step into the same rivers different and different waters flow... They scatter and ... gather ... come together and flow away ... approach and depart." (Fr. 12

Arius Didymus ap. Eusebium P.E. XV, 20 + Fr. 91 Plutarch de E. 18, 392 b).

Logos and time (*αιών*: aion) are interrelated, since during the eternal time the evident "opposites" are interchanged innumerable times (the one is transformed into the other and vice versa), therefore every moment in every place the "fiery" Logos is manifested in different forms. These evidently different forms are in essence the different appearances of the same driving force of creation, destruction (*εκπύρωσις*) and recreation for the purpose of the eternal preservation of the universe, through this circular interchange. Just like a child that plays different games of draughts by using the same round pieces in every possible combination (infinite).

" **Time (*αιών*) is a child which is playing draughts. The kingdom of a child."** (Fr. 52 Hippolytus Ref. IX, 9).

" **Thunderbolt steers all things."** (Fr. 64 Hippolytus Ref. IX, 10).

" **When the fire comes, it will judge all things and conquer them."** (Fr. 66 Hippolytus Ref. IX, 10).

The soul and the body are bound together with special proportions, and the soul provides us the sensation of the body and the faculty of perception and thinking. The structure of the soul is fine and ethereal and due to this form (warm exhalation) possesses the faculty of sensation, perception and knowledge. When it changes into water (moist soul) loses all these faculties, as we have seen, however the "dry soul" is wisest. In other words movement, sensation and knowledge are the faculties of the soul. The soul experiences the death of the body and the body experiences the death of the soul, which means the one affects the other.

" **Just as the spider stands in the middle of its web and senses immediately if a fly damages a part of it and rushes at this, as it has sensed the break of its thread, in this way the soul of a man when a part of his body is damaged, rushes at there, since it cannot bear the body's damage, with which it is bound together in a certain proportion."** (Fr. 67 a Hisdosus Scholasticus ad Chalcid Plat. Tim. Cod. Paris I 8624).

" Soul is warm exhalation of which everything else is composed." (Fr. 12 Aristotle On the Soul 405 a).

" For souls it is death to become water, for water it is death to become earth; from earth water comes to be and from water soul." (Fr. 36 Clement Strom. VI, 17, 2).

" Immortal mortals, mortal immortals, living their death and dying their life." (Fr. 62 Hippolytus Ref. IX, 10, 6).

However, according to Heraclitus, the virtuous (**slain in war**) and the wise souls (**fr.118**), since are "fiery" and "dry" do not become water, and due to their better fiery proportion, can survive death. Those souls after the death of the body join the cosmic fire (Logos) and become **daimons** (guardian angels), an element that can also be found in Hesiod's Theogony.

" Souls slain in war are purer than those (that perish) in diseases." (Fr. 136 Bodl. Ad Epictetus)

" For better deaths gain better portions according to Heraclitus." (Fr. 25 Clement Strom.IV 49, 3).

" Men's character is his daimon." (Fr. 119 Stobaeus Anth. IV 40, 23).

"To it, being there, they rise up and become guardians, wakefully of living and dead." (Fr. 63 Hippolytus Ref. IX, 10, 6).

The wise man who expresses the wisdom of Logos, goes beyond the conventional meaning of the words, as he speaks about the essence of all things. Therefore he cannot be understood by the "many", since he speaks about eternal values, beyond space and time in a symbolic, laconic and oracular style like Sibyl and Apollo.

" The Sibyl with raving mouth, according to Heraclitus, uttering things mirthless, unadorned and unperfumed, reaches over a thousand years with her voice through the god." (Fr. 92 Plutarch de Pyth. or. 6, 397 a).

" The lord whose oracle is in Delphi (Apollo) neither speaks out nor conceals, but gives a sign." (Fr. 93 Plutarch de Pyth. or. 21, 404 e).

Logos is expressed symbolically, frigidly and unadorned through the meanings of the "opposite" expressions, just like the harmony between the opposite tensions, which exists all over the universe. In this way it corroborates its wisdom.

" **An unapparent harmony** (*αρμονίη*) **is stronger than an apparent one." (Fr. 54 Hippolytus Ref. IX, 9, 5).**

As we said, when there is a total balance between opposite tensions, this ensures the coherence, the tensions are not apparent and the whole complex appears as a stable unity. For the total balance and harmony is never apparent, but is always hidden. Therefore, just as the strong harmony between the opposites, can be found hidden everywhere in nature, in the same way wisdom which the Logos reveals, is hidden within the harmony of the "opposite" expressions of a wise man, since:

" **Nature** (*φύσις*: physis, real constitution) **is accustomed to hide itself." (Fr. 123 Themistius Or. 5, p. 69 d).**

6. Parmenides (540 – 470 BC)

The founder of Eleatics, the philosophical School of the Greek city Elea on the southern coast of Italy, who is known from his saying : **"for the same thing exists for thinking and for being"** (*τό γάρ αυτό νοείν έστιν τε καί είναι*: to gar auto noein estin te kai einai) or else **"thought and being are the same"**.

While Heraclitus, as we have seen, was the initiator of the **"coming to be"** (*γίγνεσθαι*), Parmenides is considered to be the initiator of the **"being"** (*είναι*: einai), which is eternal, unmoved, indestructible and unchangeable. Therefore he was called **"stasiotes"** (*στασιώτης*: from the Greek word *στάσις*, which means immobility), since the main quality of the "being" is its immobility. He is regarded as the founder of Metaphysics and Idealism, and his philosophical thought has influenced many subsequent philosophers, like Socrates and Plato as well as **Descartes (cogito ergo sum).**

He expounded his philosophical conceptions in his hexameter poem " **Way of Truth**", which is considered to have been written by him as a response to his contemporary Heraclitus. In this poem he explains the main principles of his philosophy through allegorical symbols, and expresses his disagreement with Heraclitus' law of the eternal change.

His main doctrine is that the "**being**" (*ἐστιν*: estin), namely what truly and always exists, can be grasped only through **intellect** (*νοὺς*: nous), in other words by **thinking** (*νοείν*), which means the real and the deep thought (reflecting, reasoning, speculating, understanding). On the other hand, the "**not-being**" (*οὐκ ἐστιν*: ouk estin) – namely what temporarily exists, in other words does not exist always and therefore does not really exist – can neither be grasped through the intellect nor can be explained and told.

" **Come now and I will tell you –**
and you must carry my account away with you when
you have heard it -
the only ways of enquiry that exist for thinking;
the one way, that it is and that is impossible for it not
to be,
is the path of Persuasion, for it attends upon the
Truth;
the other, that it is-not and needs must not-be,
that I tell you is a path altogether unthinkable
for you could not know that which is-not (that is
impossible) nor utter it;"

> (**Fr. 2,** Proclus In Tim. I, 345, 18 – Simplicius In Phys. 116, 28).

" **for the same thing exists for thinking and for being.**"
(*τό γάρ αυτό νοείν ἐστιν τε καί είναι*)

> (**Fr. 3, Clement Strom. VI, 23**).

As we saw in the previous verses, Parmenides exhorts us to focus our attention on what always and truly exists, namely the "being", since this is the only truth. Because, if we focus on the transient and passing, then we will be lost and will never know it, since this is not-being, therefore it is in vain to search for the truth in it. The reason is, that what really exists (being), only this we are able to know, while the not-being we are unable to know, even if we try. For we cannot know things through negation (e.g. not-white, not-man etc., if we don't know the "white" or the "man" etc.), since only the being exists. Therefore one should focus on what really *is* and not on what *is not*.

With regards to "thinking" of Parmenides (*νοεῖν*), we could say that he is referring to the **concepts** and **terms,** which are securely and always present to the mind and not the fleeting thoughts, which come and go. Just like for example "Pythagoras", who although is dead and absent, is present to the mind of men as a concept which represents his principles and deeds. Apart from that, concepts just like "Justice", "Good", " Truth" etc. are not perceptible through the senses but only through the intellect. These concepts then, although are referring to something which is absent, exist securely on the man's mind.

> " **But look at things which, though far off**
> **are securely present to the mind;"**
> **(Fr. 4 Clement Strom. V, 15, 5).**

The "being", the objective reality and the only truth, has nothing to do with the seeming and passing material forms, which we perceive through the senses, since they come into being and pass away. But due to our habitual and empirical approach to life, which enables us to face the daily problems of life, we are prompted to pay attention to the changeable forms and as a result we cannot grasp the real and the true, namely the underlying nature of all things (being). Therefore, the attention turned to what we see and hear, and the inquiry about those, since is habitual and mechanical, is aimless. On the other hand, the judgement by reasoning of all the terms and concepts, as well as their strife-encompassed refutation, can lead one to discovering the real immaterial and intelligible entities of the "being".

> " **For never shall be this forcibly maintain that things**
> **that are not are,**
> **but you must hold back your thought from this way of**
> **enquiry**

**nor let habit, born of much experience, force you down
this way
by making you use an aimless eye or an ear and a
tongue full of meaningless sound;
judge by reason the strife-encompassed refutation
spoken by me."**
(Fr. 7 Sextus Adv. Math. VII, 114).

In this last verse, as we can see, Parmenides prompts us to focus our attention on the terms, and through judgement by reason and critical analysis, to discover the true concepts of the "being".

From all the previous mentioned, we can draw a conclusion with regards to Parmenides' method of thought. First of all, through **abstraction**, he tries to approach, not the apparent and the partial, but the whole, the eternally constant and unchangeable, which is the underlying nature of the apparent, namely the "being". This we can only perceive through the intellect (*νούς*), since is the cause of thinking and knowledge. His main assumption and presupposition then for the "being" is the fr. 3, which means "**the being is what can be grasped through the real thinking**". This assumption that Parmenides did not prove, as we are going to see, the sophist Gorgias used it to prove his "agnosticism".

After taking this assumption for granted, Parmenides proceeds to the terms and concepts which are securely and always present to the mind, namely the intelligible and eternal "Forms", which Plato also adopted as we are going to see. For the "being" is what always exists, otherwise if it was changeable and destructible, it would have been called "not-being". His second acceptance then, is that the "being" always exists and therefore its qualities are eternal, as well as the thoughts and speculations about it. In order to reach these eternal "Forms" of the "being", one must judge by reason all the concepts – by rejecting the passing and changeable ones – and through their strife-encompassed refutation to get by **abstraction** and **deduction** to the real and true concepts and entities, which are the attributes of the eternal "being". In this way one can know it and grasp the eternal truth. This

abstraction and **deductive revelation of truth** is the method of thinking of Parmenides, which influenced later the method of **Socrates** (*ἔλεγχος:* **elenchus**), as well as the **dialectic** of Plato.

As Parmenides goes on in his poem, he distinguishes the "not-being" from the "being", since the "being" lies behind the apparent and perishable material forms. For the "**being**" (*εόν*:eon) sometimes scatters everywhere with order and creates the different material forms of the universe, and sometimes draws together, without being separated from itself. With this sentence Parmenides initiates the **multiplicity** of the **One** which can also be **many** at the same time, since every part gets a share from the whole, namely the "being".

> " **But look at things which, though far off, are securely**
> **present to the mind; for you will not cut off for**
> **yourself what is from holding to what is,**
> **neither scattering everywhere in every way**
> **in order nor drawing together.**"
> **(Fr. 4 Clement Strom. V, 15, 5).**

As Parmenides returns to the same point, namely to focus our attention on the "being", he is referring to the thought of the **ordinary mortals** (*βροτοί*: brotoi), which is characterized by helplessness and dissent, since the "mortals" confuse the "being" with the "not-being". Therefore their thought is wandering and they themselves are unable to know the truth. At this point of his poem he blames the followers of "bipolar thought" of Heraclitus (*ἄκριτα φύλα*: akrita phyla, **undiscriminating hordes**), namely the "strife between the opposites", since they regard that everything in the universe follows backward turning.

> " **It is a common point from which I start;**
> **for there again and again I shall return.**"
> **(Fr. 5** Proclus in Parm. I p. 708, 16).
> " **What is there to be said and thought needs must be:**
> **for it is there for being, but nothing is not**
> **I bid you ponder that, for this is the first way of**
> **enquiry**
> **from which I hold you back, but then from that**

on which mortals wandering knowing nothing,
two-headed; for helplessness guides the wandering thought
in their breasts, and they are carried along,
deaf and blind at once, dazed, undiscriminating hordes,
who believe that to be and not to be are the same and not the same;
and the path taken by them all is backward-turning."
(Fr. 6 Simplicius in Phys. 86, 27-8, 117, 4-13).

As Parmenides proceeds with his poem unfolds all the qualities of the "**being**" (*εόν*: eon). So he describes it as **uncreated** (*αγένητον*: ageneton), **imperishable** (*ανώλεθρον*: anolethron), **of a single kind** (*μουνογενές*: mounogenes), **unshaken** (*ατρεμές*: atremes) and **perfect** (*τέλειον*: teleion).

" There still remains just one account of a way that it is.
On this way there are many signs that being <u>uncreated</u> and <u>imperishable</u> it is, whole and of a <u>single kind</u>
and <u>unshaken</u> and <u>perfect</u>."
(Fr. 8, 1-4 Simplicius in Phys. 78, 5, 145, 1).

First of all it is uncreated because it existed and will exist forever. For if once was created, this means that there was a time that it did not exist, and therefore some day it would have been perished. If it had derived from something else, this must have been the "not-being", which is impossible, since the "being" cannot be derived from the "not-being". Apart from that, if it is perishable it follows that it will be perished one day, which means that it will turn into "not-being", which is also impossible, since the "being" cannot change into "not-being". "Justice" holds the "being" fast and does not allow it to perish. At this point Parmenides introduces the term of "**Justice**" (*Δίκη*: deke), a supernatural and universal law which is a "principle" of the "being" and is responsible for the eternal preservation of the "being".

" It never was nor will be, since it is now, all together one,
continuous. For what birth will you seek for it?

How and where did it grow? I shall not allow you to say
nor to think from not being; for it is not to be said
nor thought that it is not; and what need would have driven it
later than earlier, beginning from the nothing to grow?
This must be either be completely or not at all.
Nor will the force of conviction allow anything besides it
to come to be ever from not-being. Therefore Justice has never
loosed her fetters to allow it to come to be or to perish, but holds it fast.
And the decision about these things lies in this:
it is or it is not.
But it has in fact been decided, as is necessary,
to leave the one way unthought and nameless (for it is no true way),
but the other way is and is genuine.
And how could what is be in the future? How could it come to be?
For if it came into being, it is not;
nor is it if it is ever going to be in the future.
Thus coming to be is extinguished and perishing
 unheard of."
        (Fr. 8, 5-21 Simplicius in Phys. 78, 5, 145, 5).

As he goes on with the qualities of the "being", Parmenides declares that it is not divisible, is continuous and all alike. Because if there was a void between the "being" and since the void is "not-being", then it would have been separated the "being" from itself. With this argument Parmenides rejects the concept of void, since this is not being. And as there is not void between the "being", follows that it is continuous and all alike, for if it was thinner in some parts, it would have been penetrated by the "not-being". As we can realize, through his **reductio ad absurdum,** proceeds gradually to the attributes of the "being", one by one.

" **Nor is it divisible, since it is all alike**

nor is there more here and less there,
which would prevent it from cleaving together.
So it is all continuous; for what is draws near to what
is."

    (Fr. 8, 22-25 Simplicius in Phys. 144, 29).

As he goes on with the qualities of the "being", he defines it as motionless within its limits. Since each motion is defined in relation with space and time, and the "being" remains the same through the time, without beginning and end, then it follows that it is motionless with regard to space and time. The "**strong Necessity**" (*κρατερή Ανάγκη*: kratere Anange), another "principle" of the "being", which Parmenides introduces, holds it firm and motionless within the limits of the absolute time and space, since everything is motionless in absolute terms. For **space** and **time** are relative terms, therefore in absolute terms the "being" is **motionless**. On the other hand, since Parmenides rejects the "**void**" as a term, it is impossible for one part of the "being" to approach or go away from another part of it, as everything is defined as a unity, as a continuous "being", without void between. Therefore, it makes no sense that the "being" moves within the "being", since all things are a continuous unity. Only if one assumes that exists the void, then the motion makes sense, something that Democritus introduced, as we are going to see.

    " But changeless within the limits of great bonds it
exists,
without beginning or ceasing, since coming to be and
perishing
have wandered very far away, and true conviction has
thrust them off.
Remaining the same and in the same place it lies on its
own
and thus fixed it will remain. For strong Necessity
holds it
within the bonds of a limit, which keeps it on every
side."

    (Fr. 8, 26-31 Simplicius in Phys. 145, 27).

The "being" is self-sufficient and perfect - for if it were not it would be deficient in everything - just as the thoughts that derive from it, since the "being" is the cause of thoughts which are perfect and true. While the thoughts with regard to the change and "coming to be" are deficient, as they refer to something deficient and imperfect, and therefore whatever is deficient needs to change in order to be completed.

" **Therefore it is right that what is should not be imperfect,**

for it is not deficient – if it were it be deficient in everything.

The same thing is there to be thought, and is <u>why there is thought</u>.

For you will not find thinking without what is, in all that has been said.

For there neither is nor will be anything else besides what is,

since <u>Fate</u> fattered it to be whole and changeless."

(**Fr. 8, 32-38** Simplicius in Phys. 146, 5).

As we see in the last verse, Parmenides introduces the third "principle" of the "being", namely the "**Fate**" (*Moíρα*: moira) which keeps it motionless, self-sufficient and perfect. This "principle" determines in advance everything (**determinism**) in the universe and interferes with all the changes in order to keep the universal law perfect, self-sufficient and imperishable. Therefore these three "principles" (**Justice, Necessity and Fate**) are related with one another, since all of them contribute to the eternal existence of the perfect universal law and keep the balance in the universe. These three principles are eternal, imperishable and changeless, since are the attributes of the "being", are the real and true **thoughts** (*νοεῖν*), are the "**being**" (*εἶναι*) itself.

As he goes on, Parmenides refers to the thought of the common people who are confused, since they cannot distinguish the "being" from "not-being", and believe that the "being" moves, changes and perishes, while it is changeless, motionless and imperishable. According to him it is perfect within its limits, therefore it has the shape of the perfect form, namely the well-rounded "**sphere**" (σφαίρης: spheres) which is equally balanced from the centre in every direction.

> "**Therefore it has been named all the names,**
> **which mortals have laid down believing them to be true –**
> **coming to be and perishing, being and not-being,**
> **changing place and altering in bright colour. But since there is**
> **a furthest limit, it is perfected like the bulk of the well-rounded sphere,**
> **from the centre equally balanced in every direction.**"
> (Fr. 8, 38-44 Simplicius in Phys. 146, 5).

Parmenides specifies the shape of the "being", which must be a sphere in order to be equally balanced and perfect, a view which derives from the Pythagorean belief about the "being", however his difference is that he drew this conclusion through his deductive reasoning. And as he continues the description of the "being" he returns to the initial point, namely that it is continuous and of a single kind, otherwise if it were not, it would have been penetrated and cut off from itself.

> "**For it needs must not be somewhat more or**
> **somewhat less**
> **here or there. For neither is it non-existent in such a way**
> **that there would be more being here, less there, since it is inviolate;**
> **for being equal to itself on every side, it lies uniformly within its limits.**"
> (Fr. 8, 44-49 Simplicius in Phys. 146, 5).

As he goes on Parmenides, is referring again to the views of the common people about the "being", who, since are deceived by the false senses, name the "being" and the "coming to be" as one and the same, while the latter they should not name at all. The first one is the "**aitherial flame of fire**" (αιθέριον πύρ: aitherion pyr), which is gentle and very light and is the "being" itself, the knowledge and wisdom. The other one is the "**dark night**" (νύκτα αδαής: nekta adaes), dense and heavy, which is the changeable, the ignorance and illusion itself. Thus, according to him, everything is composed of both light and night, each one equal and not mixed with the other.

> " For they made up their minds to name two forms
> which they needs must not name so much as one –
> that is where they have gone astray – and distinguished them
> as opposite in the appearance and assigned to them signs
> different one from the other – to one the aitherial
> flame of fire, gentle and very light,
> in every direction identical with itself,
> but not with the other; and the other too is in itself just the opposite,
> dark night, dense in appearance and heavy.
> The whole ordering of these I tell you, as it seems fitting,
> for so no thought of mortal men shall ever outstrip you."

> (**Fr. 8, 53-61** Simplicius in Phys. 38, 28).

> " But because all things have been named light and night,
> and things corresponding to their power have been assigned
> to this and that, <u>all is full of light and of obscure night</u> at once,
> both equal, since neither has any share of nothing."

> (fr. 9 Simplicius in Phys. 180, 8).

As the form of the "being" takes shape in Parmenides' poem, we can conclude that it is a well-rounded sphere, where there is in equal proportion light and dark, since "all is full, of light and night". Particularly Parmenides considers that the "being" is compounded of rings wound one around the other within the sphere. The one is full of light and the other is full of darkness, and between them are mixed rings. In the middlemost of the mixed rings is the **goddess** that steers all things (primary cause of movement), namely the "principles" of universal law (Justice, Necessity, Fate), which governs the "coming to be", through the attraction of the opposites, that is to say the mingling of the male with the female principle.

" Parmenides said that there were rings wound one around the other, one formed of the rare, the other of the dense; and that there were others between these compounded of light and darkness... The middlemost of the mixed rings is the primary cause of movement and of coming into being for them all, and he calls it the goddess that steers all, the holder of the keys, Justice and Necessity." (Fr. 37 Aetius II, 7, 1).

" The narrower rings are filled with unmixed fire,
those next to them with night, but into them a share of flame is injected;
and in the midst of them is the goddess who steers all things;
for she governs the hateful birth and mingling of all things,
sending female to mix with male, and again conversely the male with the more feminine."

(Fr. 12 Simplicius in Phys. 39, 14 and 31, 13).

In the midst ring then, is the **goddess** ($\delta\alpha\iota\mu\omega\nu$: daimon) who steers all things and governs the "**hateful birth**" ($\sigma\tau\upsilon\gamma\epsilon\rho\sigma\iota\sigma$ $\tau\acute{o}\kappa\sigma\upsilon$: stygeroio tokou), a characterization of birth which along with the fire, the " **hearth of the world**" ($\epsilon\sigma\tau\acute{\iota}\alpha$: hestia), as a centre of the universe, it reveals the influence of **Orphic** and **Pythagorean** beliefs upon Parmenides' thought.

Apart from that, we can realize Parmenides' notion concerning the **opposite principles**. This means that the stronger the one opposite becomes the more resistance meets from its opposite. In other words, the increase of strength of the one opposite, instead of extinguishing the other, provokes it to reveal more strength, so as to keep the balance (conversely the male with the more feminine). As for Parmenides' goddess, we could compare her to goddess Aphrodite of Greek Mythology who prompted the mixing of male with female.

" The goddess .. <first of all gods she invented Eros> and < she sends the souls sometimes from light to darkness

and sometimes the reverse.>" (Fr. 13 Simplicius in Phys. 39, 18).

As we can see, the first creature of Parmenides' goddess is Eros, namely the impulse and tendency of the opposite principles (male – female) to mingle with one another, an element that we find also in Hesiod's Theogony concerning Eros, who was the offspring of Aphrodite.

Apart from that, we can see that Parmenides' goddess (daimon) sends the souls from the light to darkness and vice versa, which means that the souls are parts of the "being", since they are indestructible and immortal, and they interchange by coming and going from light to darkness. The symbol of **light**, according to some interpreters, is the "**Being**" itself, **Knowledge**, **Wisdom** and **Truth**, namely the soul which is conscious of itself. On the other hand, **darkness** is referring to **Oblivion, Illusion** and **Ignorance**, that the souls fall into, as they are "imprisoned" in the human body and the deceptive world of the five senses. Therefore, the so-called "death" is nothing but a transition from one state of existence to another, since everything is consisted of light and darkness and the immortal soul goes from one phase of existence to the other. Another element, which reveals the influence of Orphic and Pythagorean mysticism upon Parmenides' thought, concerning the state of darkness –death of the soul – when the soul is imprisoned in the human body (grave of the soul).

As we saw in fr. 4 and 7, one should focus his attention on the eternal "forms" of the "being" and not on the deceptive reality of the senses. This means that one should guide his mind, and therefore his soul, from the darkness – oblivion, illusion and ignorance of the senses – to the light of the knowledge through the intellect, which liberates the soul from the prison of the body and the senses, just like the liberated soul leaves the body when one dies. This symbolical "death" of the soul is its release, since, when one averts his intellect from the deceptive appearances of the "not-being",- where due to the habit is attached - and leads it to the "being", namely the eternal truth and reality, releases his soul from its illusion and ignorance.

With regard to perception and knowledge, according to Parmenides, they depend on the **mixture** (*κράσιν* : krasin) of the **light** and **darkness** in the corpse and the limbs. Since everything is composed of light and darkness, in that way the human body is composed of the same mixture, therefore its perception through the senses is of like by like, namely the dark part perceives the dark part of the reality and the light part the light one. In the same way the perception of the truth through the intellect depends on the mixture of light and darkness of one's mind. The **light** part of the mind is the hot and the pure, which are the **Knowledge,** the **Truth** and the "**Being**". The **dark** part is the cold night, the **Oblivion**, the **Illusion** the **Ignorance,** the "**coming to be**" The real reasoning and reflecting then is the predominance of the light over the darkness in this mixture of one's mind.

" **As is at any moment the <u>mixture</u> of the wandering limbs,**
so intellect is present to men; for that which thinks
is the same, namely the substance of their limbs,
in each and all men;
<u>for what preponderates is thought</u>.
(Fr. 16 Aristotle, Metaphysics IV, 5, 1009 b 21).

" **The majority about general views about sensation are two: some make it of like by like, others of opposite by opposite. Parmenides, Empedocles and Plato say it is of like by like, the followers of Heraclitus and Anaxagoras of opposite by opposite.. Parmenides gave no clear definition at all, but said only that there were two elements, and that knowledge depends on the excess of one or the other. Thought varies according to whether the hot or the cold prevails, but that which is due to the hot is better and purer."**
(Fr. 46 Theophrastus De Sensu I ff).

From the last fragment of Theophrastus we can realize what Parmenides means when he refers to real thinking (*νοείν*), for when the light prevails over the darkness in one's mind, he comes closer to the "being". However, when the darkness prevails, then comes the state of oblivion, illusion, sleep and

60

death. When both are in equal proportion one can simply perceive the sensual reality. Therefore, he prompts us to the real thinking and reflecting, through the strict control of our mind and the focus of our attention on the eternal "forms" of the "being", in order to achieve the predominance of the light in our mind and grasp the truth of the "being".

To sum up, we could say that Parmenides by using only his judgement and reasoning (deduction) reached the Metaphysics, namely the discovery of the supernatural and divine "Being", therefore he is considered to be the founder of Metaphysics. For as we have seen, according to him, the true thinking and reflecting is identical to the "being".

"τό γάρ αυτό νοείν έστιν τε καί είναι." (for the same thing exists for thinking and for being).

7. Empedocles (495 – 434 BC)

Empedocles of Acragas (Sicily) was another representative of Eleatics, as well as a **Pluralist** like Anaxagoras and Democritus. He initiated more particularly the two opposite principles, which are in continuous struggling, in order to justify the continuous **coming to be** (*γίγνεσθαι*: gignesthai) and passing away. We are referring to **Love** (*φιλότης*: philotes) and **Strife** (*νείκος*: neikos).

Apart from that, he raised the question of the **four elements** (*ριζώματα*: rezomata, roots), namely **earth, water, air** and **fire**, which have been introduced at first by the Milesians. However, Empedocles regarded the elements to be indestructible and eternal, and that all things have been created by the combination of these four "**roots**".

The basic principle of his philosophy consists in the existence of the four elements, which are in the first place ungenerated, indestructible, imperishable and unchangeable. All things have been made by their association with one another, which means that each thing is composed of these four elements in different proportions among them. Therefore, there is no coming to be and passing away, but only association and dissociation of the four elements.

The impulse that drives them to come together and to be combined in varying proportions, and as a result to coming to be, is **Love** (*φιλότης*). On the other hand, the cosmic power which forces them to separation and consequently to passing away, is **Strife** (*νεῖκος*). All changes that are taking place in the universe consist in the combination and separation of the four elements, as well as of the primary combinations of them, namely the qualities: hot, cold, wet and dry. This continuous interchange of combination and separation is eternal, and generates the perpetual motion of creation and destruction of the various forms, which come into being and pass away in the universe. However, during this procedure the four elements remain imperishable, indestructible and changeless, and what comes into being and passes away is only their mixtures, namely the physical forms and structures.

All the above mentioned changes are taking place in the **Sphere** (*σφαῖρος*: spheros), similar to Parmenides supernatural being, which is ungenerated, it remains imperishable, changeless, continuous and is perfect.

Just as his predecessor Parmenides, Empedocles sets out his views in his hexameter poem "**On the Nature**" (*περί φύσεως*: peri physeos), in Ionian dialect just like Homer.

The poem is addressed to his disciple Pausanias, to whom he announces that he is going to reveal the truth, which the common "mortals" cannot grasp. Since on the one hand the senses which are spread through the body are weak, and on the other hand the common people are busy with the daily cares, therefore their thoughts are wandering in wrong paths, and as a result they form subjective and wrong opinions about life and truth. On the other hand, only through reflection and understanding he (Pausanias) could grasp the truth of his wisdom.

" And you Pausanias, son of the wise Anchites hear me.
Narrow are the powers that are spread through the body,

**and many are the miseries that burst in, blunting
thought.
Men behold in their span but a little part of life,
then swift to die, are carried off and fly away like a
smoke,
persuaded of one thing only, that which each has
chanced on
as they are driven every way; who then boasts
that he has found the whole? Not so are these things
to be seen or to be heard by men,
or grasped by understanding.
You then, since you have turned aside to this place,
shall learn: no further can mortal wit reach.**
**(Fr. 1 Diogenes Laertius VIII 60, Fr. 2 Sextus, Adv.
Math. VII 123).**

Afterwards Empedocles asks from Pausanias to approach the knowledge, which will be revealed to him, with respect and modesty, and not to let his conceit and ambition to run away with him, and pursue honour and fame, due to the wisdom that he will acquire.

As he goes on with regard to the senses, he points out that each sense reveals a small part of the truth, therefore he should not regard one sense as superior to the others. All the senses and the parts of the body (limbs) are the channels through which the truth enters a man, therefore they give us a partial perception of the reality and truth. One must unify these partial perceptions through the intellect in order to grasp the truth as a unity, and this method Empedocles promises to reveal to his disciple.

**" But come, consider with all your power how each
thing is manifest
neither holding sight in greater trust as compared
with hearing
not loud-sounding hearing above the clear evidence
of your tongue,
nor withhold your trust from any of the other limbs,
wheresoever there is a path for understanding, but
think (νόει)**

on each thing in the way by which it is manifest."
(Fr. 3 line 9, Sextus adv. Math. VII, 125).

Then he returns to the mentality of the **common people**
(*κακοίς* : kakois, wicked), and says that they cannot trust their
perception of truth which enters through the channels of the
body, namely they cannot compose the partial data of the
senses, and perceive the reality and truth as a whole. On the
other hand, Empedocles with the help of his Muse can
compose all these partial perceptions and grasp the truth as a
unity. For the truth when enters the body is dispersed into
partial sense perceptions. However, Empedocles' Muse
inspires him and guides him to the perception of **Unity** by
composing all these partial perceptions. With this fragment
Empedocles introduces his concept of **intellect** (*νούς*: nous), a
faculty that the common people do not possess, since they
cannot compose the partial perceptions and possess
understanding of truth, and consequently grasp the unity.
According to Empedocles, as we can realize, the reasoning
and understanding proceeds from the parts to the whole
(**induction**).

" **The wicked do not trust the true things, but**
as the infallible words of my Muse reveals to me
know the truth that has been broken to parts inside
you."
(**Fr.5 Clement Strom. VI, 18, 4**).

Afterwards Empedocles asks from his disciple to keep
hermetically sealed, the mysteries which he is going to reveal
to him. At this point Empedocles unlike Parmenides calls for
discretion and secrecy, just like the Pythagorean and Orphic
mysticism.

" **Keep these to yourself, in your silent thoughts.**"
(**Fr.5 Plutarch Symp. Probl. VIII, 8, 1 728 e**).

Then he introduces the four elements (roots) from which all
things are composed. Each element is corresponding to a
certain god of Greek Antiquity, namely the fire to Zeus, air to
Hera, water to Nestis and earth to Aidoneus (Hades).

" **Hear first the four roots of all things;**
shining Zeus, life-bringing Hera, Aidoneus

and Nestis who with her tears waters mortal
springs."
(Fr.6 Aetius I, 3, 20).

What follows then is the most important section of the
poem, where Empedocles presents the principal doctrines of
his philosophy concerning the **coming to be** (*γένεσις*: genesis)
and **passing away** (*απόλειψις*: apoleipsis). Double is the
procedure of birth of mortal things, as he says, since the one
comes into being from all things through the **coming together**
(*σύνοδος*: synodos), and on the other hand, through the
scattering (*δρυφθείσα*: dryftheisa) of the one all things are
separated and come into being. Therefore the coming to be
and passing away of the mortal things, is nothing but this
ceaseless and continuous interchange of coming together and
separation of the four elements.

" **A twofold tale I shall tell: at one time they grew to
be one alone
out of many, at another again they grew apart to be
many out of one.
Double is the birth of mortal things and double is
their failing;
for the one is brought to birth and destroyed by the
coming together
of all things, the other is nurtured and flies apart
as they grow apart again.
And these things never cease their continual
interchange."**
(Fr.17 Simplicius in Phys. 158, 1, 1-6).

The cosmic forces (principles), which preserve this
ceaseless interchange of coming together and scattering, are
"**Love**" (*φιλότης*: philotes) and "**Strife**" (*νεῖκος*: neikos).
Under the influence of "love" all things come together into
one, and under the influence of "strife" the one is scattered
into many. This eternal and cyclic interchange results in the
coming to be and passing away in the universe, therefore all
things have **no lasting life** (*ἔμπεδος αιών*: empedos aion).
Since this cyclic motion is repeated always, in the same way,
therefore with reference to the cycle, we can regard these

elements as changeless and **motionless in the cycle** (*ακίνητα κατά κύκλον*: akineta kata kyklon), for there is no beginning and end in a cycle, as whatever is being moved periodically, it returns always to the starting point. So, when Empedocles says that the four elements remain motionless in the cycle, he probably means that they are indestructible, imperishable and unchangeable, since the word **motion** (*κίνησις* kinesis) in a wider sense in the Ancient Greek language means corruption, destruction, alteration.

> " Now through <u>Love</u> all coming together into one,
> now again each carried apart by the hatred of <u>Strife</u>.
> So insofar as they have learned to grow one from many,
> and again as the one grows apart grow many,
> thus far they do come into being and have no stable life;
> but insofar as they never cease their continual interchange,
> thus far they exist always motionless in the cycle.
> But come hear my words, for learning increases wisdom.
> I said before in declaring the limits of my words,
> I shall tell a twofold tale: at one time they grew to be one alone out of many,
> at another they grew apart to be many out of one,
> <u>fire</u> and <u>water</u> and <u>earth</u> and the immense height of <u>air</u>."
>   **(Fr.17 Simplicius in Phys. 158, 7-18).**

Apart from the four elements and distinguished from them is the dreadful "strife", which is equally balanced, namely equivalent and proportional to their quantity. On the other hand, among them is "love", which is perfect and equally balanced. Her existence one cannot perceive through the senses (eyes dazed), but through the intellect, since the intellect enables one to unify all the partial sense perceptions and grasp the truth, therefore Empedocles' disciple must contemplate "love" with his intellect. "Love" is the motive of kind thoughts and deeds of mutual help among men, as well as of joy, love and affection, therefore it is called "**Joy**" (*Γηθοσύνη*: Gethosyne) and "**Aphrodite**" (*Αφροδίτη*). However, none of the mortals has ever realized that "love" is among the four elements and exhorts them to come together, and as a result all things come into being. Therefore, he calls upon his disciple to listen to his speech, because his words comprise the truth, since the unity of all the sense perceptions through the intellect, is undeceitful. At this point Empedocles, as we can see, disagrees with his predecessor Parmenides, who as we saw in fragment 8, he regards the views based upon the sense perceptions as deceitful.

> " **And cursed Strife apart from them, equal in every direction,**
> **and Love among them equal in length and breadth.**
> **Her you must contemplate with your mind and sit with eyes dazed;**
> **she it is who is thought innate even in mortal limbs,**
> **because of her they think friendly thoughts**
> **and accomplish harmonious deeds,**
> **calling her Joy by name and Aphrodite.**
> **She is perceived by no mortal man as she circles among them;**
> **but you must listen to the undeceitful ordering of my discourse."**
> **(Fr.17 Simplicius in Phys. 158, 19-26).**

As Empedocles goes on with reference to the four elements, he says that they are of like age, and none of them has been created before the others, and that they are equal in quantity, namely none is more than the others. However, their nature and their qualities are different, for example the earth is heavier, or the air extends to the vast height, as we saw, therefore each one prevails in different parts of the universe as the time comes around. None of them is perishable, otherwise it would have perished by now. Furthermore, nothing can be increased from the whole, since there is no source whence it could have come. And if a part of this all had perished, there is no place that it could have gone, since there is **no void** (*ουδέν έρημον*: ouden heremon). As we can realize, at this

point Empedocles shares Parmenides' view concerning the
"**being**", that it is continuous, imperishable and without void
(Fr.8).

To sum up, these four elements come together and form
different mixtures, and in accordance to their proportions in
each mixture, come into being the various material forms of
the universe. However, throughout this eternal interchange the
four elements remain indestructible and imperishable.

> " **All these are equal and coeval, but each has a**
> **different prerogative**
> **and each its own character, and they prevail in turn**
> **as time comes round. And besides them nothing**
> **further**
> **comes into being nor does anything pass. How could**
> **it in fact**
> **be utterly destroyed, since nothing is empty of**
> **these?**
> **For only if they were continually perishing would**
> **they**
> **no longer exist. And what could increase this all?**
> **Whence could it have come? No, there are just these,**
> **but running through one another, they become**
> **different things at different time,**
> **and yet ever and always the same.**"
> **(Fr.17 Simplicius in Phys. 158, 13, 26-35).**

As he goes on, Empedocles repeats Parmenides' view that
nothing can come to be from what is "not-being", as well as
that the "being" cannot result in the "not-being". The
difference is that Empedocles means by the "being", the
whole of the four elements, which remain imperishable,
throughout their continuous interchange.

> " **For it is impossible for anything to come to be**
> **from what is not,**
> **and it cannot be brought or heard of that what**
> **should be**
> **utterly destroyed; for wherever one may ever set,**
> **there it always be.**"
> **(Fr.12 Aristotle M.X.G. 2, 975 b 1).**

68

Therefore, one cannot speak about birth and death of the mortal things, since they neither come from the "not-being" nor result in that. What really occurs is, on the one hand the "mingling" (*μίξις*: mixes) and the "interchange" (*διάλλαξις*: diallaxis) of the four elements, which the mortals call **birth**, and on the other hand their "separation" (*αποκρινθώσι*: apocrinthosi) from the mixture, which is called **death** by them. And as the "roots" are mixed, come into being the races of animals or of plants or of the very men, and this event the people call it birth, while when the "roots" are separated from these mixtures, they call it death.

" Another thing I will tell you:
of all mortal things none has birth,
nor any end in accursed death, but only <u>mingling</u>
and <u>interchange</u> of what is mingled –
<u>birth</u> is the name given to these by men."
(Fr.8 Plutarch adv. Colotem 1111 f).
" And when they (the roots) are mixed in the form of a man
and come to the air, or in the form of the race of wild beasts
or of plants or of birds, then they say that this comes into being;
but when they are separated, they call this wretched faith;
they do not name them as is right, but I myself comply with custom."
(Fr.9 Plutarch adv. Colotem 1113 a-b).

Since, on the one hand the four "roots" are imperishable and indestructible, on the other hand the cosmic forces of "love" and "strife" always exist (eternal), it follows that the perpetual cycle of mingling and separation of the four elements will be eternal. Therefore, a wise man can realize that the common knowledge of life and death is wrong, since through the mingling and interchange of the "roots" the physical forms come into being, and due to their proportions in the mixture, we perceive the pleasant and unpleasant things in life. Apart from that, after their separation from the mixture all these forms are disappeared, and what remains truly is only the four elements.

> **" A man wise in such matters would not surmise in his mind**
> **that while they live what they call life, so long do they exist,**
> **and good and ill befall them, but that before they were formed**
> **as mortals and once they are dissolved, they do not exist at all."**
> **(Fr.15 Plutarch adv. Colotem 1113 d).**

Afterwards Empedocles applies his doctrine to living compounds, by referring to trees, men, women, beasts, birds and fish. Due to "love" the four immortal elements come together, and as a result the living creatures come into being. However due to "strife" they are separated and all the forms are dissolved. And everything assumes its form in accordance with the proportions of the elements in the mixture.

> **" But come look upon the witness to this former discourse**
> **of mine, should beauty have been lacking in it earlier:**
> **the sun to see and dazzling all over; all the immortals**
> **that are bathed in heat and brilliant rays; rain in all things**
> **dark and chill; and from the earth pour forth things rooted**
> **and solid. In Anger all are of different forms and separate,**
> **but in Love come together and are desired by each other.**
> **From them comes all that was and is and will be in the future-**
> **trees have sprang up and men and women, and beasts**
> **and birds and water-bred fish, and long-lived gods too,**

**highest in honour. For there are just these,
but running through each other they assume
different appearances;
so much does mixture changes them."
(Fr.21 Simplicius in Phys. 159, 13).**

Then Empedocles proceeds to the description of the eternal and supernatural Being, which is a rounded **sphere** (*σφαῖρος*: spheros), similar to Parmenides' sphere, however Empedocles uses a masculine name for describing it, in order to define its divinity. This sphere is held fast, is well rounded, unmoved, self-sufficient, perfect and rejoices its joyous solitude. Under the influence of "**Love**" it is harmonious and no limbs can be distinguished, since everything is harmonized in a perfect balance and therefore it is equal to itself.

**" No twin branches spring from its back, it has no
feet,
no nimble knees, no fertile part, but it was a Sphere,
and is equal to itself."
(Fr.29 Hippolytus Ref. VII 29, 13).**

**" Eudemus understands the immobility to apply to the
Sphere in the supremacy of Love when all things are
combined:
" There neither are the swift limbs of the sun, thus it
is held
in the close obscurity of Harmonia, a rounded
sphere rejoicing in its joyous solitude."
(Fr.28 Simplicius in Phys. 1183, 28).**

However, when "**Strife**" begins to win supremacy, then starts the movement, and as a consequence starts the timing, since the time is connected to the movement. Then the limbs begin to spring and to be distinguished, which so far were very well harmonized. This signifies the transfer of supremacy from "love" to "strife", due to the necessity and the mutual commitment (oath) between the two cosmic forces, which interchange their dominance over the universe.

**" But when great Strife had grown strong in the
limbs,
and sprang to its prerogatives as the time was**

fulfilled
which is marked for them by a broad oath."
(Fr.30 Aristotle, Metaphysics B 4, 1000 b 12).
Empedocles describes this interchange of the dominance of
the two cosmic forces as a struggle, which results in a rotation
within the sphere in the form of a **vortex**. When "strife" had
reached the zenith of its power and separated the roots, then
"love" began to advance from the centre of the cosmic
whirlpool, and "strife" was exiled outermost to the limits of
the circle. And as "love" was advancing from the centre of the
cycle to the periphery, just like a wave of light with gentle and
creative impulse, transformed the immortal roots into mortal
compounds and creatures. In this way came into being all the
countless tribes of the mortal things. And as "love" expanded
from the centre to the outer limits, "strife" retired to the
outermost.

" But I shall turn back again to the path of song I
traced before,
as I draw off one discourse after another - to that
path.
When Strife reached the lowest depth of the whirl,
and when Love comes to be in the middle of the
vortex,
there it is that all these things come together to be
one only,
not suddenly, but combining from different
directions at will.
And as they mingled countless tribes of mortal
things
poured forth; but many remained unmixed – all
those
that strife held back from above, for it yet not
retired
blamelessly to the furthest limits of the circle,
but in some of the limbs it remained while from
others
it had withdrawn. As much as it was always running
ahead

**to escape, so much was it always pursued by a gentle
immortal impulse of blameless Love. Then
straightway
those things grew mortal that before had learned
to be immortal, and those that were unmixed before
became mixed as they exchanged their paths. And as
they
mingled countless tribes of mortal things, fitted with
forms
of all kinds, a wonder to look upon."
(Fr.35 Simplicius, de Caelo 529, 1, in Phys 32, 13).**

After this cosmological description Empedocles proceeds and describes his Zoogony, by applying the same doctrine, and holds that the first generations of animals and plants were not complete, but consisted of separate limbs not joined together, as the four roots were mingled accidentally. After that period of **evolution** followed a period, when came into being monsters e.g. with two heads, ox-headed men, etc. Finally, in the last stage of evolution came into being the complete creatures of our present world. In each kind there is a different proportion of the four elements, for example in bones there are eight parts of earth, two parts of water and four parts of fire. However, in the blood the four elements have equal proportions, and therefore arose from this all the forms of flesh.

**" And earth chanced in about equal quantity upon
these,
Hephaestus (fire), rain and gleaming air (aither),
anchored in the perfect harbour of Cypris (love),
either a little more of it or less of it among more of
them.
From these arose blood and the various forms of
flesh."
(Fr.98 Simplicius in Phys. 32, 6).**

Since the four roots chanced in equal proportions and from these arose the blood, then the heart must be the dwelling place of the thought, for in this perfect mixture the four elements are in equal proportions, and the unbiased judgement can be attained through this perfect mixture.

> " The heart dwelling in the sea of blood, which surges
> back and forth, where especially is what is called thought
> by men; for the blood around men's hearts is their thought."
> (Fr. 105 Porhyrius ap. Stobaeum Anth. I, 49, 13).

With regard to the faculty of thinking, Empedocles holds that it is developed by the equal proportions of the four elements and grows in accordance with the difficulties caused by the external events, since they trigger off a further development and evolution.

> " Men's wit grows according as they encounter what is present."
> (Fr. 106 Aristotle, On the Soul 426 a, 21).

Since all things have come into being from the roots, and thought is a consequence of the perfect mixture, then the feeling of pleasure is due to "Love" among the roots and pain due to "Strife" among them.

> " Out of these things are all things fitted together and
> constructed, and by these do they think and feel pleasure or pain."
> (Fr. 107 Theophrastus de Sensu 9).

Referring to perception and thought, Empedocles points out his view that is of like by like. Therefore the procedure of learning and the faculty of knowledge follows the same way. Through the earth within us we perceive the earth, through the water we perceive the water etc. In the same way when "Love" wins supremacy in us, we perceive the "Love", and when "Strife" wins supremacy, we perceive the "Strife". Each one of us then, has a prejudice against or in favour of some things, according to the supremacy of "love" or "strife" over the roots within us.

> " For with earth do we see earth, with water water,
> with air bright air, with fire consuming fire;

with Love do we see Love, Strife with dread Strife."
(Fr. 109 Aristotle, Metaphysics B 4, 1000 b 6).

Empedocles sums up with his poem by exhorting his disciple to keep deep in his mind what has been revealed by him, and to use it as a basis for further contemplation. In this way the disciple can exercise his thought, so as to be able to perceive and understand the principles, which determine the universe and the human nature. Since all the sense-perceptions grow according to their nature in us, this will enable him to understand and grasp the truth as a unity. However, if he is attached to the ephemerals, namely what the mortals desire and blunt their thought, then he will confront the abandonment and the calamity, since all the ephemerals will abandon him, as the time goes around, to meet their dear kind, which means the mixture of their elements will be separated and search for its own and alike.

> **" If you plant them in your stout understanding**
> **and contemplate them with good will in pure**
> **exercises,**
> **these will assuredly all be with you throughout your**
> **life;**
> **and you will gain many other things from them;**
> **for of themselves they will cause each to grow**
> **in his own way, according to the nature of each.**
> **But if you reach for things of different kind,**
> **such as come in their thousands among men,**
> **evils that blunt their thoughts, then at once**
> **they will abandon you as time goes around,**
> **longing to find their own dear kind;"**
> **(Fr. 110 Hippolytus Ref. VII, 29, 25).**

In the end of his poem Empedocles returns to his initial position, that all the sense-perceptions compose the unity of understanding the truth through intellect. For each sense-perception holds a part of the whole truth, therefore his disciple must interpret and compose all these perceptions through his intellect (*νούς*: nous) in order to grasp the truth as a unity.

> **" For know that they all have intelligence and a**

share of thought."
(Fr. 110 Hippolytus Ref. VII, 29, 25)

Apart from this poem Empedocles has written another work which is called "**Purifications**" (*καθαρμοί*: katharmoi), where he is referring to the cycle of incarnation (**reincarnation**) and fallen **daimons** (*δαίμονες*), with clear influence of Pythagorean beliefs. To be more specific, there (Fr. 115, 127 of Purifications) he holds the view that the soul wanders for ten thousand years, being born throughout that time in all manners of forms of mortal things (animals, birds, fish, plants etc.). However, when the soul becomes wise then arises as a god (Fr. 146, 147 of Purifications). All these views have been subject of discussion by scholars, whether they are referring to other period of Empedocles' life or are metaphorical symbols of the nature of mortal life.

8. Anaxagoras (500 – 428 BC)

The philosopher from Clazomenae (Asia Minor) who first introduced the term of indestructible and ungenerated parts, which are infinite in smallness and in number, and he called them "**homeomerous**" (*ομοιομερή*) or else "**seeds**" (*σπέρματα*: spermata). He was taught the Ionian philosophy probably by Anaximenes, and as a young man went to Athens, where he taught philosophy for many years. Among his disciples were Archelaus (later the master of Socrates), Pericles and the poet Euripides. He is considered to be the philosopher who brought the Ionian philosophy to Athens.

According to him, everything in the universe consists of the "homeomerous", which are small things with like parts, infinite in number and their size is infinitely small.

" **All things were together, infinite in respect of both number and smallness; for the small too was infinite. And while all things were together, none of them were plain because of their smallness; for air and aither held all things in subjection, both of them being infinite; for these are the great ingredients in the mixture of all things, both**

in number and in size." (Fr. 1 Simplicius, In Phys. 155, 26).

Within all things there are parts of these "homeomerous", which cannot be perceived as distinguished parts, since they are infinite in smallness and in number, and these small particles are dispersed in the air and aither. Here we can see the influence of Anaximenes with regard to the infinite air. And as for air and aither, since they are more light than earth and water, they are separated off from the surrounding mass which is infinite in number as well.

" For air and aither are being separated off from the surrounding mass, which is infinite in number." (Fr. 2, Simplicius In Phys. 155, 31).

The homeomerous, since are indestructible, - for it is impossible from the being to turn into the not-being – they cannot be more or less, but their quantity is always equal, namely invariable, although are infinite in number.

" And when these things have been thus separated, we must know that all things are neither more nor less; for it is not possible that there should be more than all, but all things are always equal." (Fr. 5, Ibid 156, 10).

All things are infinitely divisible according to Anaxagoras, for there is always a smaller part from the small. This at first sight paradox of infinite divisibility of homeomerous we can understand it, if we think that through infinite divisibility of the unit, we never come to nought, so to say from the being we can never reach to the not-being through infinite divisibility. For example, if we divide the unit in two equal parts, it makes 1/2, then if we continue dividing in the same way for infinite times, we have: 1/4, 1/8, 1/16, 1/32, .. and so on, but we never come to nought. The same as if we multiply the unit infinite times, we have: 2, 4, 8, 16, .. and so on. For both cases then, the multitude of divisibility and multiplicity is the same.

" Neither is there a smallest part of what is small, but there is always a smaller (for it is impossible what is should cease to be). Likewise there is always something larger than what is large. And it is equal in respect of

number to what is small each thing, in relation to itself, being both large and small." (Fr. 3 Simplicius In Phys. 164, 17).

As the homeomerous combine with one another, all existing things come into being. Therefore Anaxagoras considers the coming to be, as a **composition** (*συμμίσγεσθαι*: symmisgesthai) of the homeomerous, and perishing as a **dissolution** (*διακρίνεσθαι*: diakrinesthai). With this view Anaxagoras introduced a new conception of coming to be and passing away, through the composition and dissolution of homeomerous, which are imperishable, and according to their association with one another all the existing material forms come into being and perish.

" **The Greeks are wrong to recognize coming into being and perishing; for nothing comes into being nor perishes, but is rather composed or dissolved from things that are. So they would be right to call coming into being composition and perishing dissolution.**" (Fr. 17, Simplicius In Phys. 163, 20).

Concerning the cosmogony, Anaxagoras regards the rotational motion as the originating cause of it, and through this rotation the homeomerous are composed or dissolved and as a result all the existing material forms come into being or perish. The whole rotation is controlled by "**Nous**" or else "**Intellect**"(*νούς*: mind) which is separated, all alone by itself, self-ruled, infinite and not mixed with the homeomerous.

Apart from homeomerous, as we can see, Anaxagoras introduces a second "principle" (**dualism** of Intellect and matter), which is the **primary principle** and originating cause of the rotation. This supernatural Being initiated the rotation, which separated off all the homeomerous, and led to the cosmogony. The ability of "**Intellect**" to control all things and their motion, is due to the fact that it is alone, **unmixed**, **unmoved** and **unaffected**. Although it is corporeal, owes its power to its purity and fineness. He defines two qualities of the "Intellect", the **knowledge** and the **motion**, since it has all knowledge about everything and it can also initiate the motion, therefore it can control the coming to be, the passing away, and maintain the order in the universe.

" And when **Intellect (νοῦς) initiated motion, from all that was moved Intellect was separated, and as much as Intellect moved was all divided off; and as things moved and were divided off, the rotation greatly increased the process of dividing."** (Fr. 13, Simplicius In Phys. 300, 31).

" **All other things have a portion of everything, but Intellect is <u>infinite</u> and <u>self ruled</u>, and is <u>mixed with nothing</u> but is all <u>alone by itself</u>. For if it was not by itself, but was mixed with anything else, it would have a share of all things if it were mixed with any; for in everything there is a portion of everything, as I said earlier; and the things that were mingled with hinder it so that it control nothing in the same way as it does now being alone by itself. For it is the <u>finest</u> of all things and the <u>purest</u>, it has all knowledge about everything and the greatest power; and Intellect <u>controls</u> all things both the greater and the smaller, that have life. Intellect controlled also the <u>whole rotation</u>, so that it began to rotate in the beginning. And it began to rotate first from a small area, but it now rotates over a wider area still. And the things that are mingled and separated and divided off, all are known by Intellect. And all things that were to be – those that were and those that are now and those that shall be – Intellect arranged them all, including the rotation in which now rotating the stars, the sun and moon, the air and the aither that are being separated off... But there are many portions of many things and nothing is altogether <u>separated off</u> nor divided one from another except from Intellect. <u>Intellect is all alike</u>, both the greater and the smaller quantities of it, while nothing else is like anything else.."** (Fr. 12, Simplicius In Phys. 164, 24 and 156, 13).

" **In everything there is a portion of everything except Intellect; and there are <u>some things</u> in which there is Intellect as well."** (Fr. 11, Ibid. 164, 23).

So the "Intellect" possesses knowledge and wisdom, it is infinite and eternal, maintains the order in the universe and is separated off from the homeomerous. While Empedocles regarded the two opposite powers to govern the world (love and strife), Anaxagoras initiates the Intellect which has knowledge and rules the universe. Therefore, Anaxagoras was called "Intellect" (νούς), as he considered that everything in the world is decided on the Intellect. With regard to the things where the "Intellect" is to be found, Anaxagoras considers that throughout the living beings is distributed discontinuously a part of the universal Intellect, therefore the man has the capability of knowledge, since he shares a portion of the Intellect within.

Concerning the gnoseology, Anaxagoras considers the perception through the **senses weak**, therefore it is not sufficient for understanding the truth. The only possibility for knowledge is, if one through the **intellect** tries to interpret and judge the **appearances** (φαινόμενα: phenomena), so as to be able to understand what is beyond and not perceptive through the senses (άδηλα: adela: **obscure**). Anaxagoras, like Empedocles, initiates with this conception the **inductive** method of thought, which proceeds from the parts to the whole, or else from the apparent to the not apparent.

" **Appearances are a glimpse of the obscure.**" (όψις γάρ τών αδήλων τά φαινόμενα: opses gar ton adelon ta phenomena) (**Fr. 21 a, Ibid VII, 140**).

" **From the weakness of our senses we cannot judge the truth.**" (**Fr. 21, Sextus Adv. Math. VII, 90**).

Referring to the sense perception, Anaxagoras' notion is that it is of unlike by unlike, namely by opposites, therefore each perception is accompanied by pain, for everything unlike produces pain by its contact. By warm we can identify the cold, by sweetness the bitterness and so on. According to the proportion of our **deficiency** in something we can perceive it, for like is not affected by like. The dwelling place of the senses is considered to be the brain, according to him, therefore is the first part which is formed in the embryo.

" **Anaxagoras thinks that perception is by opposites, for like is not affected by like..**" (**Theophrastus De Sensu 27 ff**).

Anaxagoras rejects the concept of determinism, since everything occurs either by necessity or as a result of chance or by free choice. Therefore it is difficult for us to find out the causes of the events.

" **According to Anaxagoras, Democritus and Stoics the cause is inconceivable for the human mind; some things occur by necessity, others by determination, others by free choice, others by chance and some incidentally. Anaxagoras says that nothing happens because of fate, and this word is meaningless."** (Aetius I, 29, 7).

Man is the wisest of all living beings, since although is inferior to them in body's strength, he possesses memory, experience, wisdom and is skilful with his hands.

" **Anaxagoras says then, that it is his possession of hands that makes man the wisest of living things."** (Fr. 102 Aristotle, De part animalium 687 a, 7).

" **Although in all these we are less fortunate than animals, we use instead our experience and memory and wisdom and skill, according to Anaxagoras.."** (Fr. 21 b, Plutarch).

Prudence is a faculty that every man can possess (potentiality), if he develops his mind, since, as we saw in the last part of Fr. 12, man has a portion of universal Intellect and that both the greater and the smaller parts of the Intellect are alike. Soul and intellect are identified and possess self-motion, sense perception and knowledge.

" **Anaxagoras considers that not all men possess prudence as faculty of mind, not because of lack of intellectual substance, but because they do not use it. Soul is characterized by the following two: mobility and cognitive power."** (Fr. 101 a).

Concerning **happiness**, Anaxagoras regards it to be bound together with wisdom, therefore he said that the happy man would seem to most people a strange person, since the happy man is considered to be by him neither the rich nor the despot. On the contrary, the most significant factor for man's happiness is the development of the intellect, through **contemplation**. (θεωρία: theoria, reflection), as it liberates the man. This **speculative activity of the intellect,** which is concerned with knowledge and comprehension of the primary principles of the universe, is similar to the "life according to intellect" of Aristotle, as we are going to see.

" **Anaxagoras also seems to have supposed the happy man not to be rich nor a despot.**" (Aristotle, Nicomachean Ethics X, 1179 a 12).

" **Anaxagoras said that the end of life is the speculative activity of the intellect and the freedom which derives from it.**" (Fr. 29, Clement Strom. II, 130).

9. Democritus (460 – 370 BC)

Democritus and Leucippus are considered to be the founders of Atomism. Democritus of Abdera was called the "**laughing**" (*γελασίνος*: gelasinos) philosopher, as he used to laugh at the people, since they are always occupied with insignificant pursuits. Basic principle of his philosophy is that every perception is subjective, and what truly exists is the atoms and void. First time after the Pythagoreans the concept of **void** (*κενόν*: kenon) is introduced more clearly by the Atomists, while all the previous philosophers regarded the matter continuous. Apart from that, the Atomists introduced the **atoms** (*άτομα*), namely the indivisible particles which collide with one another and form the four elements and all things in the universe.

" **By convention bitter, by convention hot, by convention cold, by convention colour; but in reality <u>atoms</u> and <u>void</u>.**" (fr. 9, Sextus, Adv. Mathem. VII, 135).

Atoms – Cosmogony

These primary bodies (atoms) are infinite in number, indivisible, indestructible and impassable, and they do not possess any quality of the compounds they form. As they are in perpetual motion and while they move through the void, they collide with one another, some of them become entangled, and due to the combination of atoms in special proportions are formed the four elements and furthermore all the compounds.

" **There are infinite in number primary bodies which are indivisible, impassible and move through the void. When they come close or collide with one another or become entangled, the whole appears sometimes as water or fire or plant or man..**" (Fr. 57).

The atoms hold three differences: **shape** (*ρυσμός*: rysmos), **position** (*τροπή*: trope) and **arrangement** (*διαθιγή*: diathege). Those atoms which are of congruous properties collide with one another and in this way are formed the complex of atoms and the compounds. The compounds which come into being possess different qualities from their primary bodies. For example, if two atoms have a shape **A** and **N** respectively, then **A** differs from **N** in **shape**. The compounds **AN** and **NA** differ in **arrangement**, and the atom **N** differs from **Z** in **position**. And each one has different properties from the other. As we know, by chemistry it is admitted that there are different shapes of molecules and atoms, as well as that the different shapes, position and stereochemical arrangements of the atoms give different sorts of compounds with unlike chemical properties.

" **These atoms move in the infinite void, separate one from the other and differing in <u>shapes</u>, <u>sizes</u>, <u>position</u> and <u>arrangement</u>; overtaking each other they collide, and some are shaken away in any chance direction, while others, becoming intertwined one with another according to their congruity of their shapes, sizes, positions and arrangements, stay together and so effect the coming into being of the compound bodies.**" (Simplicius De Caelo 242, 21).

The universe was a vortex, separated off from the whole, and due to the rotation all the atoms were separated off, which since they have collided with one another, effected the coming to be of the compounds and the innumerable worlds.

" **A whirl was separated off from the whole, of all short of shapes.**" (Fr. 167 Simplicius In Phys. 327, 24).

The motion is innate quality of the atoms, which as they move periodically through the void, collide with one another. As we can realize, Democritus considers the motion to be potentially in the atoms, contrary to Anaxagoras, who regarded Intellect the one that initiated the motion of homeomerous. The creation and destruction of the innumerable worlds is eternal and is determined by the "**necessity**" (*ανάγκη*: anange), according to Democritus, the sequence of rotational motion of vortex and the chain of collisions and reactions (cause and effect). Democritus introduces another "principle", the necessity, as we can see, apart from atoms, void, motion and collision of atoms.

" Democritus of Abdera regarded the universe infinite, since it has not been created by anyone... The causes of what it comes to be have no principle. In the infinite time what were to be, what is and what shall be is determined by necessity." (Fr. 39 Plutarch, Strom. 7 d).

"Nothing occurs by random, but everything for a reason and by <u>necessity</u>." (Fr. 2 Aetius I, 25, 4).

The universe has no beginning and end therefore it is infinite, since existence cannot be destroyed into non-existence, namely from being we cannot come to not-being. So, it will always be, eternally, since its "principles" are eternal (atoms, void, motion, necessity).

" Nothing derives from not-being and nothing results in not-being." (Fr. 1 Diogenes Laeritus IX, 44).

There are innumerable worlds, some of them are at their height and some are decadent, namely each world is in different stage of evolution, in this perpetual and periodical motion of creation and destruction.

" Democritus spoke as if the things were in constant motion in the void; and there are innumerable worlds which differ in size. In some worlds there is no sun and moon, in others they are larger than in our world, and in others more numerous. The intervals between the worlds are unequal; in some parts there are more worlds, in other fewer; some are increasing, some at their height, some decreasing; in some parts they are arising, in others

84

failing. They are destroyed by collision one with another. There are some worlds devoid of living creatures or plants or any moisture." (Fr. 40, Hippolytus, Ref. I, 13, 2).

Since time cannot exist as distinguished from motion and the motion is eternal, then it follows that the time is eternal, namely it is uncreated, because for each creation there is always a beginning and end.

" In fact, it is just this that enables Democritus to show that all things cannot have had a becoming; for time he says is uncreated." (Aristotle, Physics VIII, 251 b 15).

Soul

The soul consists of atoms which are mobile, therefore it originates movement in the body, and since its atoms are spherical they can permeate everywhere. The substance of soul then is material, and due to the fineness of its atoms looks like fire, therefore after the body's destruction it is dispersed. The soul and mind are identified, since the sensation of the body, the sense perception and the faculty of thought derive from the same source, which is the soul.

" This is what led Democritus to say that the soul is a sort of fire or hot substance; his forms or atoms are infinite in number; those which are spherical he calls fire and soul..

The spherical atoms are identified with soul, because atoms of that shape are most adapted to permeate everywhere, and set all the others moving by being themselves in movement.

Democritus roundly identifies soul and mind.." (Aristotle, On the Soul 404 a, 1-10, 27).

" Democritus says that the soul has not any different parts and qualities, since the sensation and thought derive from the same capability." (Fr. 105, Aetius IV, 4, 6).

„ Democritus and Epicurus consider the soul perishable, and that it is dispersed when the body is destroyed." (Fr. 109 Aetius IV, 7, 4).

Eyesight is due to the "effluences" (απορροαί: aporroai) of atoms from the seen object, which form the "images" (εἴδωλα: eidola) that affect the eyes. As for the gods, he says that they are solid images, not imperishable but hard to be perished, which travel through the air together with their thoughts and passions.

" **They attributed sight to certain images of the same shape as the object, which were continually streaming off from the objects of sight and impinging on the eye. This was the view of the school of Leucippus and Democritus.**" (Alexander De Sensu 56, 12).

" **Democritus claims that there are some solid images, which approach the people, and some of them are well-doers and some evil-doers... Apart from those images there are no gods with imperishable nature.**" (Fr. 166 Sextus, Adv. Math. IX, 19).

The two opposite powers (good and evil) co-exist within the human soul, according to Democritus (a similar view to Heraclitus), and the way of its use, can lead us either to happiness or to misfortune. Therefore, if a man guides with prudence these powers, can achieve happiness.

" **Happiness and misfortune are qualities of the <u>soul</u>.**" (Fr. 170 Stobaeus II, 7, 3).

" **Happiness does not reside in cattle or gold; the <u>soul</u> is the dwelling place of one's good or evil genius (daimon).**" (Fr. 171 Stobaeus II, 7, 3).

" **From the same things that the goods can come, could derive the evil also, but we can avoid the evil. The deep water is useful for many, but at the same time is bad, since we can drown. However, it has been found a skill which one can possess it by taking swimming lessons.**" (Fr. 172 Stobaeus II 9, 1).

Gnoseology

The knowledge of truth according to Democritus is difficult, since the perception through the senses is subjective. As from the same senses derive different impressions for each individual, then through the sense-impressions we cannot judge the truth. We can only interpret the sense data through the intellect and grasp the truth, because the **truth** (αλήθεια: aletheia) lies **at the bottom** (εν βυθώι: en bythoe).

" **And again, many of the other animals receive impressions contrary to ours; and even to the senses of each individual, things do not always seem the same. Which then, of these impressions are true and which are false is not obvious; for the one set is no more true than the other, but both are alike. And this is why Democritus, at any rate, says that either there is no truth or to us at least it is not evident."(Aristotle, Metaphysics IV, 1009 b 7).**

" **Democritus .. says: <By convention hot, by convention cold, but in reality atoms and void>, and also < in reality we know nothing, since the truth is at bottom>." (Fr. 117, Diogenes Laertius IX, 72).**

There are two kinds of knowing, the one he calls "legitimate" (γνησίη: gnesie, **genuine**) and the other "bastard" (σκοτίη: skotie, **obscure**). The "bastard" knowledge is concerned with the perception through the senses, therefore it is insufficient and subjective. The reason is that the sense-perception is due to the effluences of the atoms (απορροαί) from the objects to the senses. When these different shapes of atoms come to us, stimulate our senses according to their shape, and there from arise our sense-impressions. (Fr. 135, Theophrastus De Sensu 49-83).

The second knowledge, the "legitimate" one, can be achieved through the intellect, in other words all the sense-data from the "bastard" must be elaborated through reasoning. In this way one can get away from the false perception of the "bastard" knowledge and grasp the truth through the **inductive reasoning**. Therefore, the man after taking into account the sense-impressions, can examine the causes of the appearances, draw conclusions about the laws that govern the appearances, and find out the **causality** (αιτιολογία: aetiologia) by which they are related. This procedure of thought, from the parts to the whole or else from the apparent to non-apparent, as we saw in Empedocles' and Anaxagoras' philosophy, is the basis of the inductive method which

Democritus follows, and Aristotle also adopted, as we are going to see.

" But in the *Canons* Democritus says there are two kinds of <u>knowing</u>, one through the senses and the other through the intellect. Of these he calls the one through the intellect '<u>legitimate</u>' attesting its trustworthiness for the judgement of truth, and through the senses he names '<u>bastard</u>' denying its inerrancy in the discrimination of what is true. To quote his actual words: <Of knowledge there are two forms, one legitimate, one bastard. To the bastard belong all this group: sight, hearing, smell, taste, touch. The other is legitimate and separate from that>. Then, preferring the legitimate to the bastard, he continues: <When the bastard can no longer see any smaller, or hear, or smell, or taste, or perceive by touch, but finer matters have to be examined, then comes the legitimate, since it has a finer organ of perception>." (Fr. 11 Sextus, Adv. Math. VII, 138).

" In the Confirmations .. he says: <But we in actuality grasp nothing for certain, but what shifts in accordance with the condition of the body and of the things (atoms) which enter it and press upon it>." (Fr. 9 Sextus Adv. Math. VII 136).

" Democritus used to say that he < prefers to discover a causality rather than become a king of Persia>." (Fr.118)

The faculty of reasoning and understanding depends on the proportions of the atoms of which consists the mixture of the soul. If this mixture is harmonious, then the perception through the intellect (legitimate) functions well and one can acquire the faculty of knowledge and understanding. But, if this balance is lost, then he loses the ability of reasoning. Just like for example, when one exposes himself to extreme conditions of temperature, then this disturbs his equanimity and as a result he loses his mental perception (hallucinations, loss of memory etc.).

" Concerning the faculty of reasoning (*φρονείν*: phronein) Democritus said that one possesses it when the mixture of the soul is harmonious (*σύμμετρον*: symmetron).

**When someone is very cold or feel very warm, loses his
mental ability, what the people in the old days called
madness." (Fr. 135 Theophrastus De Sensu 58).**

Therefore, Democritus regards the balance of the soul
(harmonious mixture) very significant for acquiring
knowledge and happiness. This is the reason why the man's
end, according to him, should be the calmness (balance) of
soul through its perfection, and the state of **good spirits**
(εὐθυμίη: euthumie). Since the perfection of the soul can
correct the depravity of the body, one must take care of his
soul, for it is superior to the body. Perfection of the soul
means to him, development of one's intellect through
prudence, which takes care of the body and prevents one from
the excess and deficiency that destroy the man, as we are
going to see. For the beauty and nobility of a man is his
faculty of reasoning and understanding, just as the strength of
the body is the nobility of an animal.

" **Take care of the soul.**" (ψυχῆς .. τίθησιν: psyches
tithesin) (**Fr. 36, Democritus' Gnomai).**

" **The perfection of the soul will correct the depravity of
the body; but the strength of the body without the
reasoning does not render the soul better.**" (Fr. 187
Stobaeus III, 1, 27).

" **Vigour and strength of body are the nobility of cattle;
but the rectitude of manners is the nobility of man.**" (Fr.
57 Democritus' gnomai).

Good spirits – Virtues

In order to acquire the balance of soul and to be in good
spirits, one should live with temperate enjoyments and self-
sufficiency. As the excess and deficiency lead to the
imbalance of the soul, since both are extremes, therefore one
should live moderate life. Both the extremes **deficiency**
(ἔλλειψις: ellipse) or **excess** (ὑπερβολή: hyperbole) of
pleasures make large motions in the soul and destroy its
balance, since the one tend to turn into its opposite (from
excess to deficiency and vice versa). In other words, the
excess of pleasures destroys the body and leads to deprivation.

On the other hand, the complete deprivation of pleasures through the repress of one's impulses, leads to the other extreme, namely to the excess of pleasures. In this way the soul loses its balance, and as a result the man loses his peace of mind, and therefore his happiness.

Therefore, through **temperate enjoyment** (*μετριότητι τέρψιος*: metriotete terpsios) and **commensurate life** (*βίου συμμετρήι*: biou symmetrie) one can acquire peace of mind and be in **good spirits** (*ευθυμήι*: euthumie). In order to achieve these, one must possess prudence and self-sufficiency. Prudence in a sense, that he realizes what lies in his power and to live in accordance with it, as well as to avoid the extremes of want and satiety. Self-sufficiency, on the other hand, means that one should gain contentment by looking at the lives those in trouble, and to be satisfied with things at hand. Otherwise, if he desires always more possessions and fame by admiring those who possess more power and wealth than him, he will finally throw himself to do something illegal and irremediable in order to achieve all these quickly.

" The <u>equal</u> is beautiful in everything; but <u>excess</u> and <u>defect</u> to me do not appear so." (Fr. 102 Democritus' gnomai).

" For <u>good spirits</u> come to men through temperate enjoyment and a life commensurate. <u>Deficiencies</u> and <u>excesses</u> tend to turn into their opposites and to make large motions in the <u>soul</u>. And such souls as are in large-scale motion are neither in good balance nor in good spirits. One should keep one's mind then, on things in one's power, and be quite satisfied with things at hand, taking little notice of those who are envied or admired and not dwelling in thought upon them. One should look at the lives of those in trouble, bearing in mind how mightily they are suffering...

For he who admires those blessed with possessions and the congratulations of other men and who dwells every hour on the memory is ever compelled to plot something new and to throw himself through desire, into doing something irremediable and illegal.

For if you keep to this mind, you will both carry on in good spirits, and you will ward off some considerable curses in life – envy, jealousy and malice." (Fr. 191, Stobaeus Anth. III, 1, 210).

" The best for a man is to be more in good spirits and less in depression; and this could have been possible if one had not searched for pleasure in the mortal things." (Fr. 189 Stobaeus Anth. III, 1, 47).

In the previous fragment we can see that, Democritus regards the pleasures which arise from the "**mortals**" (*θνητοίσι*: thnetoise) as a source of depression and agitation of the soul. The reason is that the desires for sensual pleasures, acquiring wealth and winning fame, lead us to disappointment and depression, when all these are gone. Therefore, when one is attached to the "mortals" and as a result his happiness is dependent on them, that is misleading, since the mortals come and go. For a man cannot be in good spirits, when his soul is agitated by desires and passions for the "mortals", as they are accompanied with envy and jealousy of those who possess the mortal and external things. All these desires and passions, which are deep in us constitute the motives of our actions and the roots of the vice that derives from passions. Therefore, a man ought to rule over the desires, which is very difficult as we saw in Heraclitus' philosophy (fr. 85), however through prudence one can dominate over the desires, and break away of his childish and immoderate disposition.

" If you open yourself inwardly, as Democritus says, you will find stored up all sorts of evils which do not run inwards, but are like having underground sources, which the vice generates that is rife within the soul." (Fr. 149 Plutarch Psych. 550 d).

" To desire immoderately is the province of a child and not of a man." (Fr. 70 Democritus' gnomai).

" Vehement desires about any one thing render the soul blind with respect to other things." (Fr. 72 Democritus' gnomai).

" It is difficult to fight with desires, but to dominate over them shows a prudent man." (Fr. 236 Stobaeus Anth. III, 20, 56).

According to Democritus, the desires rank among the parts of the soul which can be governed, and reason is the one that can govern the other parts. Therefore, through reasoning one can analyse and grade the desires, in order to find out which of them can help him to be in good spirits. Through this process of reasoning and valuation of the desires, one can acquire **prudence** and keep his unreasonable desires under control.

" Other elements of the soul only rule, just like reason, others rule and are ruled, as anger, but others are only ruled, like desire." (Fr. 34 David Prol. 38, 14).

Prudence is not learning but broadening the perception through intellect and faculty of judgement. Therefore, those who have **great learning** (πολυμαθήι: polymathie) do not possess prudence, since only the faculty of judgement, consideration and reflection can lead one to discover the causalities of the appearances. Apart from that, prudence is distinguished from the common sense, as it goes beyond the appearances, in order to discover their causalities. This development of the **intellect** (νούς), is what distinguishes the philosophers from the common men, as we have seen.

" Many that have great learning have no intellect." (Fr. 64 Democritus' gnomai).

" It is necessary to endeavour to obtain an abundance of intellect and not pursue an abundance of erudition." (Fr. 65 Democritus' gnomai).

The **proper thought** (ορθοσύνηι : orthosynie) and the **abundance of intellect** (πολυφροσύνηι : polyphrosynie) can lead one to achieve happiness - and not the pursuit of sensual pleasures and wealth - since through these he can always be in good spirits.

" The felicity of a man does not consist either in body or in riches but in right reflection and abundance of prudence." (Fr. 40 Democritus' gnomai).

The excess of bodily pleasures on the one hand, turns a man into a brute, and on the other hand leads him to vicious circle of pleasures' pursuit, since sensual pleasures are deficient and very short. Therefore, after having fulfilled a bodily desire we usually search out another sensual pleasure, since we hope that this time we will enjoy more pleasure. However, after being disappointed with the new form of pleasure, since we cannot relish it, as we expected to do, we carry on searching the pleasure in other forms of sensual desires. In this way, one can become involved in a vicious circle of seeking bodily pleasures, and due to the continuous repetition, this attitude becomes a habit, and as a result he turns into a brute, for eventually his only end of life will be the enjoyment of the bodily pleasures.

" **Those who like worms wallow in the mud and in the mire are grazing senseless and useless pleasures, are men who look like pigs. Pigs find pleasure rather in mud than in clear water and they fall into muck.**" (Fr. 147 Clement Protr. 92, 4).

" **Those who pursue bodily pleasures and go too far in food, drink or sex, their pleasures are petty and short, and last as long as they eat and drink, while their sorrows are many. The desire for the same things exists always among those men, and when happens what they desire, the pleasure shortly goes away and nothing advantageous is left except a short delight, and then they feel again a need for the same things.**" (Fr. 235 Stobaeus Anth. III, 18, 35).

On the other hand, the pleasures of the intellect last longer, therefore a man should pursue these sorts of pleasure and develop his intellect and culture. The peace of mind, the state of good spirits lasts longer and is continuous, therefore it should be preferable. Through **prudence** one can acquire the sense of proportion and possess the virtues of justice, self-sufficiency, bravery, and as a result respect for oneself, which enables him to get rid of jealousy, envy and malice. In this way a virtuous man can act always justly and be beneficial to his fellow-men.

" Temperance increases the joy and extends the pleasure." (Fr. 211 Stobaeus Anth. III, 5, 27).

" He who loves the goods of the soul will love things more divine; but he who loves the goods of his transient habitation will love things human." (Fr. 37 Democritus' gnomai).

" The love is just which, unattended with injury, aspires after things becoming." (Fr. 73 Democritus' gnomai).

" Admit nothing as pleasant which is not advantageous." (Fr. 74 Democritus' gnomai).

" One should not prefer any pleasure, except the one which arises from the good." (Fr. 207 Democritus' gnomai).

" The great pleasures arise from the observation of the good deeds." (Fr. 194 Stobaeus Anth. III, 2, 46).

Temperate enjoyment of course does not mean that one should get to the other extreme, and deprive of every pleasure, but it actually means the golden mean, just like in the saying "all things in moderation" of Thales.

" Life without feasts is a long way without inn." (Fr. 230 Stobaeus Anth. III, 17, 25).

" If one goes too far, the most pleasant things can turn into the most unpleasant ones." (Fr. 233 Stobaeus Anth. III, 17, 38).

The opposite powers, namely good and evil, as we saw, co-exist within us and derive from the same source (Fr.170,173), and in accordance with the way we use them, they can guide us either to misfortune or to happiness. This way of use defines the man of **prudence** and wisdom, who can escape from the influence of **chance,** and administer his own affairs. However, the imprudent man attributes everything to bad luck in order to justify his own lack of foresight. But chance is uncertain and unstable, contrary to prudence, which enables him due to foresight to avoid the misfortunes of life.

" They do not praise prudence as being fortunate, but chance as being wisest. In a few instances does chance intrude upon the wise man, but reason has administered his greatest and most important affairs, and will continue to do so throughout his life." (Fr. 119 Dion. Alex. XIV, 27,5).

The motive of our actions, according to Democritus, is the pursuit of pleasure and the avoidance of displeasure (**pleasure – pain**). Through that process, and in order to achieve this aim, one can acquire better perception and judgement, more foresight and knowledge. Therefore the difficulties in life spark off more reasoning and as a result more prudence and understanding. On the other hand, the easy acquisition of material comforts and the fulfillment of all one's desires, lead to shallow thought and lack of judgement, as well as to the continuous pursuit of pleasure which results in the vicious circle, as we have mentioned. Because, when one is used to easy life of pleasure, he will always try to satisfy his bodily desires by making the lesser possible efforts, which will inevitably lead him to act unjustly and illegally.

" **Pleasure and lack of pleasure is the criterion of advantageous and not advantageous." (Fr. 188 Stobaeus III, 1, 46).**

" **The worst master of youth has been easiness. It generates the pleasures from which arises the vice." (Fr. 178 Stobaeus III, 1, 56).**

" **Fools frequently become wise under the pressure of misfortunes." (Fr. 54 Democritus' gnomai).**

" **Not argument but calamity is the preceptor of children." (Fr. 76 Democritus' gnomai.).**

" **It is better that foresight should precede actions than that repentance should follow them." (Fr. 66 Democritus' gnomai).**

" **Neither art nor wisdom can be acquired without learning." (Fr. 59 Democritus' gnomai).**

" **Good scarcely presents itself even to those who investigate it; but evil is obvious without investigation." (Fr. 108 Democritus' gnomai).**

Through this process of learning one can possess prudence, and escape from the level of the "**fools**" ($\alpha\xi\acute{v}\nu\varepsilon\tau o\iota$: axynetoi) and as a result to have a sense of the truly **good** ($\alpha\gamma\alpha\theta\acute{o}\nu$:

agathon). Because the main obstacle to a man's knowledge and understanding is the pursuit of pleasure and the avoidance of pain, since he judges the good and evil through this criterion. However, this criterion, namely "good and true is what is pleasant", is absolutely subjective, and can lead one to vice.

" **For all men the good and the true is one and the same; the pleasant is different.**" (Fr. 69 Democritus' gnomai).

Significant virtue, according to Democritus, apart from **moderation** and **self-sufficiency**, is the **justice** (*δικαιοσύνη*: dikaiosyne) since it is the basis of the whole virtue. The sense of justice, according to him, should be associated with the respect for oneself and for the others, for the man ought not to act justly only for the fear of punishment by the law. Certainly all these virtues are associated with one another, since when one is self-sufficient and moderate, is aware of his desires through **prudence**, he has a control over them, and does not go to the extremes of excess and deficiency, and as a result he does not do an injustice to the others, as he is not greedy. He understands the needs of his fellow-men and tries not to wrong them, just because he wants to satisfy his unreasonable desires on them. When one has respect for himself, takes care of himself, and does not allow to be ruined by the remorses or the fear of punishment for his injustice, as well as by the poison of envy and jealousy for the fortunate and successful people. **Respect for oneself** also means that, one does not deceive himself by pretending to be a just man, when the others do not realize his injustice, but since he takes care of himself, tries to improve himself, therefore he chooses the virtuous life, and not for the sake of public acknowledgement. Through this process one can acquire esteem for himself because of his virtues, and not to hate him for his weakness and vices.

" **It is great thing to be wise where we ought in calamitous circumstances.**" (Fr. 42 Democritus' gnomai).

" **Sin should be abstained from, not through fear, but for the sake of becoming.**" (Fr. 41 Democritus' gnomai).

" He who is perfectly vanquished by riches can never be just." (Fr. 50 Democritus' gnomai).

" It is good not only to refrain from doing an injury, but even from the very wish." (Fr. 62 Democritus' gnomai).

" A man who is in good spirits is led to just and legal acts and he is happy while being awake or asleep and strong without anxieties. Whoever does not rely on justice and does not do what he ought to do, for him everything is displeasant and whenever he remembers something of these he is fearful and troubles himself." (Fr. 174 Stobaeus II, 9, 3).

" Reward for justice is the courage and fearlessness of one's convictions, while the result of injustice is the fear of calamity." (Fr. 215 Stobaeus III, 7, 31).

The respect for oneself is a basic component of the social consciousness, according to Democritus, and derives from true love and care about oneself and leads to the virtuous life and the state of good spirits. Therefore the man should focus his efforts to improve himself and not the others, namely to take care of and respect himself.

" It is better to reprove your own errors, than those of the others." (Fr. 60 Democritus' gnomai).

" An envious man is the cause of molestation to himself, as to an enemy." (Fr. 88 Democritus' gnomai).

" Even when you are alone, do not say or do anything bad. Learn to respect yourself more than the others." (Fr. 244 Stobaeus III, 31, 7).

" One should not respect the others more than himself, and not to do an injury when it comes to none's notice more than when it comes to anyone's notice. On the contrary one should respect mainly himself and this must be a law for his soul so as not to do anything improper." (Fr. 264 Stobaeus IV, 5, 46).

The fear of death, according to Democritus, is a significant factor, which determines the motives of the human behaviour. The men who are aware of their bad disposition, lose their peace of mind, and due to the fear which arises from their unjust behaviour and comes upon them, they invent fictions about life after death to console themselves, or even worse throw themselves into the pursuit of bodily pleasures in order to forget these fears and the very fear of death. In this way they get involved in a vicious circle of pleasures' pursuit which gets them nowhere, since afterwards they live a life of short enjoyments, as we saw in fr. 235. Therefore their life becomes a continuous "death", namely an endless pursuit of pleasure without success. On the other hand, the man of prudence who has peace of mind and is in good spirits, is not afraid of death, since after having lived a happy life, departs from life satisfied and without a need for eternal life.

At this point we can realize that Democritus meets Heraclitus' view, concerning the "continuous death" of the life of the "**sleepers**" (Fr. 20 Heraclitus), however he himself calls them "**fools**" (*αξύνετοι*). And in general, all the philosophers, as we have seen, dissociate themselves from the common people (many, sleepers, fools), whose common sense is not sufficient to enable them to comprehend the principles which govern the universe and by extension the human nature.

" **Some people since they do not know that the mortal nature is dispersed and as they are conscious of their bad behaviour in life, are troubled and agitated and have fear while they live and invent ungrounded fictions about the time after death.**" (Fr. 297 Stobaeus IV, 50, 22).

" **Fools although hate life, they want to live for the fear of Hades.**" (Fr. 199 Stobaeus III, 4, 73).

" **Fools while are trying to avoid death they pursue it.**" (Fr. 203 Stobaeus III, 4, 77).

" **Fools desire life because of fear of death.**" (Fr. 205 Stobaeus III, 4, 79).

" **Democritus said that life without prudence, temperance and piety is not only bad life but death that lasts long.**" (Fr. 160 Porphyrious IV, 21).

The above mentioned virtues can lead one to possess **wisdom**, since through the right reason and prudence can possess all the virtues of the Greek Antiquity (justice, nobility, bravery, piety, continence, temperance etc.). However the deficiency of these virtues transforms the life into "continuous death", since the benumbed soul by the desires of pleasure or by the sorrow of their non-fulfillment, is led to that vicious circle, which does not make for happiness.

" **You should refute the unreasonable depression of your benumbed soul with reason."** (Fr. 290 Stobaeus IV, 44, 67).

To sum up with the matter of **happiness** (*ευδαιμονία*: eudaimonia), which Democritus also calls 'euesto' (*ευεστώ*), one can achieve it through peace of mind and good spirits, and this can only happen, when there is no defect or excess of pleasures, and by means of prudence, which can help him to lead a virtuous life and to act properly.

" **Athena (goddess) the Tritogeneia is considered to be by Democritus prudence. For from prudence derive the proper thought, the proper speech and the proper action."** (1b,Tritogeneia, Democritus ET. OR. 153).

Whoever possesses prudence can become a wise man and overcome the fear of death, as we saw in fr. 295. Therefore, for Democritus the **fearless wisdom** (*άθαμβος σοφία*: athambos sophia) is the precious good, since the fear leads one to postpone his self-improvement, and as a consequence to the vice.

" **Fearless wisdom is of great worth since it is precious."** (Fr. 216 Stobaeus III, 3, 74).

According to him the wisdom of nature, is greater than the one of man, since nature is self-sufficient, has assurance, its criterion is the necessity and it always rewards the best.

" **Chance is generous but uncertain, while nature is self-sufficient. Therefore with its little but certain forces wins the greater ones, which hope promises."** (Fr. 176 Stobaeus II, 9, 5).

" **When an animal needs something, knows its need, while when a man needs he does not know his need."** (Fr. 198 Stobaeus III, 4, 72).

" **By nature the authority belongs to the best."** (Fr. 267 Stobaeus IV, 6, 19).

A man by **teaching** (*διδαχή*: didache) can be transformed gradually into a completely different nature, namely he can be transformed from "fool" into a prudent man. Just like in nature, each element can be transformed into another in accordance with its mixture of atoms, in the same way through teaching changes the mixture of the atoms of a man's soul into harmonious one.

" **Nature is similar to teaching, since teaching transforms a man and by transforming him creates a new nature.**" **(Fr. 33 Clements Strom. IV, 151).**

Very significant was his study of matters concerning social and political consciousness, which Democritus presents in his work "**Little-world system**". In this work he analyses the development of the first social consciousness among the people, which he attributes to the "necessity" of survival of the human beings, that prompted them to join together in order to be able to confront the wild animals and the natural forces. As we can realize, the "**necessity**" (*ανάγκη*), which is the driving force of creation and destruction in the universe, has prompted the men to the social co-existence and by extension to the development of their social consciousness.

" **.. As for the earliest people.. because the animals used to charge at them, their interest taught them the mutual help and as the fear prompted them to live in gathering, they started to know each other..**"

" **.. In general, master of the mankind has been the necessity, which led to the knowledge of everything the most endowed by nature creature (man), whose collaborators have been his hands, reason and intelligence..**" **(4c, Little-world system, Diodorus I, 8,1).**

We consider very significant the contribution of Democritus to the philosophy and the physical sciences, as well as to the education and politics (democracy). Therefore Socrates called him "pentathlete" of philosophy. We quote some of his sayings, which we regard as well timed even nowadays.

" **The ignorance of what is excellent is the cause of error.**" **(Fr. 83).**

" A man given to contradiction and very attentive to trifles is naturally unadapted to learn what is proper." (Fr. 85 Democritus' gnomai).

" Education is adornment for the happy ones and refuge for the unhappy ones." (Fr. 180).

" The association with the vicious increases the predisposition to the vice." (Fr. 184).

" The hopes of cultured are better than the wealth of the ignorants." (Fr. 185).

" Most become noble by learning and not by nature." (Fr. 242).

Democritus believed deeply in freedom of speech and choice, in political rights and all the democratic institutions, therefore he considered them more important than the prosperity of the authoritarian regimes, since he regarded respect for oneself and justice as the most significant virtues.

" Hunger in democracy is more preferable from the so-called prosperity of the authoritarian regimes, just as freedom is from slavery." (Fr. 251).

" Because the state which is governed properly is the greatest protection and everything lies in this. When the state is safe everything is safe and when it is destroyed everything is destroyed." (Fr. 252 Stobaeus IV, 1, 42-43).

" It is hard to be governed by those who are worse than ourselves." (Fr. 49).

" It is shameful thing for a man to be employed about the affairs of others, but to be ignorant of his own." ((Fr. 80).

" It is beautiful to impede an unjust man; but if this be not possible, it is beautiful not to act in conjunction with him." (Fr. 38).

In conclusion, we quote a fragment of Democritus philosophy, which we regard as a quintessence of his philosophical attitude to the very meaning of our existence.

" - The world is a scene; life is a transition. You came, you saw, you departed.

- The world is a mutation; life a vain opinion.

- **A little wisdom is more precious than a glory for a great folly."** **(Fr. 115 Democritus' gnomai).**

10. The Sophists (5th century BC)

The sophists were wandering teachers of Greece who taught mainly rhetoric, which aimed at persuasion but not truth, since at this time was a need for these skills to the ordinary citizens in order to participate in public assemblies and to win over opinion in courts of law. Sophism it is not considered to be a philosophical doctrine, but a social movement which contained men of genuine intellectual eminence such as Protagoras and Gorgias, whose characteristics were mainly the skepticism of the intellect and the relativity of truth.

Protagoras of Abdera claimed that " **man is the measure of all things**", which means that true is what it seems to each man to be, namely each perception is subjective and relative, an argument which he based upon the relativity of the sense-perceptions by ignoring their interpretation through the intellect. Therefore he was the one who tried to make the weak argument stronger and the strong argument weak.

Gorgias of Leontini (Sicily) reacting to Parmenides' view that "the same thing exists for thinking and Being" (Fr.3), and as he took no account of his clarification "the things which are securely present to the mind" (Fr.4), he concluded that **"Nothing exists; if anything did exist, it would be unknowable; and if it were knowable, it would be incommunicable"**. On this argument Gorgias based his "agnosticism" and his **moral relativity**.

Most of the sophists challenged the objectivity of Greek morality, since they believed in cultural relativity, just like many modern sociologists do, and that the basis of morality lies in custom and law. This belief inevitably resulted in the view that all moral standards are subjective and relative to the individual, therefore nothing is either right or wrong. This intellectual and moral skepticism contributed to further development of philosophy with Socrates' moral philosophy and Aristotle's logic, as we are going to see.

*At this point we complete the presentation of **Presocratics**, who associated their philosophy with the study of nature, and their conclusions drawn by this study were used as principles of their philosophy. However, philosophy with Socrates and afterwards, took a turn from the study of nature for the study of man and morality.*

B. Socrates (470 – 399 BC)

Socrates was a disciple of Archelaus, the disciple of Anaxagoras, and he is known by his saying " **one thing I know that I know nothing**" (*έν οίδα ότι ουδέν οίδα*: en oida oti ouden oida), since Socrates wanted to emphasize that the method of searching for the truth, must be followed without prejudice, in other words, nothing has to be taken for granted.

The basic method of approaching the truth for Socrates was: a) The **midwifery** (*μαιευτική*: meaeutiki), which he used to apply in a discussion by questioning his interlocutors about their definition of terms and concepts, and never expressing his own views, in order to elicit the truth from them, the truth that the others could discover within themselves and bring forth into the light, due to this method.

" **And the most important thing about my art (midwifery) is the ability to apply all possible test to the offspring, to determine whether the young mind is being delivered by phantom, that is an error, or a fertile truth.**" (Plato, Theaetetus 150 c).

b) The **controlling** method (*έλεγχος*: elenchus), which consisted in the strict control and the cross-examination of all the philosophical concepts, without prejudice and by means of refutation, in order to reach to the real and true concepts, as we also saw in Parmenides' method of truth.

Socrates did not write anything, and everything we know about his teachings, is what **Plato** wrote in his Dialogues. Plato met Socrates when he was a very young man, and became his disciple for eight years until Socrates' death. As we know, Socrates was sentenced to death and volunteered to drink the hemlock, and died faithful to his principles, concerning the compliance with state's laws, as we can see in the following answer, that he gave to his disciple Crito, when the latter proposed him to escape from the prison.

".. **If the laws and the state came and confronted us and asked: <Tell me Socrates, what are you intending to do?**

Do you not by this action you are attempting intend to destroy us, the laws and indeed the whole city, as far as you are concerned? Or do you think it possible for the city not to be destroyed if the verdicts of its courts have no force, but are nullified and set at naught by private individuals?" (Plato, Crito 50 a, b).

We are going to examine Socrates' teachings together with Plato's, since in all Plato's dialogues appears Socrates to explain his philosophical principles. Apart from Plato, another significant disciple of Socrates was **Antisthenes** (445-365 BC), who disagreed with Plato upon the matter of education, and then he founded the philosophical School of the **Cynics**. He believed, like Socrates, that the purpose of life must be the achievement of virtue and the release from bodily pleasures. Therefore, the Cynics rejected the conventional lifestyle, and castigated the dissolute life, hypocrisy and arrogance of their contemporaries. Other well-known Cynics were **Diogenes** of Sinope and **Zeno** who afterwards became the founder of **Stoicism**.

C. Plato (427 – 348 BC)

Plato was born in Athens of distinguished Athenian parentage, and in the beginning he took up poetry, until he met Socrates in the age of twenty years, and then he dedicated his life to philosophy. He is considered to be the founder of **Idealism**, since he introduced the existence of the eternal and unchangeable "Forms" or else **"Ideas"** (*Ιδέαι*) of the **"Being"** (*Είναι*: einai), as well as the method of knowing it through **"dialectic"** (*διαλεκτική*). His philosophy is mainly influenced by his master Socrates, but also includes some principles of Orphic and Pythagorean teachings, as well as the Parmenidean views about the unchangeable concepts of the "Being". In 387 BC he founded his philosophical School in Athens, the well - known **"Academy"**, which lasted until the 6th century AD. His thought has influenced most of the following philosophers of the West until nowadays.

Basic principle of his philosophy is the existence of the divine, immaterial and eternal Forms (Ideas), which are: Justice, Goodness, Equality, Love, Knowledge, Beauty etc., and they derive from the Idea of the "**Good**" (*Aγαθόν*: Agathon, God). The Ideas of the "Good" can only be apprehended by "**reason**" or "**intellect**" (*νούς*: nous), since the "Good" resides in the world of Knowledge.

According to "Platonic" Socrates exist two different worlds, the "**visible**" (*ορατός*: horatos), which is the material world and we can perceive through the **senses,** and the "**intelligible**" (*νοητός*: noetos), which is immaterial and we can only understand through "**intellect**". The "intelligible" world is the true and the eternal one, since it belongs to the "**Being**", while the "visible" is ephemeral and false, as it belongs to the "**coming to be**". The relation between the two worlds is compared to the relation between object and reflexion in the water. In other words, the "visual" world is the reflexion in the water or in the mirror of the "intelligible" world. Since the truth can be found in the "intelligible" world and not in the "visual" one, therefore we should focus our attention on the eternal and real "**being**" (*όv*: on) in order to acquire knowledge, and not on the changeable and ephemeral "**coming to be**" (*γίγνεσθαι*: gignesthai), of which we can only have an assumption and "**belief**" (*δόξα*: doxa). From all the above-mentioned principles is apparent the influence of Parmenides (Fr.2) on Platonic Socrates.

" **Well understand the soul in the same way. When it focuses on something illuminated by truth, and what is (όv), it understands, knows and apparently possesses understanding (νούν), but when it focuses on what is mixed with obscurity, on what comes to be (γίγνεσθαι) and passes away, it opines and is dimmed, changes its opinions (δόξα) this way and that, and seems bereft of understanding.**" (Plato, Republic VI 508 d).

HANDBOOK OF GREEK PHILOSOPHY

Cosmogony

Referring to the creation of the "visible" world, Plato in his Dialogue *Timaeus*, states his views about the creation of the universe by the God, with the use of geometrical patterns and numbers, in order to create the "**four elements**" in such way that the one can be transformed into the other. To be more specific, the molecules of **fire** have the solid form of the **tetrahedron**, constructed out of equilaterial triangles, which are combined together. The solid form of **air** is the **octahedron** constructed out also of the same triangles. The element of **water** has the solid form of the **icosahedron**, which is made up of a combination of one hundred and twenty of the elementary triangles with twenty equilaterial triangles. Finally the element of **earth** is made up of isosceles triangles combined in the solid form of the **cube** (Timaeus 55 a, b). All the above mentioned solids can be inscribed in the sphere, and the fifth inscribed in the sphere solid is the **dodecahedron,** which is made up of **pentagons,** and it has been used for the shape of the **universe** (Timaeus 55 c). By this combination of infinite varieties in shape and size of triangles have been created the four primary bodies, therefore it allows them to transform one into another eternally and without being passed away (Timaeus 57 d). These views of Plato are referred to the Pythagorean views about the creation of the Universe.

God has created the "visible" world after its pattern of the eternal "intelligible" world, and this "visible" is the only one and unique model.

" **So, in order that this living thing should be like the complete Living Thing (Intelligible world) in respect of uniqueness, the Maker made neither two, nor yet an infinite number of worlds. On the contrary, our universe came to be as the one and only thing of this kind, is so now and will continue to be so in the future." (Plato, Timaeus 31 b).**

The soul, according to Plato, is immortal and immaterial, therefore the Creator mixed three components in order to make the soul. One from the changeless and indivisible "Being", one from the changeable which "comes to be" in the corporeal realm, and a third one, intermediate form of being derived from the other two. Then he made a single mixture, from which, after dividing in many parts and mixing again through geometrical proportions, he made the final compound and sliced it in the form of **X**. Then, after he had bent the two lines of X back in a circle, he made two concentric circles one vertical to the other. The **outer** circle was of the "**Same**" (**Being**) and the **inner** was of the "**Different**" (**coming to be**), and next he made a movement of the "Same" revolve toward the right and the movement of the "Different" toward the left by way of the diagonal. We could compare this simultaneous rotation of the two circles to the transmission of **electromagnetic wave**, where the wave of electric field moves simultaneously and vertically to the wave of the magnetic field carrying messages, data and pictures. Then the Creator divided further the inner circle to make seven unequal circles, corresponding to the orbits of seven planets (Timaeus 35b-36b).

In this way the soul started from the centre and spread all over the universe, revolving within itself in eternal rotation. Therefore, the visible world has a body and is material, while the soul is immaterial and invisible.

" **The soul was woven together with the body from the center on out in every direction to the outermost limit of the universe, and covered it all around on the outside. And revolving within itself, it initiated a divine beginning of unceasing intelligent life for all time. Now, while the body of the universe had come to be as a visible thing, the soul was invisible.**" (Plato, Timaeus 36 e).

Since the soul is a mixture of these three components, when comes into contact, has the faculty of knowing both, the divisible and changeable - which is related to "coming to be" – and the changeless and indivisible, that belongs to the "Being". As we can see, according to Plato, the capacity for knowledge is of like by like (through the same, ὅμοιον: omoion), just like Parmenides' and Empedocles' view about knowledge (Empedocles fr. 109). The way of perception of the changeable (Different) follows straight line but the knowledge of the changeless (Same) follows the rotation of the circle of the Same. The perception, on the one hand, of the "visible" world can lead to true "opinions" (δόξαι) and "convictions" (πίστεις: pisteis), and on the other hand the perception of the "intelligible" world results in "understanding" (νόησις: noesis) and "knowledge" (ἐπιστήμη: episteme).

" Because the soul is a mixture of the Same, the Different and Being, because it was divided up and bound together in different proportions, and because it circles round upon itself, then whenever it comes into contact with something whose being is scatterable or else with something whose being is indivisible, it is stirred throughout its whole self. It then declares what exactly this thing is the same as, or what it is different from, and in what respect and in what manner, as well as when, it turns out that they are the same or different and are characterized as such."

".. Whenever the account concerns anything that is perceptible, the circle of the Different goes straight and proclaims it throughout its whole soul. This is how firm and true <opinions> and <convictions> come about. Whenever, on the other hand, the account concerns any object of reasoning, and the circle of the Same runs well and reveals it, the necessary result is <understanding> and <knowledge>." (Plato, Timaeus 37 a, b, c).

As Plato goes on with the description of the creation of the universe, he says that the Creator made the heaven, the planets and the stars, and then he set in motion the planets, in order to create the "time" in succession, and to make an eternal image of the model of "intelligible" world. Then he gave birth to the gods like Zeus, Hera etc. to supervise the universe, and in the end he created the human beings by mounting each soul in a carriage, and in particular the number of souls was equal to the number of the stars. Since the souls consist of this immortal mixture, can survive after the death of the human body, and through repeated reincarnations can acquire virtue and true knowledge of the "Being", and then return to its dwelling place in his companion star, to live a life of happiness (Timaeus 37d-42d). From all the above mentioned, it is evident that Plato with Timaeus initiates in philosophy the natural **Theology**, with apparent influences from the Orphics and Pythagoreans, as well as the religious beliefs of Egyptians and Judeans.

Parts of the soul – Gnoseology

Concerning the parts of the soul and the faculty of knowledge, the "Platonic" Socrates holds the view that exist three different parts of the soul, the rational part, the spirited part and the appetitive part. The "**appetitive part**" (*επιθυμητικόν*: epithemetikon) is related to the desires, instincts and indulgences; therefore it is referring to the bodily pleasures. This part he calls it also "**irrational**" (*αλόγιστον*: alogiston), since it is completely unreasonable.

The "**spirited part**" (*θυμοειδές*: thymoeides) is referring to the emotions and is related to joy, hope, sorrow, anger, fear, disappointment etc. He regards it as the courageous part of the soul, for it can lead one to bravery when is guided by the reasonable part.

The most significant part, according to Socrates, is the "**rational part**" (*λογιστικόν*: logistikon), which is related to the faculties of reasoning, judgement, thinking (*λογισμός*: logismos), opinion, conviction, knowledge, understanding, nous (*νούς*).

" **Hence it is not unreasonable for us to claim that they are two, and different from one another. We'll call the part of the soul with which it calculates, the** rational part**, and the other part with which it lusts, hungers, thirsts and gets excited by other appetites, the** irrational appetitive part**, companion of certain indulgences and pleasures."** (Plato, Republic IV 439 d).

" **Is the** spirited part **a third thing in the soul, that is by nature the helper of the rational part, provided that it has not been corrupted by a bad upbringing? It must be a third."** (Plato, Republic IV 441 a).

" **Then would not these two parts also do the finest job of guarding the whole soul and body against external**

enemies – reason by planning, spirit by fighting, following its leader, and carrying out the leader's decisions through its courage? – Yes, that's true." (Plato, Republic IV 442 b).

In each person the relationship among the three parts is determined by his upbringing, in other words his character. Since the "spirited part" is the most powerful (concerning the energy), prompts the man to certain actions, following the orders either of the "appetitive" or of the "rational" part, according to his character.

When one feels fear, sorrow or anger to a large extent as he hungers or thirsts or is deprived of any other bodily pleasure, and on the other hand, he is overjoyed (spirited part), when he enjoys all the bodily pleasures (food, drink, sex etc.) - and he always thinks up (rational part) lawful and unlawful means in order to satisfy his insatiable desires for bodily pleasures - we could say about this person, that his "appetitive part" has become very strong, due to the excessive fulfillment of the bodily pleasures, and rules over the other two parts. This is the case of the **self-indulgent** man, who in order to satisfy all of his desires for bodily pleasures, and by using his "rational part" for this purpose, he ends up in subservience, deception, corruption, crime etc.

On the other hand, someone else can stand with courage (without fear, sorrow, despair or anger) all the hardships and deprivations of the bodily pleasures, without becoming unjust in order to satisfy his bodily pleasures. In this case we are referring to the **moderate** and abstemious man, whose "rational" part rules over the other two parts harmonically, which in turn agree to follow the orders of the "rational" part.

" And these two (rational and spirited part), having been nurtured in this way, and having truly learned their own roles and been educated in them, they will govern the appetitive part, which is the largest part in each person's soul and is by nature the most insatiable for money. They will watch over it, to see that it is not filled with the so-called pleasures of the body and that it does not become so big and strong, that it no longer does its own work but attempts to enslave and rule over the classes it is not fitted

to rule, thereby overturning everyone's whole life." (Plato, Republic IV 442 a, b).

" And it is because of the spirited part I suppose that we call a single individual courageous (*ανδρείος*: andreios), namely when it preserves through pains and pleasures the declaration of reason (*λόγος*: logos), about what is to be feared and what is not." (Plato, Republic IV 442 c).

" And is not he moderate because of the friendly and harmonious relations between these same parts, namely when the ruler and the ruled believe in common that the rational part should rule and don't engage in civil war against it?" (Plato, Republic IV c, d).

As we can see, the moral virtues that correspond to the three parts of the soul are, as for the "**appetitive**" part **moderation** (*σωφροσύνη*: sophrosini) and abstinence, and as for the "**spirited**" one **courage** (*ανδρεία*:andreia). Concerning the "rational" part, Socrates defines **prudence** (*φρόνησις*: phronesis) and **wisdom** (*σοφία*: sofia) as its virtues, which are the ones that must guide a man in his actions. These three parts, when they collaborate harmonically and each one does its own work that is fitted to it, then the man can be called **just** (*δίκαιος*: dikaios), according to Socrates. Therefore "justice" comprises the three virtues which we previously mentioned. However, before we analyse justice, we are going to refer to the rational part of the soul and the faculty of knowledge through the reason.

As we have seen, according to Plato, the **visible** world is a model of the intelligible, therefore the perception of that is inadequate, since it is perceptible by the senses, and as a result we can only have true **opinions** and **beliefs** about it. On the other hand, the **intelligible** world is true and eternal, therefore we can only acquire **understanding** and **knowledge** about it by reasoning.

" What is that which always is (*όν αεί*) and has no becoming, and what is that which becomes but never is (*όν ουδέποτε*). The former is grasped by understanding which involves reasoned account (*νοήσαι μετά λόγου*: noesai meta logou). It is unchanging. The latter is grasped by opinion,

which involves unreasoning sense perception. It comes to be and passes away but never really is." (Plato, Timaeus 28 a).

Beginning with the view that there are many beautiful and good things, Socrates concludes that there is only one good and beautiful, which is the "**Good itself**" (*αυτό αγαθόν*: auto agathon), therefore it is desirable for its own sake and not for the sake of anything else, and from this derive all the other goods. The "Good itself" is the cause of existence, knowledge and truth, which reigns in the "intelligible world". Then he draws a parallel between the Sun of the "visible" world, and the Good of the "intelligible" world. As the sun brings the visible things into existence and gives the light to be seen, in the same way the Good is the source of knowledge, truth and existence of the "intelligible" world. The power to see the objects of the "visible" comes from the light of the sun, while the power to know the intelligible things comes from the Good, the Being that enables us to understand the objects of knowledge, which means the intelligible "Forms" (**Ideas**). Following up the analogy further, the means of sight in the "visible" world are the eyes, while the means of understanding the intelligible is reason (**nous**). The faculty of perceiving the "visible" is the eyesight, while the faculty of grasping the "intelligible" is the understanding power of intellect. We can perceive then the "visible realm" through the senses, but not through the intellect, while on the contrary we cannot perceive the "intelligible" realm through the senses, we can only understand it by the reason, through the intelligible Forms (Ideas). We quote an index of the correspondences between the intelligible and visible world.

Visible world	Intelligible world
Sun	Good itself
Light	Truth
Sight	Understanding power of intellect
Eyes	Intellect (*νούς*)
Visible things, colours	Objects of knowledge (*νοήματα*), Ideas

The Good, although is not identified with knowledge and truth, is the source of knowledge and truth through the reason. The Good is more beautiful and superior than knowledge and truth, since it is the Being itself, therefore is perfect, and from it derive the "visible" realm, the virtues, and anything that is beautiful and good in the universe.

" - **The sun is not sight, but isn't it the cause of sight itself and seen by it?**

- **Certainly.**

- **Let's say then, that this is what I called the offspring of the Good, which the Good begot as its analogue. What the Good itself is in the intelligible realm, in relation to understanding and intelligible things, the sun is the visible realm in relation to sight and visible things." (Plato Republic VI 508 b, c).**

" **And Beauty itself and Good itself and all the things that we set down as many, reversing ourselves, we set down according to a single Form (Idea) of each, believing that there is but one and calling the <being> of each.**

And we say that many beautiful things and the rest are visible but not intelligible, while the forms are intelligible but not visible." (Plato, Republic VI 507 b).

From all the above mentioned it is apparent that, when the soul focuses on what always exists (**being: όν**) and is illuminated by the **light** of truth, then it possesses **knowledge** (*επιστήμη*: episteme), **understanding** (*νόησις*: noesis) and **intelligence** (*νούς*: nous). On the other hand, when the soul focuses on what "**comes to be**" (*γίγνεσθαι*) and passes away, where there is **obscurity** and **dim**, it cannot see clearly, therefore it can only have **opinion** (*δόξα*: doxa) and **belief** (*πίστις*: pistis), since it has a lack of understanding and intelligence. At this point, we can realize that Socrates adopts Parmenides' view, as we saw in fr.2 of Parmenides, where he declared that the truth can be found out in the "Being" and not in what "comes to be".

" **Well, understand the soul in the same way. When it focuses on something illuminated by the truth and what is** (being), achieves understanding and knowledge and is apparently in possession of intelligence, but when it focuses on what is mixed with obscurity, on what comes to be and passes away, it has only opinions and seems bereft of understanding.." (Plato, Republic VI 508 d).

Plato in his middle Dialogue **Republic**, analyzes his epistemological notions by the use of the example of the divided line The faculty of knowledge, both of the "intelligible" and "visible" realm can be graphically represented by a straight line, divided in four sections, as follows:

	Visible	//	Intelligible world	
	Opinion	//	Knowledge	
B	D	C	E	A
/-------/-----------//-----------------/--------------------------------/				
Imagination/ Belief	// Thought	/ Understanding	/
(eikasia) / (pistis)	// (dianoia)	/ (noesis)	/

Ratio BD/DC = BC/CA and CE/EA = BC/CA, and BD/DC = CE/EA.

The section of the straight line **BC** refers to the perception of the **visible** world, and the part **CA** refers to the perception of the **intelligible** world. The section **BC** of the visible world is divided in two subsections **BD** and **DC**. The first one **BD**, refers to the **sense-impressions**, which Socrates calls images, or shadows or reflections, since through the senses we perceive the **reflections** (impressions) of the objects and not the objects themselves. The section **DC** corresponds to the **objects** themselves of the visible world, namely the originals of these images that we perceive. Since our perception of the visible is based upon the reflections and not upon the real objects (originals), it is called **imagination** (εικασία: eikasia) and corresponds to the section **BD**. Our perception of the whole of the objects which compose the visible world (section **DC**), he calls it **belief** (πίστις: pistis), since we simply believe that the reality of the visible world is the one that we perceive through these images (impressions), without being sure and without any reasoning, for we base this perception only upon the images of the objects and not upon the objects themselves (originals). The total line section **BC** corresponds to the so-called **opinion** (δόξα), namely the perception of the visible world as a whole, of which the highest capability for us is to have a clear picture of the visible world, namely **true opinion** (*doxa alethes*), as we have seen.

" **It is like a line divided in two unequal sections. Then divide each section – namely that of the visible and that of the intelligible – in the same ratio as the line. In terms now of relative clarity and opacity, one subsection of the <u>visible</u> consists of <u>images</u>. And by images I mean, first shadows, then <u>reflections</u> in water and in all close-packed, smooth and shiny materials, and everything of that sort, if you understand.**

In the other subsection of the visible, put the <u>originals</u> of these images, namely the <u>animals</u> around us, all the <u>plants</u> and the whole class of <u>manufactured things</u>.

Would you be willing to say that, as regards truth and untruth, the division is in this proportion. As the opinable is to knowable, so the likeness is to the thing that is like." (Plato, Republic VI 509 e, 510 a).

As for the section of the intelligible that corresponds to **CA**, namely **knowledge** (ἐπιστήμη: episteme), it is also divided in two subsections **CE** and **EA**. The section **CE** corresponds to **thought** (διάνοια: dianoia), namely conception by the use of intelligible entities. The images of the first section **BD** are used as a basis to form the first hypotheses, the first conclusions, after intellectual interpretation of these images. In other words, by using these sense-data (images) and through the intellectual interpretation of them, one proceeds, starting first with hypotheses and then he draws conclusions, which means laws and principles, which determine the appearances. On this process, some assumptions must be rejected, and some other, the confirmed ones, must be accepted. The whole procedure is intellectual by using the images as a basis for the assumptions. This section **CE**, corresponds to the nowadays **scientific** inquiry, the searching out of the laws, which determine the phenomena.

" – Consider now how the section of the intelligible is to be divided. - How? – As follows: In one subsection the soul, using as images the things that were imitated before, is forced to investigate from <u>hypotheses</u>, proceeding not to a first principle, but to a <u>conclusion</u>." (Plato Republic VI 511 a).

" This then, is the kind of thing that, on the one hand, I said is intelligible, and on the other, is such that the soul is forced to use hypotheses in the investigation of it, not travelling up to a first principle, since it cannot reach beyond its hypotheses, but using as images those very things of which images were made in the section below, and which, by comparison to their images, were thought to be cleared (*εναργέσιν*: enargesin) and to be valued as such." (Plato, Republic VI 511 a).

The last section of the perception of the intelligible **EA**, corresponds to the **understanding** (*νόησις*: noesis), and is considered to be the highest level of knowledge, since it refers to the knowledge and comprehension of the **first principle** (*τού παντός αρχήν*: tou pantos archin), which determines all things in the universe. Those laws and principles that we concluded in the previous stage of **thought** (**CE**), we must consider now as hypotheses, in order to reach the first principle, which means the "Being itself". Because all the previous principles are consistent with one another, therefore they can be deduced in one **first principle**, from which derive all the others and whose they are part. So, the laws and the principles of mathematics, physics, astronomy etc. can be **abstracted** to one principle, of which they are the various forms of manifestation. The method that one must follow to approach that first principle is **dialectic**, which consists in knowing and understanding the intelligible forms (Ideas), therefore through dialectic one can reach the first principle, the Good itself, the Being. After having grasped the first principle, then by **deduction** one can apply this knowledge of the first principle on each subject of knowledge and everyday life. The whole procedure is also here (**EA**) completely intellectual, but without the use of any image as in the previous stage (thought), but only by the use of intelligible Forms and Ideas. When one fathoms these forms by reasoning, can reach the first principle and achieve understanding and true knowledge of the Good.

" In the other subsection, however, it makes its way to a **first principle**, that is not a hypothesis, proceeding from hypothesis but without the images used in the previous subsection, using forms themselves and making its investigation through them." (Plato Republic VI 510 b).

" Then also understand that, by the other subsection of the intelligible, I mean that which reason itself grasps by the power of **dialectic**. It does not consider these hypotheses as first principles but truly as hypotheses – but as stepping stones to take off from, enabling it to reach the unhypothetical first principle of everything. Having grasped this principle, it reverses itself and keeping hold of what follows from it, comes down to a conclusion without making use of anything visible at all, but only of forms themselves, moving on from forms to forms and ending in forms." (Plato, Republic VI 511 b).

" Thus there are four conditions of the soul, corresponding to the four subsections of our line. **Understanding** for the highest, **thought** for the second, **belief** for the third and **imaging** for the last." (Plato, Republic VI 511 d).

Further to epistemology, Plato presents the well-known allegory of the **Cave**, in order to give a vivid account of knowledge and happiness in the intelligible realm, compared with the ones in the visible realm. He likens the visible realm to a cave, where people live since they were born and they are chained by the leg and by the neck, so they can see only what is in front of them. The only light in the cave comes from a fire burning behind them, and it enables them to see their shadows, thrown by the fire-light on the wall of the cave facing them. Between the fire and the prisoners is a track with a parapet built along it, and behind this parapet, persons are carrying along various artificial objects, including figures of men or animals in wood or stones or other materials, which project above the parapet. So, the prisoners the only things they know is their own shadows and those passing shadows of the objects.

If someone of the prisoners had been released from the chains and come out to light, he would have been able to see the real light of the sun, the real objects and not the figures, the sun and the stars themselves, and even to realize that the sun produces the seasons and the life on earth. Certainly, he would need some time to grow accustomed, before could see the sunlight. However, he would count himself very happy for the liberation from the chains, the miserable life and illusion, therefore he would never like to get back to his previous life. (Plato Republic 514-516).

The allegory of the Cave, as we can realize, refers to the **visible** world, in which since we are enslaved by the **chains** of the **senses**, we have limited capability of knowledge, for we perceive only the shadows and the figures (sense-impressions) of the objects and not the objects themselves. When we manage to escape from the world of senses and to come to the **intelligible** realm, through **reasoning**, then we will be liberated from the chains of the senses, which have forced us to see only in one direction (limited perception). Afterwards we can achieve universal and true **knowledge** of the real substance of all things, and grasp the Idea of the **Good** (light), which is the cause of everything (sun). This liberation from the chains of ignorance give us joy and happiness, which cannot be compared to the pleasures of life in the Cave (sensational pleasures).

" **The whole image Glaucon, must be fitted together, with what we said before. The visible realm should be likened to the prison dwelling, and the light of the fire insight to the power of the sun. And if you interpret the upward journey and the study of things above as the upward journey of the soul to the intelligible world, you'll grasp what I hope to convey, since that is what you wanted to hear about.**" (Plato, Republic 517 b).

Since the human soul, when once was in the intelligible world acquired knowledge of all the divine things, desires to stay there forever. However, if by some reason it is forced to come down to the visible world, then it will be burnt with desire and **love** of **wisdom**, of **beauty** and **immortality**, which it met and saw in the intelligible realm of the Good, and will not have peace until it meets again, what has experienced in the realm of the Good. That desire and love of immortality is manifested as a creative impulse, which means that we, the human beings, always want to leave something new behind, before we become older and die, e.g. offsprings, creations, reputation etc. The desire for beauty and strife for immortality and self-completion in a form of creativity is also manifested as creativity of the mind in a form of love of wisdom, which can only be fulfilled, when the soul grasps the knowledge of the beauty and the truth of the "Being". Upon this view Plato bases his doctrine, that the knowledge of the Forms (Ideas) of the Good is a **recollection** (*ανάμνησις*: anamnesis) of what the soul knew in the past, when it was in the intelligible world. Therefore, according to him, each human being has an inborn impulse to search for beauty, virtue and truth.

" **For among the animals the principle is the same as with us, and mortal nature seeks so far as possible to live forever and be immortal. And this is possible in one way only: by reproduction, because it always leaves behind a new young one in the place of the old.**" (Plato, Symposium **207 d).**

" **So don't be surprised if everything naturally values its own offspring, because it is for the sake of** immortality **that this eagerness and** Love **attends upon all.**" (Plato, Symposium **508 b).**

" **But the lover is turned to the great sea of beauty and gazing upon this, he gives birth to many gloriously beautiful Ideas and thoughts, in unstinting** Love of wisdom**, until, having grown and been strengthened there, he catches sight of Knowledge, and it is the Knowledge of such Beauty.**" (Plato, Symposium **210 d).**

However, Plato in his later Dialogues *Theaetetus* and *Sophist* changes his definition of knowledge. Knowledge: *true belief with an account* was proved not sufficient enough in the

Theaetetus, while in the *Sophist* dialectic is the understanding of the five Great Kinds (*Being, Rest, Change, Sameness* and *Difference*) and of their capability of blending.

Immortality of the soul

Plato proves the immortality of the soul, so to say the persistence of the soul after the death of the body, in his early Dialogue *Phaedo*, by the use of four arguments: The cycle of opposites, the theory of recollection, the resemblance to the true and eternal Forms, and the exclusion of the opposite eternal Forms.

In the "**argument of the opposites**" Plato points out that each thing comes to be from its opposite, for those forms that exists an opposite. For example, the larger comes from the smaller, just from the unjust, sleeping from being awake and vice versa. In the same way, the living comes from the dead and the dead from the living. Therefore, the souls of the dead come to life again in this cyclical change, otherwise if everything endowed with life were to die and remain in the state of death, ultimately everything would have to be dead in the universe and nothing alive (Plato Phaedo 71 – 72).

" **In the same way my dear Cebes, if everything that partakes of life were to die and remain in that state and not to come back to life again, would not everything ultimately have to be dead and nothing alive?" (Plato, Phaedo 72 d).**

The reason why particularly the soul persists after the death of the body, Plato tries to explain with his second "**argument of recollection**". Beginning with the common knowledge that everything that we can recollect, we must have previously learned, he draws attention to the faculty of mind concerning the **similarity** and **equality** of the objects. So, he claims, when we perceive the visible objects through the senses, we are in a position to compare these objects and conclude that e.g. this one is similar to that, or equal to the other or larger than this one etc. This means that we possess the knowledge of the **Equal** itself, **Greater** itself and **Smaller** itself, long before our senses allowed us to perceive the visible objects of wood or stone etc. After we have perceived the objects, we are able to compare them and to conclude that, this piece of wood for example is larger than the other one, or equal to this one. This knowledge of the forms of Equality, Smallness and so on, since we possess it from our birth, means that we have acquired it in the past before our birth, for knowledge is a recollection of what we have previously learned. As we can realize, this knowledge is similar to the **a priori** knowledge of **Kant**.

" **Consider, he said, whether this is the case: we say that there is something that is equal. I do not mean a stick equal to a stick, or a stone to a stone, or anything of the kind, but something beyond all these, the Equal itself** (*αυτό τό ίσον* : auto to ison). **Shall we say that this exists or not?**

And do we know what is this? – Certainly.

Where have we acquired this knowledge?" (Plato, **Phaedo 74 a, b).**

In combination now with the first argument, we can conclude that the human soul coming from a previous death does not lose this knowledge, which remains as a recollection, but recovers it by the use of senses. However, we must consider the fact that, when we recall something from the visible things, during this recollection we always realize that what we recall e.g. a person, object etc., is always an inferior copy of the real person, object etc.

" **When the recollection is caused by similar things, must one not of necessity also experience this: to consider whether the similarity to that which one recollects is deficient in any respect or complete?"**(Plato, Phaedo 74 a).

From all the above considerations we can conclude that, our soul after having acquired the knowledge of Equality itself, and while seeing the visible objects, realizes that these objects appear to be the same with the original equal (perfect), however they are always inferior, just like the memories are always inferior to the objects themselves.

" **Whenever someone, on seeing something says to himself: <the thing I am looking at wants to be like**

122

something else but falls short and cannot be like the other, since it is inferior copy>." (Plato, Phaedo 74 d).

To sum up, as we had possessed the knowledge of the Equal itself before birth, and since after birth we have the ability of perception through the senses, we try to refer these sense-data of equal objects to this Ideal Equal, but we realize that although they are inclined to be equal, are always inferior to that Ideal.

" Then before we began to see and hear or otherwise perceive, we must have possessed knowledge of the Equal itself if we were about to refer our sense perceptions of equal objects to it, and realized that all of them were eager to be like it, but were inferior." (Plato, Phaedo 75 b).

This previously mentioned knowledge of the Ideal Forms that the soul has acquired in the intelligible realm of the Good, remains in its memory, and is manifested as a faculty of comparison of all the perceptible things with the ideal and perfect original Forms, which the soul once has learned in the intelligible realm. That particular knowledge does not only concern the knowledge of the **Equal**, Greater and Smaller, but also the knowledge of the **Beautiful itself** (*καλόν*: kalon), the **Good** (*αγαθόν*: agathon) itself, the **Just** (*δίκαιον*: dikaion) and the **Pious** (*όσιον*: osion), which are called intelligible **Forms** or **Ideas**. These **Forms** are the **eternal** attributes of the Good itself, of the unchangeable and divine **Being**. Therefore, the **recollection** (*ανάμνησις*) of all these intelligible Forms of the Being is the knowledge of the truth, of what really exists, of "**what it is**" (*αυτό ó έστι*: auto o esti). This knowledge can only be recalled through **dialectic**, as we are going to see later on.

" Therefore, if we had this knowledge, we knew before birth and immediately after not only the Equal, but the Greater and the Smaller and all such things, for our present argument is no more about the <u>Equal</u> than about the <u>Beautiful</u> itself, the <u>Good</u> itself, the <u>Just</u>, the <u>Pious</u> and, as I say about all those things which we mark with the seal of <what it is>." (Plato, Phaedo 75 c, d).

Referring now to the well-known argument that the soul is a **harmony** that persists, Plato argues that each harmony is composed of elements, which are in the same state, so if the soul were a harmony, would not have existed before its elements. Furthermore, since the wise soul rules over the elements of which it is composed, which means the appetitive and the spirited part, it is impossible to be a harmony, in which as we know, none of its composing elements can rule over the others.

" **On the other hand we previously agreed that if the soul were a harmony, it would never be out of tune with the stress and relaxation and the striking of the strings or anything else done to its composing elements, but it would follow and never direct them?" (Plato, Phaedo 94 c).**

Further to the matter of immortality of the soul, Plato refers to the imperishable Ideas and distinguishes them from the other pairs of opposites, mentioned in his first argument. These Forms although have opposite qualities (e.g. warm – cold, odd – even etc.), they neither can tolerate the coming to be from one another, nor admit the opposite Form, but when that Form advances upon them, they either perish or withdraw. For example, the odd number three (3) cannot be transformed into the even number two (2), but each one retaining its quality, perishes or gives way. The same as, when the cold snow approaches the hot fire they cannot change the one into hot snow and the other into cold fire.

" **Look now. What I want to make clear is this : not only do those opposites not admit each other, but this is also true of those things which, while not being opposite to each other, yet always contain the opposites, and it seems that these do not admit that Form which is opposite to that which is in them; when it approaches them, they either perish or give way." (Plato, Phaedo 104 b).**

According to this argument of the **exclusion of the opposite Forms**, since the immortal soul is within a body which is alive, when death comes, the body will change from **alive** into its opposite **dead** (first category of the opposites), while the soul since it is an imperishable Form, will give way to death and will leave safe and indestructible for another place. As the **body** possesses the quality of **mortal** can be transformed from **alive** into its opposite **dead**. However, as the **soul** possesses the quality of **immortal Form,** cannot be transformed into its opposite **mortal**, but it simply gives way to death and it **goes away.**

" **Then when death comes to man, the mortal part of him dies, it seems but this deathless part goes away safe and indestructible, yielding the place to death.**" (Plato, Phaedo 106 e).

In his Dialogue *Phaedrus* Plato adds one more argument of the immortality of the soul, concerning its capability of **self-motion.** To be more specific, whatever moves itself is the source and spring of motion, and therefore has no beginning and end, otherwise if it had come to a stop, it would have a need of something else to cause the motion again, But since it is always in motion and never stops, then the very soul is the source of motion. The same as the universe is without beginning and end, since it is a self-mover and therefore it is immortal. Concerning the human body, on the one hand the body moves itself, however on the other hand, the soul which is inherent in the body, is the source of its motion, therefore the soul has no beginning and end, which means is immortal.

" **Every soul is immortal. That is because whatever is always in motion is immortal, while what moves, and is moved by, something else stops living when it stops moving. So it is only what moves itself that never desists from motion, since it does not leave off being itself. In fact this self-mover is also the source and the spring of motion in everything else that moves and a source has no beginning...**

And since it cannot have a beginning, then necessarily it cannot be destroyed...

And if this is so – that whatever moves itself is essentially a soul – then it follows necessarily that soul should have neither birth nor death." (Plato, Phaedrus 245 c, d, e).

In the myth of Er, which Plato presents in his Dialogue *Republic*, he associates the immortality of the soul with reincarnation. According to this myth, the soul reincarnates many times into an animal or human body, according to its deeds of the previous existence on earth, in order to pay penalty or to be rewarded for its wrongdoings or good deeds respectively. So, the souls after the death of the body, some of them, the injust ones, are thrown into Tartarus to pay the penalty, while the just souls go to heaven and enjoy the beauty and the happiness of the intelligible world. Afterwards, all of them must return to the earth, after having chosen themselves the life to which they would be bound then by necessity, from different models of lives which had been presented before them (Plato Republic 614-621). With that myth Plato introduces the matter of free choice and will, which means each one of us is personally responsible for the way of his life, and therefore his personal choices, decisions and actions are in parallel to the Law of Necessity (Destiny).

" **The one who has the first lot will be the first to choose, a life to which he will then be bound by necessity. Virtue knows no master; each will possess it to a greater or lesser degree, depending on whether he values or disdains it. The responsibility lies with the one who makes the choice; the god has none.**" (Plato, Republic 617 e).

" **After that, the models of lives were placed on the ground before them. There were far more of them than they were souls present, and they were of all kinds, for the lives of animals were there, as well as all kinds of human lives.**" (Plato Republic 618 a).

Ideas – Dialectic

The human being through its immortal soul has the capability to know what truly exists (Being), since its soul has learned once the truth in the intelligible realm, and it only requires to recall to the mind (**recollection**) the eternal and absolute intelligible Forms of the Being.

" **But a soul that never saw the truth cannot take a human shape, since a human being must understand the** language of the Forms, passing from a plurality of perceptions to a unity gathered together by reasoning. That process is the recollection of the things our soul saw when it was travelling with the god." (Plato Phaedrus 249 c).

A man, in order to be able to recollect that knowledge of the Good, must be prepared for "seeing the light of the sun", for as we saw in the allegory of the Cave, it takes some time for the man of the cave, to become used to the light. This means that, the perception of the Forms of the Good demands **preparation,** on the one hand **intellectual**, which means the knowledge of the intelligible Forms (Ideas) through **dialectic**, and on the other hand **moral**, namely the possession of the **virtues** of prudence, courage and moderation, as we have already seen. Afterwards, only the one who is prepared he will be able to understand the Idea of the Good itself, which is the source and the cause of everything beautiful, good and just, as well as the source of knowledge and truth.

Dialectic needs training, so as to enable us to distinguish between all the terms and the forms the true Ideas of the Good, namely the concepts of the true Beauty, Love, Justice and the Goodness itself. Therefore, the principles and the laws that one has concluded at the stage of "**thought**" (διάνοια) (page 115) or the so-called sciences, he must consider them now as hypotheses, and while proceeding to be prepared to abandon some of them, if they are inconsistent with the ultimate hypothesis, which includes all the previous principles, so as to be able to reach finally the first principle, which steers all things in the universe, and from which derive all the other principles and laws of the different sciences.

At this point we can refer to **Antisthenes**, who after having adduced Socrates' teaching, he argued with Plato about the way of approaching to the first principle (Being). According to Antisthenes, one can reach the first principle through the inquiry into the deeper sense of the words, in order to find out the true Forms of the Being within the names. Therefore he disagreed with Plato on the matter of scientific education, since he believed that the single principle of education should be the searching out the meaning of the words. Therefore he is considered to be the pioneer of **nominalism**.

Further to dialectic, one must judge by reason all the concepts in order to find out the true and eternal Ideas, rejecting everything that is apparent, changeable and temporary. The concepts, which sustain the premises, must be judged by reasoning, so as to enable us to establish true hypotheses, whose consequences are consistent and not contradictory, and which will be used for approaching the ultimate true principles (Ideas). These are the attributes of the Good, and after understanding them, one can grasp the Idea of the Good itself. So, through dialectic one can approach the first principle and reach the state of understanding (*νόησις*), which is the knowledge and understanding of the Being, the Good, the Deity.

" **If someone then attacked your hypothesis itself, you would ignore him and would not answer <u>until you had examined whether the consequences that follow from it, agree with one another or contradict one another</u>. And when you must give an account of your hypothesis itself, you will proceed in the same way; you would assume more ultimate hypothesis, the best you could find and continue until you reached something satisfactory.**" (Plato, Phaedo 101 d).

" **Therefore, dialectic is the only enquiry that travels this road, doing away with hypotheses and proceeding to the first principle of all, so as to make sure of confirmation there. And when the eye of the soul is really buried in a sort of barbaric bog, dialectic pulls it out and leads it upwards, using the crafts we described to help it and cooperate with it in turning the soul around. From force of habit, we have often called these sciences or kinds of knowledge, but they need another name, clearer than opinion (*δόξα*), darker than knowledge (*ἐπιστήμη*). We called them thought (*διάνοια*) somewhere before.**" (Plato, Republic 533 d).

" **Then, do you call someone who is able to give an account of the being of each thing dialectical?**"

" Then the same applies to the Good. Unless someone can distinguish the Form of the Good from everything else, can survive all refutations, as if in a battle, striving to judge things not in accordance with opinion, but in accordance with being, and come all through this with his account still intact, you'll say that he doesn't know the Good itself or any other good. And if he gets hold of some image of it, you'll say that it is through opinion (δόξα), not knowledge (ἐπιστήμη), for he is dreaming throughout his present life.." (Plato, Republic 534 b, c).

As we can see, Plato regards as real science (ἐπιστήμη: **episteme**) the knowledge of the first principle of all, namely the Good, therefore he places philosophy, which teaches dialectic, on the top of all "sciences". The so called "sciences" can lead us only up to the first stage of knowledge, which he calls "**thought**" (διάνοια), however, the unification of all the principles and laws of all the sciences in one principle, the **first principle of all**, can be achieved only through **dialectic**. In this way we can reach the highest rung of knowledge, which is "**understanding**" (νόησις).

Virtue of the Good itself – Justice

Referring now to the moral part of preparation for seeing the Good, when someone has been trained in dialectic, without having possessed the virtues of the Good, is led to arrogance and vanity, misuses dialectic for the purpose of humiliating and torturing the others, in order to parade his wit and rhetorical skill. And as a result he forgets and departs from his aim, which is the knowledge of the Good.

" I don't suppose it has escaped your notice that, when young people get their first taste of arguments, they misuse it by treating it as a kind of game of contradiction. They imitate those who have refuted them by refuting others themselves, and like puppies, they enjoy dragging and tearing those around them with their arguments." (Plato, Republic 539 b).

" And when we said before that those allowed to take part in arguments should be orderly and steady by nature, not as nowadays, when even the unfit are allowed to engage in them – wasn't all that also said as a precaution?" (Plato, Republic 539 d).

Further then to the moral part of Socrates' teaching, concerning the virtues of the Good, as we have seen the main virtue is considered to be the justice, since it is the combination of all the virtues of the irrational and the rational part of the soul. Socrates is beginning to examine the matter of justice, in Plato's dialogue *Republic*, with the saying of Simonides of Ceos that: **"just is to give to each what is owed to him"**, and he is trying to find out its meaning, and is also wondering why justice is the most useful for the human soul.

Then he proceeds with the Sophists' claim that: **"justice is nothing than the advantage of the stronger"** and sets out the arguments of their saying. The unjust, according to the Sophists, is more advantageous in life than the just, since by deceiving the others and disguising himself as a just, can live a comfort and pleasant life, after having gained social estimation and personal profit by committing crimes in secret.

Socrates argues that, if a state applies this principle (advantage of the stronger), then inevitably will conflict with the other states, and apart from that, in the bosom of that state will be disunity, since each citizen will try to serve his own interest and to do injustice to the others, As a result, they will not be able to act in common, therefore the state will be ineffective and weak.

" If the effect of injustice is to produce hatred wherever it occurs, then whenever it arises, whether among free men or slaves, won't it cause them to hate one another, engage in civil war, and prevent them from achieving any common purpose?" (Plato Republic 351 d).

Furthermore, the unjust man is a split personality, since each part of himself is fighting and hating the other, and as a result the man is incapable of achieving anything in his life.

" And even in a single individual, it has by its nature the very same effect. First it makes him incapable of achieving anything, because he is in a state of civil war and not of

one mind; second it makes him his own enemy, as well as the enemy of just people." (Plato, Republic 352 a).

On the other hand, the just people both as individuals and when acting together, are more capable in doing things, since they live in harmony with themselves and with the others.

" We have shown that just people are cleverer and more capable in doing things, while unjust ones aren't even able to act together.." (Plato, Republic 352 b).

Concerning the matter of **happiness** (*ευδαιμονία*: eudaimonia) in relation to **justice** (*δικαιοσύνη*: dikaiosini), Socrates argues that each **being** (*όν*: on) is happy when performs its **function to which is assigned** (*αυτού έργον*: autou ergon). And when it performs **well** this action, this means that it possesses **its own virtue** (*οικεία αρετή*: oikeia areti), but when it performs this action **badly**, then it possesses **vice**. Just like for example with the eyes, the function to which are assigned is the sight, and their virtue is the good sight. On the analogy of the eyes, the human soul is assigned to **taking care of things** (*επιμελείσθαι*: epimelisthai), **ruling** (*άρχειν*: archein) and **deliberating** (*βουλεύεσθαι*: vouleuesthai). The virtue then of the soul is justice, since by means of it the soul can perform well all the above mentioned functions and lead a happy life.

" Is there some function of a soul that you couldn't perform with anything else, for example, taking care of things, ruling, deliberating and the like? Is there anything other than a soul to which you could rightly assign these, and say that they are its peculiar function?" (Plato, Republic 353 d).

" Doesn't follow then, that a bad soul rules and takes care of things badly and that the good soul does all these things well?

It does.

Now, we agreed that justice is a soul's virtue and injustice is its vice?

We did.

Then it follows that a just soul and a just man will live well and an unjust one badly." (Plato, Republic 353 e).

Plato likens the complex human soul to a State (*Republic*: **Politeia, Πολιτεία**), and is trying through this comparison to approach this concept of the Justice itself (Idea of Justice), as an attribute of the Good itself, by applying faithfully the method of **dialectic**.

" But I've yet to hear anyone defend <u>justice</u> in the way I want, proving that is better than injustice, I want to hear praised <u>by itself</u>, and I think that I'm most likely to hear this from you." (Plato, Republic 358 d).

The human soul is multiform and each form represents one desire associated with the relevant emotion and thought. The desires as we have seen, refer to the irrational **appetitive** part, the emotions to the spirited, and the reasoning to the rational part of the soul. Each desire is related to the instincts, which are assigned to perform the bodily functions, for example nutrition, reproduction, preservation etc. By analogy, in the State there must be a class which is assigned to produce food, make clothes, be in business etc., which Socrates calls it **craftsmen** (*δημιουργοί*: demiourgoi) or **money making** class. The virtue of this part of the soul and the relevant class of the state is **moderation**, which means no greediness, no avarice and no indulgence, so as to enable the members of that class to be just in their dealings, and respectively this part of the soul, to perform well its function of body's good preservation.

The second part of the soul, as we have seen, is the spirited part, which refers to the emotions, and its analogue to the state is the class of **guardians** (*φύλακες*: phylakes), who are assigned to protect the city from invaders and mutineers. The virtue of this part of the soul and the relevant class of the State is **courage**, which means no cowardice, no excessive ambition, so as to enable the guardians to maintain law and order without seeking for coming to power for personal profits, and all these presuppose of course the virtue of **moderation** as well.

" -The physical qualities of the guardians are clear, then.

-Yes.

-And as far as their souls are concerned, they must be courageous.

-That too.

-But if they have nature like that, Glaucon, won't they be savage to each other and to the rest of the citizens?"
(Plato, Republic 375 b).

" Then do you think that our future guardians, besides being courageous, must also be by nature philosophical?"
(Plato, Republic 375 e).

Therefore, the rulers of the State must be very attentive to the upbringing and education of the guardians, in order to enable them to fulfill their obligations successfully, since it will be the class with the most power. For this reason, the patterns of their education must be courageous, self-controlled, moderate, pious and free men. So, the good words combined with harmonious music and rhythm during their upbringing, can develop good and noble characters. On the analogy of the spirited part of the soul, it requires attentive and appropriate culture in order to enable one to acquire positive and noble sentiments. For this special part of *Republic* Plato was blamed for initiating censorship in the Arts, and that he prepared the ground for the "committed art", as well as for the arts' censorship in authoritarian regimes. We could point out that, each one of us chooses a specific form of art or entertainment in accordance with his temperament, character, principles or ends. So, in our private life, one way or another, we make a choice in the matter of culture.

" If they do imitate, they must imitate from childhood what is appropriate for them, namely, people who are courageous, self-controlled, pious and free and their actions." (Plato Republic 395 c).

" Then fine words, harmony, grace and rhythm follow simplicity of character – and I do not mean this in the sense in which we use <simplicity> as a euphemism for <simple-mindedness> - but I mean the sort of fine and good character that has developed in accordance with an intelligible plan." (Plato, Republic 400 d, e).

Concerning now the third part of the soul, the **rational** one, this is the analogue of the class of **rulers** (ἄρχοντες: archontes) or **kings** (βασιλείς: basileis). This class will arise from the guardians, since that class will have the most appropriate and attentive upbringing. Those from the guardians who have love for learning, will be selected and then will be educated to become rulers. Therefore, they must be taught all the sciences for some years in order to develop the faculty of "thought", and then dialectic in order to develop the faculty of "understanding". Afterwards, they must take command in matters of war in order to prove their ability in practical matters. Those who are proved capable of these matters, can enter upon office as highest government officials and become rulers. The virtue that refers to this class and to the relevant rational part of the soul is **prudence** and **wisdom**, since it is essential for a man to be able to rule a State or oneself. Certainly, this capability presupposes the possession of the other two virtues, namely moderation and courage.

" **And the kings in this city must be those among them who have proved to be best, both in philosophy and warfare.**" **(Plato Republic 543 a).**

Therefore, wisdom is the capability of ruling oneself and a whole city respectively with justice. This capability arises from the knowledge (ἐπιστήμη), which guides by reason the just ruling of the city and of oneself. This is a faculty of the rational part of the soul, therefore it is considered to be the most essential part.

" **He binds together those parts and any other there may be between, and from having been many things he becomes entirely one, moderate and harmonious. Only then does he act. And when he does anything, whether acquiring wealth, taking care of his body, engaging in politics or in private contracts – in all of these he believes that the action is just and fine and preserves this inner harmony and helps achieve it, and calls it so, and regards as wisdom the Knowledge that oversees such actions.**" **(Plato Republic 443 d, e).**

To sum up, the definition of justice according to Plato is: each class to do its own work to which is assigned by nature, and not to meddle with the other's work. This means that the rulers must rule, the guardians must maintain law and order and the craftsmen produce goods, without one class pointing out to the other its work and responsibilities. And in this way Plato interprets the saying of **Simonides**, namely to give to each class what is suited to have, so to say what is owed to do.

By analogy, if we apply this principle in the parts of the soul, since **justice is an inner state**, then each part must do its own work, and not to meddle with each other. So, the **rational** part must take the decisions and rule with **wisdom**, the **spirited** must execute the orders and defend the rational's decisions with **courage**, and the **appetitive** must obey the decisions of the rational with self-control and **moderation**. In this way there is a harmony among the three parts, since each part does its own work and the two lower parts acknowledge the authority of the rational, and obey it without rebelling against it. On the other hand, the rational part having the **knowledge** (*επιστήμη*) of what is advantageous for each part and for the whole soul, makes its declarations and rules with wisdom. This concord and harmony of the three parts of the soul is called justice in us, according to Plato, and therefore it acquires the possession of the three virtues, namely moderation, courage and wisdom.

" **Therefore, isn't it appropriate for the rational part to rule, since it is really wise and exercises foresight on behalf of the whole soul, and for the spirited part to obey it and be its ally?" (Plato Republic 441 e).**

" **And in truth** <u>**justice is, it seems something of this sort. However, it isn't concerned with someone's doing his own eternally, but with what is inside him, and what is truly himself and his own.**</u> **One who is just does not allow any part of himself to do the work of another part or allow the various classes within him to meddle with each other. He regulates well what is really his own and rules himself. He puts himself in order, is his own friend, and harmonizes the three parts of himself like three limiting notes in a**

musical scale – high low and middle." (Plato Republic 443 c, d).

On the other hand, **injustice** (*αδικία*: adikia) is the opposite state, and this means that each part of the soul rebels against the other in order to rule the whole soul, a state which is contrary to their nature. To be more specific, the appetitive part for example, which by nature is suited to serve and to be ruled, wants to become a ruler of the whole soul, and as result turmoil and confusion prevails in the whole soul. This dominance of **vices** (*κακίαι*: kakiai) in each part of the soul is the injustice, when instead of moderation arises **licentiousness** (*ακολασία*: akolasia) in the appetitive part, instead of courage in the spirited one arises **cowardice** (*δειλία*: deilia), and instead of wisdom in the rational **ignorance** (*αμαθία*: amathia) prevails.

This sort of ignorance, lack of knowledge, arises from the false estimation of excess or deficiency, concerning pleasure and pain. Since one has a false judgement of the passing or the long-term pleasant, advantageous and good for the human nature, goes astray and gives in the passing bodily pleasure, which ultimately is not advantageous and good for him, and so he becomes a dissolute. In the same way, the cowardly has a false judgement of the disgraceful fear and the honourable courage, and therefore he chooses cowardly actions and avoids the courageous ones, even if it is for the good of the people and ultimately for himself. On the other hand, the courageous since he has knowledge about what is to be feared or not, chooses always the courageous deeds, even if they are fearful, because they are right and good and as a result appropriate and pleasant.

" For you agreed with us that those who make mistakes with regard to the choice of pleasure and pain, in other words, with regards to good and evil, do so because of lack of knowledge and not merely a lack of knowledge but a lack of that knowledge you agreed was measurement. And the mistaken act done without knowledge you must know is one done from ignorance. So this is what <being

136

overcome by pleasure> is – ignorance in the highest degree.." (Plato, Protagoras 357 d, e).

" So then, knowledge about what is and is not to be feared is the opposite of ignorance."

" And this ignorance is cowardice?"

" So the knowledge about what is and is not to be feared is courage and is the opposite of the ignorance?" (Plato, Protagoras 360 d).

From the above mentioned fragments it is evident that injustice is ultimately ignorance, lack of knowledge, lack of wisdom and contrary to nature . On the other hand, justice is in accordance with our nature, since each part of the soul does its own work, to which is assigned **by nature** to do.

" **Surely it must be a kind of civil war between the three parts, a meddling and doing of another's work, a rebellion by some part against the whole soul in order to rule it inappropriately. The rebellious part is by nature suited to be a slave, while the other part is not a slave but belongs to the ruling class. We'll say something like that, I suppose, and that the turmoil and straying of these parts are injustice, licentiousness, cowardice, ignorance, and in a word, the whole of vice.**" (Plato, Republic 444 b).

In order to make a graphic description of the three parts of the soul, Plato represents the complexity of the human soul with different animals. Particularly, he represents the rational part with a human face, the spirited part with a lion and the appetitive with a multicolored beast with a ring of many heads of gentle and savage animals, and each one of them is relevant to a particular desire. And all, the three of them are joined so that they can grow naturally together.

" **Well then, fashion a single kind of multicolored beast, with a ring of many heads that it can grow and change at will – some from gentle, some from savage animals.**

Then fashion one other kind, that of a lion, and another of a human being. But make the first much the largest, and the other second to it in size.

**Now join the three of them into one, so that they
somehow grow together naturally." (Plato, Republic 588 c,
d).**

The one who considers **injustice** to be **profitable** and
advantageous for him, simply feeds the multiform beast and
the lion within him, and on the other hand, the human being
within is starving and weakening, and as a result the two
beasts maintain control over the whole of the soul, and
sometimes they fight and bite one another in order to take the
control of it. On the other hand, the one who praises **justice**,
he will insure that this human being within (**rational part**)
has the most control, and will take care of the many-headed
beast (**appetitive part**), so as to feed the gentle heads and to
prevent the savage ones from growing, and all these can be
done by the power of lion (**spirited part**), which will be his
ally and will supervise the whole soul, so as to be harmonious
community (Plato Republic 589 b, c).

In conclusion, the just man does not commit excesses,
neither due to avarice and licentiousness of the appetitive part,
nor due to softness, cowardice or extreme ambition of the
spirited part. He binds together the three parts of himself
harmonically, with wisdom, courage and moderation he
creates a just State in him, where all the three parts work in
concord for the raising of the human being to the divine level.
This raising and becoming as like God (*theo homeiosis*), Plato
calls "escaping" from the earth to heaven, and can only be
achieved when one possesses the virtues of justice, piety and
knowledge with understanding.

" **That is why a man should make all haste to escape
from earth to heaven; and escape means becoming as like
God as possible; and a man becomes like God when he
becomes just and pious with understanding." (Plato,
Theaetetus 176 b).**

Pleasure – Happiness

Concerning the matter of **happiness** (*ευδαιμονία*:
eudaimonia) in relation to **pleasure** (*ηδονή* : hedone), Plato
associates it with the three parts of the soul and their functions

to which are assigned by nature. Taking into account that pleasure is a kind of filling up of a particular deficiency, Plato points out that each part of the soul has its own pleasure.

To the **appetitive** part corresponds the **pleasure** of **profit**, since this part likes the good food, drink, sex etc., and those desires can only be fulfilled by means of money, therefore he calls it also **money-loving** which corresponds to the **profit-loving** person.

" **Hence we called it appetitive part, because of the intensity of its appetites for food, drink, sex, and all the things associated with them, but we also called it money-loving part, because such appetites are most easily satisfied by means of money." (Plato, Republic 580 e).**

To the **spirited** part corresponds the **pleasure** of **fame**, since this part has as a purpose to conquer, to win and to achieve high reputation. Therefore, it corresponds to the **victory-loving** and **honour-loving** person.

" **What about the spirited part? Don't we say that it is wholly dedicated to the pursuit of control, victory and high repute?" (Plato, Republic 581 a).**

As for the **rational** part, its **pleasure** is the one which arises from **wisdom**, since it is always interested in learning and knowing where the truth lies and despises money and reputation, therefore it corresponds to the **learning-loving** person and the friend of wisdom (**philosophic**).

" **Then wouldn't it be appropriate for us to call it learning-loving and philosophical?"**

" **And doesn't this part rule in some people's souls, while one of the other– whichever it happens to be – rules in other people's?"**

" **And isn't that the reason we say there are three primary kinds of people: philosophic, victory-loving and profit-loving?"**

" **And also three forms of pleasure, one assigned to each of them?" (Plato, Republic 581 b, c).**

So, each part of the soul pursues its own pleasure, considering the pleasure of the others worthless. The appetitive part, for example, neither is interested in reputation nor in learning. The spirited part, on the other hand, is not interested in learning and money. And as for the rational part, considers the pleasure of making money to be vulgar and the one of honour nonsense, and it is only interested in learning the nature of the things, and in achieving knowledge and wisdom. However, since the rational part is the one, which takes care of the whole soul, knows the particular needs of each part and rules, therefore as a matter of fact the man should prefer the pleasure of this part to the others' pleasure.

" **Then of the three pleasures, the most pleasant is that of the part of the soul with which we learn, and the one in whom that part rules, has the most pleasant life." (Plato, Republic 583 a).**

However, people have illusions about pleasure, when they satisfy the desires of the other lower parts, for they have not savoured the true pleasure. Since the fulfillment of those pleasures relieves them of pain temporarily, they regard them as pleasures, because they do not know the real pleasure. Furthermore, the intermediate state between pain and pleasure, namely the calm state, is considered to be pleasure, since it is preferable to the pain.

" **However, most of the so-called pleasures that reach the soul through the body, as well as the most intense ones, are of this form – they are some kind of relief from pain." (Plato, Republic 584 c).**

" **But when the calm is next to painful it appears pleasant, and when it is next to pleasant it appears painful." (Plato, Republic 584 a).**

Therefore, the intermediate state between pleasure and pain, as well as the absence of pain are the **idols** and **phantoms** of **pleasure**, and cannot be compared with true pleasure. But the man who has not known the true pleasure, he considers those states more desirable and calls them pleasures.

True pleasure, on the contrary, means to fill the soul with something that is appropriate to it by nature, and as the soul is immortal and true (being), then it must be filled with something which is immortal and real, and not mortal and changeable. The care of the body then, since it participates lesser in being and truth than the soul, it is of lesser importance compared to the soul's care. Apart from that, the fulfillment of bodily pleasures is less important than the filling up of the highest part of the soul with real, true and immortal things, which is knowing and understanding the Good itself.

" **Therefore, if being filled with what is appropriate to our nature is pleasure, that which is more filled with things that are, enjoys more really and truly a more true pleasure, while that which partakes of things that are less is less truly and surely filled, and partakes of a less trustworthy and less true pleasure." (Plato, Republic 585 e).**

However, most of the people are interested only in bodily pleasures (appetitive part) and they never taste the real, true and stable pleasure, since throughout their life move down and then back up to the middle, and they cannot even imagine that higher up there is a true pleasure. Therefore, due to their insatiety for bodily pleasures, they kick and kill one another. In this way they live their lives, having the illusion that they have tasted real pleasures, but in reality their pleasures were always mixed with pain, and they have only known the **images** (*εἴδωλα*: eidola) and shadow-paintings of true **pleasures**. The mad erotic passions and the false delights appear to them intense, and they fight for them, as they fought over the **phantom of Helen** (*Ελένης εἴδωλον*: Eleni's eidolon) at Troy, while the real Helen was not there.

In the same way, some other people try to satisfy their passion for victory, honour (spirited part), by hook or by crook, namely by using intrigues and envy for the sake of reputation, violence for the sake of victory, and anger because of failure in their aims. In all cases, as we can realize, there is no prudence and understanding, which could help them to realize, which pleasures are suited to the human being, and in which way they should be fulfilled (Plato Republic 586 a, b, c).

But when the desires associated with the profit-loving part and the honour-loving part follow the philosophical one, and through argument and reason are satisfied by the criterion of the achievement of knowledge and the attainment of the truest possible pleasures, then one can enjoy true pleasure.

" **Therefore, when the entire soul follows the philosophic part, and there is no civil war in it, each part of it does its own work exclusively, and is just, and in particular it enjoys its own pleasures, the best and the truest pleasures possible for it." (Plato, Republic 586 e).**

On the contrary, when another part of the soul gains the control, it forces the other two parts to pursue a pleasure which is not suited, therefore is alien to them, and also untrue and ephemeral, and as a result a man becomes unhappy, since the most parts of his soul are unfortunate.

As Plato corresponds each part of the soul to different regimes, and by comparing each one of them to the ideal Republic, he tries to show the magnitude of the pleasure, which each part enjoys, when it fulfills only its own pleasure, in comparison with the enjoyment of pleasure of the entire soul.

Ideal Republic of the philosopher king (**aristocracy**) corresponds to the **rational** part, **timarchy** to the honour-loving **spirited** part and **oligarchy** to the money-loving **appetitive** part. The appetitive part has three different aspects, therefore it corresponds to three different regimes, starting with **oligarchy** corresponding to **money-loving** and ending to **tyrany** corresponding to **indulgence**, with **democracy between** these two.

Thus, the tyrant enjoys only one part of the pleasure of the oligarch (appetitive), if we assume that the oligarch enjoys fully the pleasures of the appetitive part. In order to enjoy these pleasures the oligarch uses his rational part to find different ways so as to get more profit in his dealings, and he admires and honours (spirited) only great wealth, so his only ambition is to acquire great wealth. He also controls all the desires of the appetitive part, which are contrary to the achievement of this aim. As a result, all the three parts are compelled to enjoy these sort of pleasures. The pleasure then, that a **money-loving oligarch** enjoys will be three squared, namely $3X3 = 9$ times more than the one that a **dissolute**

142

tyrant enjoys. So a tyrant enjoys the **1/9** of the pleasure of an oligarch. On the same basis, an **honour-loving timocrat** will live **9X9 = 81** times more pleasantly than an **oligarch**. And finally the pleasure of a **wise king** (aristocrat) is the **cube** of the pleasure of an **oligarch**, which means that the **wise man** lives **9X9X9 = 729** times more pleasantly than a **dissolute tyrant**.

" A tyrant is somehow third from an oligarch, for a democrat was between them."

" Then, if what we said before is true, doesn't he live with an image of pleasure that is third from an oligarch's with respect to truth?"

" Now an oligarch, in turn is third from a king, if we identify a king and an aristocrat."

" So a tyrant is three times three times removed from the true pleasure."

" But then it's clear that, by squaring and cubing this number (3), we'll discover how far a tyrant's pleasure is from that of a king."

" Then, turning it the other way around, if someone wants to say how far a king's pleasure is from a tyrant's, he'll find, if he completes the calculation, that a king lives seven hundred and twenty nine times more pleasantly than a tyrant and that a tyrant is the same number of times more wretched." (Plato, Republic 587 c, d, e).

The man of knowledge and wisdom, as we have seen, lives seven hundred twenty nine (729) times more pleasantly than the dissolute man, since the latter forces all the parts of the soul to pursue pleasures, which are not suited by nature to them (rational, spirited part), and as a result these parts are displeased and consequently unhappy, as well as the entire soul is.

On the other hand, the just man who possesses prudence and wisdom, takes care of the entire soul, allows each part to taste the truest possible pleasures, which are suited to each one of them, by pursuing the aim of knowledge of the Good, and possession its virtues. In this way one can taste the **true**

pleasure of the Good, achieve true **happiness** (*εὐδαιμονία*) and resemble God.

Concerning the number (**729**), it corresponds to the 729 days and nights of a calendar year, namely 364 ½ days and 364 ½ nights, as well as the expectation of life, which means 729 months that is mentioned in the **Cosmogony** of the Pythagorean **Philolaus** (*Μέγας Ενιαυτός*: megas eniautos). This number, according to the Pythagoreans is true, since it corresponds to the data of the visible world (days, nights, months etc.). The use of this number by Plato, shows the Pythagorean influence, as well as that the virtue of justice – each part of the soul does its own work and enjoys its own pleasure – is a pure human virtue and appropriate to human life.

" Yet it's a true number, and one appropriate to human lives, if indeed days, nights, months and years are appropriate to them." (Plato, Republic 588 a).

" Then, if a good and just person's life is that much more pleasant than the life of a bad and unjust person, won't its grace, fineness and virtue be incalculably greater?" (Plato, Republic 588 a).

To sum up, happiness can be achieved only through justice, which presupposes the virtues of moderation in the appetitive part, courage in the spirited one, and prudence and wisdom in the highest rational part. On that condition the three parts are able to collaborate harmoniously, guided by the rational part, since it is by nature the one, which due to its faculty of knowledge and understanding, can take care of the entire soul and rule it.

D. Aristotle (384– 322 BC)

Aristotle was born at Stagira in Macedonia, Northern Greece, and at the age of seventeen became student of Plato's Academy in Athens, where he stayed for twenty years until Plato's death in 348. Then he left Athens and settled in Assos, in the Troad in Asia Minor, where he started developing his own philosophy. After three years he left Assos and settled in Lesbos until 342 BC. Then he was invited by the king of Macedonia Philip to his court at Pella, to undertake the education of the apparent heir Alexander, who was to become in a few years the conqueror of the world, known as Great Alexander. When Alexander succeeded to the throne in 336, Aristotle left Pella and returned to Athens, where he founded his own philosophical School, known as **Lyceum** or else **Peripatetic** School.

His philosophical thought, as we are going to see, was influenced mainly by **Anaxagoras** (concerning the Unmoved Mover '**God-Intellect'**), **Democritus** (concerning **inductive** method and the **mean state**) and of course by his master **Plato** (concerning the **virtue** and the **good itself**). He left a large number of writings behind, concerning physics, mathematics, astronomy, physiology, psychology, politics and of course logic, aesthetics, ethics and philosophy. His thought has influenced the later scientific and philosophical thinking of the Western civilization, and contributed substantially to its development. In the present study we are going to examine the main philosophical and ethical principles of Aristotle, since the detailed presentation of his views on all subjects of his studies, goes beyond the purpose and the limits of the present writing.

Cosmogony

Referring to the principles of creation and the so-called "**four elements**" by Empedocles, namely **Fire, Air, Water and Earth**, Aristotle considers that the primary **elements** (*στοιχεία*: stoicheia) are the "contrary qualities" or else "**contrarieties**" (*εναντιώσεις*: enantioseis), namely "hot" (*θερμόν*: thermon), "cold" (*ψυχρόν*: psychron), "moist" (*υγρόν*: ygron) and "dry" (*ξηρόν*: xiron). As for the others he calls them "**apparently simple bodies**". From the coupling of two different elements (contrarieties) - and the matter regarded as a substratum receptive to those contrarieties - derive the simple bodies. By a combination of **hot** with **dry** is generated the **fire**, of **hot** with **moist** is generated the **air**, **cold** with **moist** is generated the **water**, and **cold** with **dry** gives the **earth**. The other two combinations are impossible, namely hot with cold and dry with moist. Therefore the coupling of the four contrarieties can give only four 'apparently simple bodies' (fire, air, water and earth). All the changes that are taking place in the universe, can be explained through this interchange of the four main principles (contrarieties), since the **coming to be** (*γένεσις*: genesis) and **passing away** (*φθορά*: fthora) is ceaseless and eternal, because the coming to be of one thing is the passing away of another and the other way around.

" **Why then, is this form of change necessarily ceaseless? It is because the passing away of this is a coming to be of something else, and the coming to be of this a passing away of something else.**" (Aristotle, On Generation and Corruption 318 a 24-26).

As Aristotle begins his enquiry with Anaximander's principle - that there is an eternal change in the universe due to the continuous and ceaseless recycling of the primary bodies - he points out that "**what is**" (being) (*όv*: on) cannot vanish into "**what is not**" (not-being) (*μη όv*: mi on), otherwise the universe would have been vanished away long ago. Therefore, the coming to be and passing away are interchanged continuously and eternally.

" **If in fact what passes away vanishes into what <is not> and what is not is nothing (since what is not is neither a thing, nor a possessed of a quality or quantity nor in any place). If then, some one of the things which <are> is constantly disappearing, why has not the universe been used up long ago and vanished away – assuming of course that the material of all the several comings-to-be was finite?**" (Aristotle On Generation and Corruption 318 a 14-19).

Then he proceeds with the definition of the terms growth, diminution, locomotion and alteration, and he distinguishes the coming to be and passing away from all the previous ones, since after these two changes nothing persists of which the resultant is a property.

" When the change from contrary to contrary is in quantity, it is a growth and diminution, when it is in place, it is locomotion, when it is in property, i.e. in quality it is alteration; but when nothing persists of which the resultant is a property (or an accident in any sense of the term), it is coming to be, and the converse change is passing away. Matter in the most proper sense of the term is to be identified with the substratum which is receptive of coming to be and passing-away." (Aristotle, On Generation and Corruption 319 b 30 - 320 a 4).

However, since the coming to be and passing away takes place after continuous changes of growth, diminution, alteration, action and motion in general, and as in every motion there is one part that "**acts upon**" (ποιείν: poiein) the others, and another that "**suffers action from**" (πάσχειν: paschein) the others, then it must be defined, which of the contrary qualities (**contrarieties**) are "active" (ποιητικά: poietika) and which are "**susceptible**" (παθητικά: pathetika). On the base of this classification can only be explained the continuous coming to be and passing away, since the contrarieties are combined and transformed into one another, as the one acts upon the other, and the other suffers action from that. In this way Aristotle classifies as "**active**" ones the **hot** and the **cold** and as "susceptible" ones the **dry** and the **moist**.

" On the other hand, hot and cold, and dry and moist are terms, of which the first implies <u>power to act</u> and the second pair <u>susceptibility</u>. Hot is that which associates things from the same kind (for dissociating, which people attribute to Fire as its function is associating of the same class, since its effect is to eliminate what is foreign), while cold is that which brings together, i.e. associates, homogeneous and heterogeneous things alike." (Aristotle, On Generation and Corruption 329 b 23-30).

As we said before, from the association of the four contrarieties derive the four simple bodies, namely Fire which is hot and dry, Air that is hot and moist, Water which is cold and moist and Earth which is cold and dry.

" The <u>elements</u> are four, and any four terms can be combined in six couples. Contraries however, refuse to be coupled; for it is impossible for the same thing to be hot and cold, or moist and dry. Hence it is evident that the couplings of the elements will be four: hot with dry, and moist with hot, and again cold with dry, and cold with moist. And these four couples have attached themselves to the <u>apparently simple bodies</u> (Fire, Air, Water and Earth) in a manner consonant with theory. For Fire is hot and dry, whereas Air is hot and moist (Air being a sort of vapour); and Water is cold and moist, while Earth is cold and dry." (Aristotle, On Generation and Corruption 330 a, 30 – 330 b, 5).

The process of conversation into one another, will be easier and quicker between those simple bodies, who possess only one of the two qualities contrary, for example, Fire (hot-dry) and air (hot-moist) possess the same quality (hot) and have one contrary quality (dry opposite to moist). Therefore, the transformation from Fire into Air is quick, since they are akin. On the other hand, for example Fire (hot-dry) and Earth (cold-moist) have both contrary qualities, therefore the conversation from Fire into Earth is slow and requires intermediate phases of transformation. So the coming to be and passing away includes the change from one quality into its opposite (from dry into moist in our example of transformation Fire into Air).

" For coming to be is a change into contraries and out of contraries, and the elements all involve a contrariety in their mutual relation, because their distinctive qualities are contrary." (Aristotle, On Generation and Corruption 331 a, 14-16).

" For, though all will result from all, both the speed and the facility of their conversation will differ in degree. Thus the process of conversation will be quick between those which tally with one another, but slow between those which do not." (Arist. On Generation and Corruption 331 a, 20-25).

In that way, the transformation of the simple bodies is continuous and is as follows: from Fire into Air, Air into

148

Water, Water into Earth, and Earth into Fire again. On the contrary, the changes from Fire into Water and Air into Earth are impossible to take place in one phase. The reason is, as we said, that it is easier to change first the one quality, and then the other one. To be more specific, starting with Fire (hot-dry), first if the dry be overcome by the moist then from Fire will result Air (hot-moist). Afterwards, if the hot be overcome by the cold, then there will be Water (cold-moist). In this way, according to Aristotle, the coming to be and passing away can be ceaseless and continuous, therefore he dissociates himself from Empedocles' view. Because the transformation of the simple bodies from one into another (Fire, Air, Water, Earth) cannot be explained by "Love" and "Strife" of Empedocles but rather by the changes of the contrarieties.

To sum up, the coming to be and passing away of the simple bodies is a **circular motion**, as we have seen, therefore it is continuous and ceaseless, and that motion is the **principle** of transformation of the contrarieties, for it is prior to coming to be. So, we have to examine it as a circular motion, since it is the only one that is continuous and ceaseless.

" **Now that which is being moved is, but which is coming to be is not; hence motion is prior to coming to be. We have assumed and have proved that coming to be and passing away happen to things continuously and we assert that motion causes coming to be.**"

" **The cause of this as we often have said is the circular motion, for that is the only motion which is continuous.**" **(Aristotle, On Generation and Corruption 336 a, 20-25, 337 a, 1-2).**

However, in the ceaseless and eternal circular motion, as Aristotle analyses in his work "Physics" (book VIII), there must be something which initiates that movement, namely the "**mover**" (κινούν: kinoun), which must be "**single**" (ἐν: en), "**unmoved**" (ακίνητον: akineton), "**ungenerated**" (αγένητον: ageniton) and "**incapable of alteration**" (αναλλοίωτον: analoioton), which also must not be mixed with anything, in order to be able to control the circular movement (rotation). These are the same attributes of the **God-Intellect**, who controls the rotation in the universe, as we also saw in **Anaxagoras'** philosophy (fr. 11, 12, 13), where **"Nous"** or else **"Pure Intellect"** (*Νοῦς*) is the "first mover" of the circular movement. He is infinite, ungenerated, self-ruled and not mixed but alone by himself, in order to be able to supervise and control the eternal change, without a need for intervention.

" **But if there is to be a movement, as we have explained elsewhere in an earlier work (Physics VIII), there must be something which initiates it; if there is to be movement always, there must always be something which initiates it; if the movement is to be continuous, what initiates it must be single, unmoved, ungenerated and incapable of alteration.**" **(Aristotle, On Generation and Corruption 337 a, 16-20).**

" **But the** <u>first mover</u> **causes a motion that is eternal, and causes it during an infinite time. It is clear therefore, that is indivisible, and is without parts and without magnitude.**" **(Aristotle, Physics VIII 267 b 25).**

" **Now <being> (we have explained elsewhere the variety of meanings we recognize in this term) is better that <not-being>; but not all things can possess being, since they are too far removed from this principle. God, therefore, adopted the remaining alternative, and fulfilled the perfection of the universe by making coming-to-be uninterrrupted.**" **(Aristotle, On Generation and Corruption 336 b 30-35).**

In these last fragments we can see, that Aristotle assumes that God is the first mover, who has created the universe in such a way, by making the coming to be and passing away a continuous and ceaseless process, through the circular motion, which he has initiated, without a need for him to intervene, since it is perfect and uninterrupted. So, as we can realize, Aristotle rejects the terms of fate and determination, contrary to Plato and the Stoics.

Goods - Virtue

Referring to the moral philosophy of Aristotle, as matter of course, is based upon the **"free choice"** (προαίρεσις: prohairesis), since as we have seen he rejects any concept of fate. The **Chief** (άριστον: ariston) and **Complete** (τέλειον: teleion) **Good** (αγαθόν: agathon), according to him, is **Happiness** (ευδαιμονία: eudaimonia), because we choose it for itself (**good itself**) and not for the sake of something else. Although there are many goods, according to the end of each one (for example in medicine the good is health, in strategy victory, in architecture a house etc.), there are some, which are chosen for the sake of them, and happiness is one of them. So, Aristotle disagrees with Plato on the question, that there is one eternal Good (the Good Itself), since according to him, each science and art has its own good, as we saw (health, victory, house etc.). However, happiness is considered to be a chief good, since we choose it for its sake and somehow includes all the other goods.

" **Clearly the good cannot be something universally present in all cases and single; for then it would not have been predicated in all the categories. Further, since of the things answering to one Idea, there is one science, there would have been one science of all the goods, but as it is there are many sciences that fall under one category, e.g. of opportunity (for opportunity in the war is studied by strategy and in disease by medicine.." (Aristotle, Nicomachean Ethics I, 1096 a, 28-35).**

" **Clearly then, goods must be spoken of in two ways, and some must be good in themselves, the others by reason of this."**

" **But the chief good is evidently something complete. Therefore, if there is only one end, this will be what we are seeking, and if there more than one, the most complete of these will be what we are seeking." (Aristotle, Nicomachean Ethics I, 1096 b, 13-15, 1097 a, 27-30).**

" **Now such a thing (good) happiness, above all else, is held to be; for this we choose always for itself and never for the sake of something else, but honour, pleasure,** reason and every virtue we choose indeed for themselves (for if nothing resulted from them, we should still choose each of them), but we choose them also for the sake of happiness, judging that through them we shall be happy. Happiness on the other hand, no one chooses for the sake of these, nor in general, for anything other than itself." (Aristotle, Nicomachean Ethics I, 1097 b, 1-7).

Aristotle divides the goods into three classes, the external goods, those that relate to the body, and those to the soul. As all things have a **function** or **activity**, the **good** resides in their good function. For example, the function of a lyre player is to play the lyre, and his good is to play well, and as a result the "**virtue**" or the "**excellence**" (*αρετή*: arete) of the lyre player is the good performance of that action. Since life is alertness and activity, the work of the soul and the work of the virtue is to produce good life. **The work then of the complete virtue is happiness.** As a result, the complete good is a rational activity of the soul in conformity with the best and most complete virtue. For, what distinguishes the virtue is the action, since the deeds are the ones that can be blamed or praised, as they prove the understanding or no of the virtue. On the other hand, when some one is asleep, neither can we give an opinion of his virtue, nor to mark him as a happy man.

" **Human good turns out to be activity of soul in conformity with virtue, and if there are more than one virtue, in conformity with the best and most complete.**" (Aristotle, Nicomachean Ethics I, 1098 a, 15-17).

" **Therefore, happiness would be the activity of a complete life in accordance with complete virtue.**" (Aristotle, Eudemian Ethics II, 1219 a 37-39).

However, in order to understand the activity of the soul which implies a rational principle, we have to analyze the meaning of terms "**soul**" (*ψυχή*: psyche) and "**rational**". According to Aristotle, the soul has two parts: the "**rational**" part or else the one that "**possesses reason**" (*λόγον ἔχον*: logon echon) and the "**irrational** (*ἄλογον*: alogon) part. The one that has reason consists of the "**intellective**" (*νοητικόν*:

noetukon) and the "**deliberating**" (*βουλευτικόν*: bouleutikon) part, as we are going to see later in detail.

The parts of the soul

The **soul** is defined by Aristotle as "**substance in one kind of what is**" or else "**actuality of the first kind of a natural body having life potentially in**". In order to be able to follow this definition, we must analyze the terms "substance", "potentiality" and "actuality.

All the **beings**, according to Aristotle, are classified by **substance** (*ουσία*: ousia), in the sense of **matter** (*ύλη*: hyle), and in the sense of **form** (*μορφή*: morphe) or **essence (kind:** *είδος*: eidos). The substance is what really defines each being, e.g. man, horse, etc. It is neither said of a subject, nor in a subject.

" **A substance – that which is called substance most strictly, primarily and most of all – is that which is neither said of a subject nor in a subject e.g. this given man, this given horse." (Aristotle, Categories 5, 11-15).**

All the beings can be defined apart from **substance** (e.g. horse), by **quality** (white), **quantity** (four foot), **relative** (larger), **place** (in the Agora), **time** (yesterday), **end, function, potentiality, actuality**. Referring to "**potentiality**" (*δύναμη*: dynamei), is what a thing is 'capable' of doing, or being acted upon, if it is not prevented from something else. For example, a seed of a plant in the soil is "**potentially**" (*δυνάμει*) plant, and if is not prevented from something, it will become a plant. Potentially beings can either "**act**" (*ποιείν*: poiein) or "**be acted upon**" (*πάσχειν*: paschein), as well as can be either innate, for example the eyes possess the **potentiality** of sight (**innate - being acted upon**), or come by practice or learning, e.g. the **capability** of playing the flute, which can be possessed by learning (**exercise - acting**).

" **As all potentialities are either innate, like the senses, or come by practice like the power of playing the flute, or by learning, like that of the arts, those which come by practice or by rational formula we must acquire by previous exercise, but this is not necessary with those**

which are not of this nature and which imply passivity."
(Aristotle, Metaphysics IX 1047 b, 30-35).

Referring now to "**actuality**" (*εντελέχεια*: entelecheia), this
is the fulfillment of the end of the potentiality. Because the
end (*τέλος*: telos) is the principle of every change, and for the
sake of the end exists potentiality, therefore actuality is the
end. Referring then to our previous example, we could say
that the actuality of the seed is accomplished when it becomes
a plant.

" **For that for the sake of which a thing is, is its
principle, and the becoming is for the sake of the end; and
the <u>actuality</u> is the <u>end</u>, and it is for the sake of this that
the <u>potentiality</u> is acquired. For animals do not see in
order that they may have sight, but they have sight that
they may see.**" (Aristotle, Metaphysics IX, 1050 a, 5-10).

Returning now to the question of the soul, the "**matter**" of
the soul is its "**potentiality**" and the "**kind**" is its "**actuality**".
Actuality is of two kinds, one is the "**knowledge**" (*επιστήμη*:
episteme) and the other is "**reflecting**" (*θεωρείν*: theorein). In
other words, the soul as a "substance" is completed, when its
rational part which is within a "living" body (potentiality),
acquires the faculty of "knowledge" and "reflection"
(actuality).

" **Now matter is potentiality and kind is actuality; and
actuality is of two kinds one as knowledge and the other
reflecting.**" (Aristotle, On the Soul II, 412 a 10).

" **Hence soul must be a substance in the sense of the
form of a natural body having life potentially within it.
But substance is actuality, and thus soul is actuality of a
body as above characterized. Now there are two kinds of
actuality corresponding to knowledge and to reflecting.**"
(Aristotle, On the Soul II, 412 a, 20-25).

Aristotle divides the soul into more than three parts,
contrary to Plato (rational, spirited and appetitive part).
According to him, as we have seen, at first there are two main
parts: the **rational** part which "**possesses reason**" (*λόγον
έχον*) and the "**irrational**" (*άλογον*) part, namely without
reason. The one which **possesses reason** is divided further in

154

two parts, namely the "**intellective**" (*νοητικόν*) and the "**deliberative**" (*βουλευτικόν*) part. As for the **irrational** part is further divided into three parts, namely the "**nutritive**" (*θρεπτικόν*: threptikon) part, which is related to the faculty of the nutrition of the body, the "**sensitive**" (*αισθητικόν*: aisthetikon) part related to the sensation of the body, and the "**appetitive**" (*ορεκτικόν*: orektikon) or else "**desiring**" (*επιθυμητικόν*: epithemetikon) part, corresponding to the appetites and desires. Afterwards Aristotle is inquiring into the following matter: which part of the soul initiates the movement of the body, as well as which one can be separated from its body and which not.

" **Those who distinguish parts in the soul, if they distinguish and divide in accordance with differences of power, find themselves with a very large number of parts, a <u>nutritive</u>, a <u>sensitive</u>, an <u>intellective</u>, a <u>deliberative</u>, and now an <u>appetitive</u> part; for these are more different from one another than the faculties of desire and passions.**" (Aristotle, On the Soul III, 433 b, 30).

" **From this is clear that the soul is inseparable from its body, or at any rate that certain parts of it are (if it has parts) – for the actuality of them is the actuality of the parts themselves. Yet some may be separable, because they are not the actualities of any body at all.**" (Aristotle, On the Soul II, 413 a, 4-8).

Apparently the nutritive faculty and the capability of the body's sensation are inseparable from the body, they cannot exist without it, and they also do not initiate its movement. But the rest of the parts are associated with one another and can initiate the movement of the body. Particularly the **appetitive** part is one of the parts which is source of movement, as it is associated with the imagination and practical thought. The process is as follows: the "**object of appetite**" (*ορεκτόν*: orekton) stimulates the appetitive part, which by the use of imagination (impressions) moves towards this aim, namely to taste the object of appetite, then it stimulates the practical thought, which ultimately gives rise to the body's movement, and this stage is the last in the process of thinking and the beginning of the action. On the other hand, the **practical thought** (*πρακτικός νούς*: practikos nous) which is different from the **theoretical (speculative) thought** (*θεωρητικός νούς*: theoretikos nous : **reflection**), as we are going to see, can also give rise to the bodily movement, by following the theoretical thought, and not the appetitive part, in order to transform the reflection into will and action. Therefore, sometimes the practical thought can originate movement contrary to appetitive part, since the appetitive moves towards sensational pleasure, but the practical thought fights against it, and does not originate the movement of the body towards this aim (abstinence).

" These two at all events appear to be sources of **movement**: **appetite** and **thought** (if one may venture to regard **imagination** as a kind of thinking: for many men follow their imagination contrary to knowledge, and in all animals other than man there is no thinking or calculation but only imagination).

Both of these then are capable of originating local movement, thought and appetite: thought, that is, which calculates means to an end, i.e. **practical thought** (it differs from **speculative thought** in its character of its end)." (Aristotle, On the Soul III, 433 a 10-15).

" For the end of **theoretical knowledge** is truth, while that of **practical knowledge** is action." (Aristotle, Metaphysics II, 993 b, 20-22).

Referring to "**imagination**" (*φαντασία*: phantasia) (impressions) can be either "**calculative**" (*λογιστική*: logistiki) or "**sensitive**" (*αισθητική*: aisthetiki). When the appetite uses it, is called "sensitive", while when the speculative and practical thought uses it, is called "calculative".

"And all imagination is either calculative or sensitive. In the latter all animals partake." (Aristotle, On the Soul III, 433 b, 25).

The "intellective" part as we have seen, consists of practical and theoretical thought, which we are going to examine in detail in Gnoseology of Aristotle. The calculative imagination is a thought associated with images, because the soul never thinks without an image. And when thought is concerning matters of action (practical), through these images it can decide about the pursuit or avoidance of the action. When it is concerning the reflection (theoretical), these images serve as sensuous contents in order to understand the forms and the objects of thought.

All the parts of the soul, according to Aristotle, cannot be separated from its body, apart from the active thought, which is a part of theoretical thought, as we are going to see in his Gnoseology.

Virtues of each part of the soul – The "mean"

One part of the "**irrational**" part of the soul, as we have seen, is related to nutrition and growth and in general to the survival and preservation of a living being, which Aristotle also calls it "**vegetative**" (φυτικόν: phytikon) and consists of "nutritive" and "sensitive" part. The "vegetative" part have in common both animals and plants, and that is what we call nowadays instinct of survival, therefore it does not share in reason. However, the other part of the "irrational", the one that he calls "**appetitive**" or else "**desiring**" part shares in reason, and therefore sometimes is contrary to reason, and sometimes can listen to the "rational" part and obey it. This fact we can realize, if we liken the young child, which has not developed its reason, to the "appetitive" part. This child is always paying heed and listening to its father, just like the "appetitive" part listens to the reason. Therefore the appetitive part, although is sometimes contrary to the reason, it can follow advices and comply with the commands of reason, as in that case of a moderate man, whose appetitive part is in accordance with his rational one.

Referring to the part that "**possesses reason**", as we have said, is divided in two parts, namely the "**intellective**" and the "**deliberating**", which corresponds to the "will" or else "**volition**" (βούλησις: boulesis). Since the virtue is associated with activity of the soul, then to each part of the rational part must correspond certain virtues (excellences). Therefore, there are two kinds of virtues, **intellectual** (*διανοητικαί*: dianoetikai) corresponding to the "intellective" part, and **moral** or **ethical** (*ηθικαί*: ethikai) corresponding to the "deliberating" one, and as a matter of course to a man's character. For example, wisdom, understanding and prudence are intellectual virtues, while calmness and temperance are moral or ethical ones.

" Therefore the irrational element appears to be two-fold. For the vegetative element in no way shares in reason, but the appetitive and in general the desiring element in a sense shares in it, in so far as it listens to and obeys it. This is the sense in which we speak of paying heed to one's father or one's friends, not that in which we speak of the 'rational' in mathematics."(Aristotle, Nicomachean Ethics I, 1102 b 30-35).

" And if this element also must be said to have a reason, that which <has reason> also will be two-fold, one subdivision having it in the strict sense and in itself, and the other having a tendency to obey as one does one's father.

Excellence (virtue) too is distinguished into kinds in accordance with this difference; for we say some virtues are intellectual and others moral. Philosophic wisdom and understanding and prudence being intellectual, liberality and temperance moral. For in speaking about a man's character we do not say that he is wise or has understanding but that he is a good-tempered or temperate; yet we praise the wise man also with respect to his mental state. And of states we call those which merit praise virtues." (Aristotle, Nicomachean Ethics I, 1103 a, 1-10).

As Aristotle proceeds further in analyzing these two parts, he begins with the moral virtues which refer to the volition, and he points out that both moral virtue and habit concern the man's character. Since the Greek word "*ήθος*" (**ethos: moral virtue**) derives from the word "*έθος*" (**aethos: habit**), it is obvious that the moral virtue comes about as a result of habit, namely of repeated and continuous exercising of a certain

158

state of the soul, which becomes habit and afterwards a man's character. Therefore, someone becomes e.g. just after having practiced just acts, which also correspond to a certain state of mind. So moral **virtue** derives from a **habit** of certain actions, which means, habit of a certain **state** of mind that leads to a certain end, e.g. to be just or brave etc.

" **While moral virtue comes about as a result of habit, whence also its name is one that is formed by a slight variation from the word for habit (_ἔθος_).**"

" **But virtues we get by first exercising them, as also happens in the case of the arts as well.**" (Aristotle, Nicomachean Ethics II, 1103 a, 16-19, 30-33).

" **This then, is the case with the virtues also; by doing the acts that we do in our transactions with other men we become just or unjust, and by doing the acts that we do in the presence of danger, and being habituated to feel fear or confidence, we become brave or cowardly. The same is true of appetites and feelings of anger; some men become temperate and good-tempered, others self-indulgent and irascible, by behaving in one way or the other in the appropriate circumstances.**" (Aristotle, Nicomachean Ethics II, 1103 b, 12-20).

Referring now to the aim of those habits or the states of mind, namely the moral **virtues**, Aristotle claims that their aim is the avoidance of "**defect**" (_ἔλλειψις_: elleipsis) and "**excess**" (_ὑπερβολή_: hyperbole). Because everything in nature is destroyed by the extremes while it is preserved by the "**mean**" (_μεσότης_: mesotes). Deficiencies and excesses, as we also saw in Democritus' philosophy (fr.191), overthrow the balance of the soul, destroy the man's body and health, and ultimately the man himself, while the "mean" preserves them. Therefore, virtue aims at the intermediate state between the excess and deficiency, for example to be just is the middle state between being unfair to and being hard done by someone.

" **First then, let us consider this, that it is the nature of such things to be destroyed by <u>defect</u> and <u>excess</u>, as we see in the case of strength and of health (for to gain light on** things imperceptible we must use the evidence of the sensible things); both excessive and defective exercise destroys the strength, and similarly drink or food which is above or below a certain amount destroys the health, while that which is proportionate both produces and increases and preserves it. So too is it then, in the case of temperance and courage and the other virtues. "

" Temperance and courage then, are destroyed by excess and defect, and preserved by the <u>mean</u>." (Aristotle, Nicomachean Ethics II, 1104 a 10-25).

The **criterion** of measuring our actions, and as a result our habits, is "**pleasure**" (*ηδονή*: hedone) and "**pain**" (*λύπη*: lype), since our upbringing is based upon them. For the instinctive drive, which we have in common with animals, is the pursuit of pleasure or the avoidance of pain. During our upbringing we are habituated by our educators, to do certain things and to avoid others, because we have been praised for some actions (pleasure), and been blamed or punished for some others (pain). Therefore, all our actions and habits are accompanied by feelings of pleasure or pain. In this sense, since the moral virtue is associated with our habits, then follows that virtue will be concerned with pleasure and pain. So the virtue is referring to the mean state, between deficiency and excess, namely the best concerning pleasures and pains. To exercise then this state of mean, is to feel delight (pleasure) when we do proper and good things, and pain when we do the improper and bad ones, in other words to delight in and to be pained by the things that we ought.

" We must take as a sign of states the pleasure or pain that supervenes on acts."

" For moral virtue is concerned with pleasures and pains; it is on account of pleasure that we do bad things, and on account of pain that we abstain noble ones."

" We assume then, that moral virtue is the quality of acting in the best way in relation to pleasures and pains, and vice is the opposite." (Aristotle, Nicomachean Ethics II, 1104 b, 4, 10-11, 26-28).

The mean state, as we have seen, namely the intermediate between the deficiency and excess, is the virtue, and it is concerned with both one's feelings and one's actions. Referring to the **emotions** (*πάθη*: pathe) that accompany pleasure and pain, these are for example fear, confidence, anger, pity, love, hatred etc. The mean state with regard to the emotions is that one has the appropriate feeling, for the right purpose, at the right time, towards the right people and in the right way, namely never with excess or deficiency. For example, with reference to anger, we stand badly if we feel it violently or too weakly, and well if we feel it moderately. Referring to the actions, the "mean" is lying for example in the intermediate between intemperance and insensibility, which is the temperance, or between lavishness and meanness which is the liberality etc. However, the "mean" is not the same for all people, but relative to each one, since due to our different upbringing, some of us are closer to one extreme of deficiency or excess than others. But since feelings and actions presuppose the relevant state of mind, which derives from the habits, we can then define the virtue as follows: *Virtue is a disposition of the mind being determined by reason and choice in order to come to a mean between deficiency and excess, which is relative to us.* This state of mind can be acquired after continuous practice and is accompanied by respective feelings and actions.

" <u>Virtue</u> (*αρετή*) **then, is a <u>state</u> concerned with choice, lying in a mean relative to us, this being determined <u>by reason</u> and in the way in which the prudent man would determine it. Now it is the <u>mean</u> between the two vices, that which depends on <u>excess</u> and that which depends on <u>defect</u>; and again it is a mean because the vices respectively fall short of or exceed what is right in both <u>feelings</u> and <u>actions</u>, while virtue both finds and chooses that which is <u>intermediate</u>."** (Aristotle, Nicomachean Ethics II, 1107 a, 1-5).

As we can realize, after having read the definition of moral virtue by Aristotle, virtue is an intermediate state between deficiency and excess. For example between the irascible (excess of anger) man and the unfeeling (deficiency) one is the gentle one (mean), between the foolhardy (excess) and the cowardly (deficiency) is the brave man, between the intemperate (excess) and the insensible (deficiency) is the temperate and moderate man etc. We quote the following list, which consists of the vices that correspond to excess and deficiency, and of the respective virtues, which correspond to the "mean" between them.

Excess	Deficiency	Mean
irascibility	lack of feeling	good-temper
foolhardiness	cowardice	bravery
shamelessness	shyness	modesty
intemperance	insensibility	temperance
envy	(unnamed)	right indignation
gain	loss	the just
lavishness	meanness	liberality
boastfulness	self-depreciation	sincerity
habit of flattery	habit of dislike	friendliness
servility	stubbornness	dignity
luxuriousness	submission to evils	endurance
vanity	meanness of spirit	greatness of spirit
extravagance	pettiness	magnificence
cunning	simplicity of mind	prudence.

(Aristotle, Eudemian Ethics II, 1221 a, 1-15).

Since virtue is concerned with **"choice"** (*προαίρεσις*: prohairesis), we have to define choice and its relation to **"voluntary"** (*εκούσιον*: ekousion) and **"involuntary"** (*ακούσιον*: akousion) actions. First of all, an action is considered involuntary, when it takes place under **compulsion** (*βία*: bia) due to external circumstances, and the person is acted upon. Another case of involuntary action is the one which takes place owing to **ignorance** (*άγνοια*: agnoia). On the matter of ignorance Aristotle distinguishes two kinds of ignorance, from which only the one is involuntary, namely when the man who has done something bad and produced pain, regrets about this action. The one who does not regret, acts voluntarily but in ignorance. Therefore, the one who acts

162

in rage or drunk even though he acts in ignorance, he does not act involuntarily. On the other hand, the voluntary action takes place, when the one who acts is aware of the particular circumstances of his action.

" **The compulsory then, seems to be that whose moving principle is outside, the person compelled contributing nothing.**"

" **Of people then, who act by reason of ignorance he who regrets is thought an involuntary agent..**"

" **Since that which is done under compulsion or by reason of ignorance is involuntary, the voluntary would seem to be that of which the moving principle is the agent himself, he being aware of the particular circumstances of the action. Presumably acts done by reason of anger or appetite are not rightly called involuntary.**" **(Aristotle, Nicomachean Ethics III, 1110 b, 15-17, 22-24, 1111 a, 21-25).**

Referring now to the relation between choice and voluntary, they seem to be the same but they are not, since children and animals act voluntarily but not after choice, for they do not possess reason. Because **choice involves reason and thought**, therefore it is not appetite or anger or will or a kind of opinion.

At first, **appetite** and **anger** are characteristics of animals as they do not possess reason. Secondly, as we know, an incontinent man acts with appetite and anger, while the continent man on the contrary acts with choice, but not with appetite and anger. Therefore, anger and appetite are contrary to choice since are closer to pleasure and pain.

" **Choice then, seems to be voluntary, but not the same thing as voluntary, the latter extends more widely. For both children and other animals share in voluntary action, but not in choice..**"

" **Those who say it is appetite or anger or will or a kind of opinion do not seem to be right. For choice is not common to irrational creatures as well, but appetite and anger are.**" **(Aristotle, Nicomachean Ethics III, 1111 b 5).**

Referring to **will** (*βούλησις*: boulesis), although it seems to be close to choice, it is not, since will is also related to what is not in our power or to impossibles, and apart from that is related rather to the end, while choice refers to what contributes to that end.

" **Again will relates rather to the end, choice to what contributes to the end; for instance, we wish to be healthy, but we choose the acts which will make us healthy..**" (Aristotle, Nicomachean Ethics III, 1111 b, 26).

Finally concerning **opinion** (*δόξα*: doxa), it is distinguished by its falsity or truth, while choice by its badness or goodness. Furthermore, sometimes although we have an opinion about what is good, we choose the contrary. Therefore, choice and opinion are not identical.

" **And we choose what we best know to be good, but we opine what we do not know at all; and it is not the same people that are thought to make the best choices and to have the best opinions, but some are thought to have fairly good opinions, but by reason of vice to choose what they should not.**" (Aristotle, Nicomachean Ethics III, 1112 a, 7-10).

To sum up, choice involves reasoning and thought for what is in our own power, in order to find out the means that contribute to the end, which the will determines. And what is in our own power, is what does not depend on nature, necessity or luck. Referring now to the definition of **moral virtue**, we could say that **will** decides the end which is the good, namely the "**mean**", and **deliberation** and **choice** finds out what contributes to this end, by reasoning and thought. Therefore **virtue** is **voluntary** and according to **choice**, as well as vice is voluntary and according to choice.

" **For choice involves reason and thought.**"

" **We deliberate about things that are in our power and can be done; and these are in fact what is left.**"

" **Now since the end is the object of the will, the things contributing to the end are what we deliberate and choose, actions concerning to the latter must be according to choice and voluntary. Now the exercise of the virtues is**

164

concerned with these. Therefore virtue also is in our own power, and so too vice." (Aristotle, Nicomachean Ethics III, 1112 a, 15-16, 30-31, 1113 b 1-6).

Gnoseology

Since then moral virtue involves reasoning and thought, we can now proceed to the analysis of the second part of the soul which "possesses reason", namely to the "**intellective**" part. This part is distinguished from the "**deliberative**" or **moral** part, which is concerned with the **will,** as we previously mentioned. But, as we said, the action to get to the mean state presupposes both intellect and will, since virtue is concerned with voluntary choice determined by reason.

" **Whereas that which is or may be done is an end in itself, because acting well is an end in itself, and this is the object of the will; and so moral choice is either intellect out in a position of will-ing or intellectual pursuit, and such an origin of action is a man." (Aristotle, Nicomachean Ethics VI, 1139 b, 1-5).**

The function of the "intellective" part is the possession of truth, and this end can be achieved by five ways: a. **Art** (τέχνη: techne), b. **Scientific knowledge** (ἐπιστήμη: episteme), c. **Prudence** or else **practical wisdom** (φρόνησις: phronesis), d. **Philosophic wisdom** (σοφία: sofia) and e.**Comprehension** or else **pure intellect** (νοῦς: nous). Apart from these is the **belief** (ὑπόληψις: hepolepsis) and the **opinion** (δόξα: doxa), which if they are not confirmed can be mistaken and deceive us.

" **Let it be assumed that the states by virtue of which the soul possesses truth by way of affirmation or denial are five in number, i.e. art, knowledge, practical wisdom, philosophic wisdom, comprehension; for belief and opinion may be mistaken." (Aristotle, Nicomachean Ethics VI, 1139 b, 15-20).**

Knowledge is concerned with the principles of truth, which means the **science** that studies the objects of knowledge, which exist of necessity, therefore it is eternal and ungenerated, namely the being. This study starts from what is

already known and proceeds through **induction** (*επαγωγή*:
epagoge) and **deduction** or **syllogism** (*συλλογισμός*).
Induction, as we have seen in Democritus' philosophy,
proceeds from the appearances to the imperceptible, it starts
from the first principles, and can draw a conclusion about the
universal laws. On the other hand, deduction proceeds from
the whole to the parts, namely from universals to the first
principles. Both deduction and induction are apt to
demonstrate.

" **Knowledge is then a state of capacity to demonstrate,
and has the other limiting characteristics which we specify
in the Analytics (Posterior Analytics I, 1); for it is when a
man believes in a certain way and the principles are
known to him that he has knowledge, since if they are not
better known to him than the conclusion, he will have his
knowledge only incidentally.**" (Aristotle, Nicomachean
Ethics VI, 1139 b, 30-35).

With regard to the **art**, it is related to the creation
(making:*ποίησις*, poiesis) and a thing made, of which the
origin is the maker, namely the man, but neither the necessity
nor nature. Therefore it is a state of capacity to make, and
involves reasoning as well, since without reason it would not
be possible to be made such a thing.

" **Art then, as has been said, is a state concerned with
making, involving a true course of reasoning, and lack of
art on the contrary is a state concerned with making,
involving a false course of reasoning.**" (Aristotle,
Nicomachean Ethics VI, 1140 a, 20-25).

Referring to **prudence,** Aristotle points out that prudence is
the quality of a man of prudence who possesses the faculty of
reasoning with regard to the human goods. Therefore, the
object of prudence is what is good and bad for the human
being, and the end of it is to find out and choose the means to
act for the human goods. For this reason prudence itself is a
virtue of the rational part of the soul.

" **Prudence then, must be a reasoned and true state of
capacity to act with regard to human goods.**" (Aristotle,
Nicomachean Ethics VI, 1140 b, 20).

The faculty of the **pure intellect** (*νοῦς*) is the comprehension and grasping of the first principles of the universe, since as we saw in the beginning, Aristotle regards the pure intellect as a divine part, which is the only one that can achieve deep and true understanding, for it goes beyond the scientific knowledge. Science (*ἐπιστήμη*) on the one hand, allows us to realize the existence of the laws and principles in the universe and their effects upon nature, and therefore enable us to use these principles for the human prosperity. However, on the other hand, only through the pure intellect one can grasp the primary and ultimate principles and definitions of the universe.

".. **And it cannot be any of the three (i.e. prudence, scientific knowledge, or philosophic wisdom), the remaining alternative is that it is** pure intellect (*νοῦς*) **that grasps the first principles."** (Aristotle, Nicomachean Ethics VI, 1141 a, 6-8).

" **And pure intellect (comprehension) is concerned with the ultimates in both directions; for both the primary definitions and the ultimates are the objects of comprehension and not of argument, and in demonstrations the pure intellect** (*νοῦς*) **grasps the unchangeable and primary definitions.."** (Aristotle, Nicomachean Ethics VI, 1143 b 1).

" **If** pure intellect (*νοῦς*) **is** divine, **then in comparison with man, the life according to it is divine in comparison with human life."** (Aristotle, Nicomachean Ethics X, 1177 b 30).

".. **Since not only the pure intellect** (*νοῦς*) **is the best thing in us, but the objects of intellect are the best of knowable objects.."** (Aristotle, Nicomachean Ethics X, 1177 a 20).

The pure intellect, as it possesses the faculty of contemplating, must be **impassive** and not mixed with anything else, as Anaxagoras also said. Apart from that, the intellect before it thinks is potentially being. The object of thought (*νοητόν*: noeton: **thinkable**) sparks off the process of transformation of intellect from **potentially** being (capability of thinking) into **actually** being, which means when the intellect finally possesses scientific (*επιστήμη*) and speculative knowledge (*θεωρείν*), as we saw in the chapter concerning the parts of the soul. Just like the light which transforms the colours from potential into actual beings. On the other hand, thinking in the sense of perceiving, is a process in which the intellect is "acted upon", which means intellect must be **passive**. In order to solve this problem, namely on the one hand impassive intellect and on the other hand passive, Aristotle introduced the two kinds of intellect, namely the pure and impassive intellect, and the passive one (Aristotle, On the Soul 429 a-430 a)..

Passive intellect can become all things, while the active intellect can make all things. Just like the craftsman, who as being the originating cause makes the use of matter (potential) to make the material objects (actual), in the same way active intellect being the originating cause creates the objects of thought. Passive intellect can perceive the thinkables, while impassive intellect transforms the objects of thought (thinkables) from potential into active, the same as we said with the light and colours. For **impassive intellect** (*απαθής νούς*: apathes nous), as being the **productive cause** (*ποιητικόν αίτιον*: poietikon aition) or "principle" of the objects of thought, it cannot be related or identified with the matter, just like all the "principles", and therefore it is **separable** from its body, **unmixed**, **immortal** and **eternal**. On the other hand, the **passive intellect** (*παθητικός νούς*: patheticos nous) is related to the matter, since it is susceptible and perceives like the senses do, therefore it is **perishable** and dies with the body, since it cannot be separated from its body, and cannot think without the impassive intellect.

" **Since in every class of things, just as in the whole of nature, there is something which is their matter, which is potentially all the individuals, and something else which is their <u>productive cause</u> in the sense that it makes them all – the two being related as an art to its material – these distinct elements must be present in the soul also.**

Intellect in the passive sense is such because it becomes all things, but intellect has another aspect in that it makes all things; this is a kind of positive state like a light; for in a sense light makes potential into actual colours. <u>Intellect</u> in this sense is <u>separable, impassive, unmixed</u> since it is essentially activity, for always the <u>active</u> is superior to passive factor and the <u>originating cause</u> to the matter.

Actual knowledge is identical with its object. Potential is prior in time to actual knowledge in the individual, but in general it is not prior in time. (Impassive) intellect does not think intermittently. When separated it is alone just what it is, and this <u>alone</u> is <u>immortal</u> and <u>eternal</u> (we do not remember because, while this is impassive, <u>passive intellect is perishable</u>), and without this nothing thinks." (Aristotle, On the Soul III, 430 a, 10-25).

Referring now to **philosophic wisdom**, this involves the comprehension of the first principles of the universe (intellect), combined with the knowledge of their effects upon nature (scientific knowledge), therefore it is considered to be the highest form of understanding the nature of all things. Wisdom is distinguished from prudence (practical wisdom), since the latter is concerned with the human goods and the man's own interests, while wisdom is theoretical, and possesses the understanding and knowledge of the first principles, and also what follows from them.

" From what has been said it is plain then, that <u>wisdom</u> is knowledge combined with comprehension, of the things that are highest by nature. This is why we say Anaxagoras, Thales and men like them have wisdom, but not practical wisdom, when we see them ignorant of what is to their own advantage.." (Aristotle, Nicomachean Ethics VI, 1141 b, 1-5).

Ultimately, there is a **judiciousness** (σύνεσις: synesis) which is similar to prudence, since they are both concerned with the human goods, however judiciousness is theoretical since is the faculty of judging what is good or bad for the man, while prudence is practical, commanding and concerned with acts for its ends. As for **judgement** (γνώμη: gnome), it is concerned with the right judgement of the equitable, therefore it is a part of judiciousness.

" Hence <u>judiciousness</u> is about the same objects as <u>prudence</u>, but are not the same. For prudence is commanding since its end is what ought to be done or not to be done; but judiciousness only judges." (Aristotle, Nicomachean Ethics VI, 1143 a, 6-10).

After having examined the most significant aspects of the "intellective" part of the soul, we can proceed our inquiry, in order to find out how all these parts are related to the good, the moral virtue and to happiness, since this is the end of a man's life. Drawing first a comparison between prudence and wisdom, we conclude that wisdom does not contemplate with what makes for happiness, since it is not interested in human goods and personal advantages, but prudence is. Therefore prudence helps the wise man, after having possessed knowledge of the divine, the just, the noble and the good for a man, to act in accordance with virtue, since virtue makes the choice right, and prudence shows the things leading to this aim. So, the three of them (wisdom, prudence and virtue) contribute to complete the function of a man, and produce happiness (actuality).

" For <u>wisdom</u> will contemplate none of the things that will make a man happy (for it is not concerned with any coming into being), and through <u>prudence</u> has this merit, for what purpose do we need it? Prudence is the quality of mind concerned with things just and noble and good for man, but these are the things which it is the mark of a good man to do." (Aristotle, Nicomachean Ethics VI, 1143 b, 19-24).

" So does <u>wisdom</u> produce <u>happiness</u>, for being a part of virtue entire, by being possessed and by actualizing itself it makes a man happy. Again the function of man is accomplished only in accordance with prudence, as well as with moral virtue; for <u>virtue</u> makes the aim right, and <u>prudence</u> the things leading to it." (Aristotle, Nicomachean Ethics VI, 1144 a, 5-9).

Virtue then, as being a natural disposition to the "mean", through the possession of intellect and knowledge - that the wise man has - will become a virtue in the strict sense. Just like the children, due to their upbringing have a natural disposition to virtue (true opinion), but when they develop reason this disposition becomes more conscious. So, with the natural disposition to virtue, when one acquires intellect (*νούς*), becomes conscious of the "mean", and through prudence he finds the means to possess the virtue.

" **If a man once acquires intellect that makes difference in action; and his state, while still like what it was. Will then be virtue in the strict sense." (Aristotle, Nicomachean Ethics VI, 1144 b 13-14).**

To sum up, moral virtue and prudence always co-exist, since the one cannot be without the other, for the right choice implies prudence, and virtue shows the right aim to be achieved by prudence.

" **It is clear then, from what has been said, that it is not possible to be good in the strict sense without prudence, nor prudent without moral virtue." (Aristotle, Nicomachean Ethics VI, 1144 b, 30-32).**

Pleasure – Happiness

After having examined the relation between the "intellective" part (prudence, wisdom, intellect) and the "deliberative" (moral virtues) rational part of the soul, we can proceed to the matter of **happiness** (*ευδαιμονία*: eudaimonia). However, in order to define happiness, we must first inquire into the question of **pleasure** (*ηδονή*: hedone), so as to be able to make clear whether happiness is related to pleasure or not. First of all, it is plain that the natural tendency of a man is the pursuit of pleasure and the avoidance of pain.

" **But in fact people evidently avoid the one (pain) as evil and choose the other (pleasure) as good." (Aristotle, Nicomachean Ethics X, 1173 a, 12).**

As Aristotle examines pleasure, at first he disagrees with Plato upon this question, namely that pleasure is the **replenishment of lack** of that, which is according to its nature. His argument is that, no one chooses to live with a mind of a child throughout his life, but chooses instead the learning, although he does not get enjoyment from being satisfied with the pleasures, that a child could get. According to him there are different sorts of pleasure, since pleasure is produced in respect to each sense, therefore there are pleasant sights, pleasant sounds etc.

" That pleasure is produced in respect to each sense is plain; for we speak of sights and sounds as pleasant." (Aristotle, Nicomachean Ethics X, 1174 b, 26-28).

Pleasure, as he argues, accompanies our activities and in particular completes the activities, since we always try to improve our activities in order to feel more pleasure. Therefore, pleasure and activity are bound up together, and as well as activity is bound up to life, since life is an activity. Life then is completed by pleasure, and this is the reason why pleasure is desirable.

" Therefore, <u>pleasure</u> also is not continuous; for it accompanies <u>activity</u>."

" One might think that all men desire <u>pleasure</u> because they all aim at life; <u>life</u> is an <u>activity</u>, and each man is active about those things and with those faculties that he loves most; e.g. the musician is active with his hearing in reference to tunes, the student with his mind in reference to theoretical questions, and so on in each case; now <u>pleasure perfects the activities</u>, and therefore life which they desire." (Aristotle, Nicomachean Ethics X, 1175 a, 5, 11-17).

Since then, activities are bound up to pleasures, and there are activities worthy to be chosen and others to be avoided, it is evident that there are pleasures to be chosen and to be avoided respectively. Profligate activities will produce pain to a virtuous man and pleasure to a profligate, while activities in accordance with virtue will produce pain to a profligate and pleasure to a virtuous man. Therefore, there are different kinds of pleasure, since <u>there are different kinds of beings, and each being has a proper function to which corresponds a proper</u>

pleasure, since "**asses would prefer hay to gold**" as we saw in Heraclitus' philosophy.

" **Now since activities differ in respect of goodness and badness, and some are worthy to be chosen, others to be avoided, and others neutral, so too are the pleasures, for each activity there is a proper pleasure.**" (Aristotle, Nicomachean Ethics X, 1175 b, 24-26).

" **Each animal is thought to have a proper pleasure, as it has a proper function.**"

" **But of those that are thought to be good what kind of pleasure or what pleasure should be that proper to man?**" (Aristotle, Nicomachean Ethics X, 1176 a, 4, 23-25).

The pleasures that are proper to a man, are in accordance with his nature, and could lead him to achieve happiness, should be the ones that perfect the activities of the complete and blessed man.

" **Whether then, the complete and blessed man has one or more activities, the pleasures that complete these activities, will be said in the strict sense to be pleasures proper to man.**" (Aristotle, Nicomachean Ethics X, 1176 a 25).

After having examined pleasure in relation to virtue and life, we can proceed to the question of **happiness**, since this is the end of Aristotle's inquiry. At first, happiness is not a state of mind but an activity, which as it has been said, is desirable not for the sake of something else but for itself, therefore it is self-sufficient.

" **We said then, that happiness is not a state; for if it were, might belong to some one who was asleep throughout his life, living the life of a plant..**"

".. **and we must rather class happiness as an activity..**" (Aristotle, Nicomachean Ethics X, 1176 a, 32-35).

Pleasant amusements are chosen also for themselves, however we receive more harm than profit from them. So of this kind (chosen for their own sake) are only the noble and good deeds in accordance with virtue, as well as the activity of pure intellect (reflecting). The complete and blessed man chooses the activities, which are in accordance with virtue, and the pleasures that accompany them, since those are the pure and generous pleasures and proper to man.

" For <u>virtue</u> and <u>intellect</u> (*νοῦς*) from which good activities flow, do not depend on despotic position; nor, if these people, who have never tasted pure and generous pleasure, take refuge in the bodily pleasures, should these for that reason be thought more desirable." (Aristotle, Nicomachean Ethics X, 1176 b 18-21).

" For happiness does not lie in such pastimes (bodily pleasures), but as we have said before, in activities which are in accordance with virtue." (Aristotle, Nicomachean Ethics X, 1177 a, 9-10).

Since happiness is an activity in accordance with virtue, then it should be in accordance with the highest virtue, which is proper to the best part within us. At this point we can see that Aristotle meets Plato's view, namely that the pleasure of the best part of the soul is the highest, and therefore it is happiness. Since the best part in us is the **intellect** (*νοῦς*), for it is the divine and noble element within us, then it follows that the **activity** in accordance with its proper virtue will be the highest pleasure, namely **happiness**. This activity of intellect, as it has been said, is **reflecting** (*θεωρεῖν*: speculating, contemplating), because this is the "actuality" of intellect. At this point, as we can realize, Aristotle meets Anaxagoras' view, that happiness is the reflecting and freedom which arises from that (fr. 29).

" If happiness is activity in accordance with virtue, it is reasonable that it should be in accordance with the highest virtue; and will be that of the best thing in us. Whether it be intellect or something else that is this element which is thought to be our natural ruler and guide and to take thoughts of things noble and divine, whether it be itself also divine or only the most divine element in us, the activity of this in accordance with its proper virtue will be complete happiness. That this activity is speculative we have already said."

" For this activity is the best, since not only is intellect the best, but the objects of intellect are the best of

174

knowable objects; and secondly it is the most continuous, since we can contemplate truth more continuously than we can do anything." (Aristotle, Nicomachean Ethics X, 1177 a, 10-23).

Philosophy can offer marvelous pleasures through reflecting and speculating, but wisdom offers the highest pleasure due to its purity and endurance, since the one who possesses knowledge and comprehension is self-sufficient. For the virtuous man e.g. the just or the brave needs the other people in order to act justly or bravely, but the wise man is self-sufficient, because the **speculative activity of the intellect** is superior in **worth**, aims only at itself (**good itself**) and has its **pleasure** proper to itself, therefore it leads to **complete happiness**.

" But the activity of the pure intellect, since it is speculative, seems both to be superior in worth and to aim at no end beyond itself and to have its pleasure proper to itself..."

" It follows that this activity will be the complete happiness of man." (Aristotle, Nicomachean Ethics X, 1177 b 18-25).

Since the intellect is the divine element within us, the life according to intellect is divine, therefore intellect is the only element that can make ourselves immortal so as to become like gods. And as the proper thing to man by nature is the intellect, then the **life according to intellect** (*κατά νούν βίος*: kata noun bios) will be in accordance with his nature, therefore the best and the most pleasant, namely the happiest.

" If pure intellect is divine, then in comparison with man, life according to it is divine in comparison with human life." (Aristotle, Nicomachean Ethics X, 1177 b, 30).

" And what we said before will apply now; that which is proper to each being is by nature best and most pleasant for each one; for man, therefore, the life according to intellect is best and pleasantest, since intellect more than anything else is man. This life therefore is the happiest." (Aristotle, Nicomachean Ethics X, 1178 a, 5-9).

However, since our nature is composed by both divine and human element, both elements must have its proper pleasure. The divine element in us, as we said before, is happy through the **speculative activity of the pure intellect**. But our human element in a secondary degree, is happy through the activities which are in accordance with moral virtue. In that way theory harmonizes with facts, the intellect with deeds, otherwise this knowledge - that the wise man possesses and does not apply - is only meaningless words about the good. So, the wise man since he lives with other people, he acts in accordance with virtue, by choosing noble and great deeds. Therefore he needs prudence, which helps him to choose the right acts and the means to be accomplished.

To sum up, on the one hand the activity **in accordance with virtue** of the "mean" through prudence, leads a happy life, for a man is a social being, and on the other hand life **according to intellect**, through the speculative activity of the pure intellect, leads to the highest pleasure, which is distinguished from all the others in power and worth. The **composite nature** of a man then, needs both activities in order to achieve happiness.

" **Being connected to the feelings also, the moral virtue must belong to our composite nature; and the virtues of our composite nature are human; so, therefore are the life and the happiness which correspond to these. But the virtue of the pure intellect is separate and distinct."** (Aristotle, Nicomachean Etthics X, 1178 a, 20-23).

We have seen then, in which way the "intellective" part of the soul (prudence, wisdom, intellect) is related to the "deliberating" one (moral virtues), as well as how they are bound up together and contribute to a man's happiness. The wisdom through reflecting and speculating gives the highest pleasure to the wise man, while the noble deeds according to virtue of the "mean" through prudence and right choice, make for his happiness in everyday life.

The " mean" into action

Now we can proceed further to the elaboration of the moral virtues and the state of the mean, taking into consideration the different parts of the soul and their functions. Since the moral virtue is a state of the mean between excess and deficiency and is concerned with choice, which means involves reason, then it is guided by prudence. In this sense we can examine in detail the virtues of the "mean", together with their corresponding vices (deficiency, excess), that we quoted in the relevant list.

As we said **bravery** (*ανδρεία*: andreia, courage) is the mean between **foolhardiness** (*θρασύτης*: thrasytes) (excess) and **cowardice** (*δειλία*: deilia) (deficiency). Civic bravery is not considered to be the virtue of bravery, since it is due to the fear of punishment by the laws. Military courage cannot be considered virtue either, since on the one hand it is due to experience in the matters of war, and on the other hand as men are driven by passion in the war, that makes them ignorant of the danger. Therefore, bravery because of ignorance of danger (e.g. children), is not considered to be a virtue either. Passion itself (lust, anger, etc.) drives people to rush on danger without foreseeing any of the perils, therefore is not bravery either. In all the above mentioned cases, neither is choice involved to act for the sake of the noble, nor act according to reason, therefore we cannot consider them as virtuous actions which imply bravery, although they resemble courageous activities.

However, the virtue of bravery enables a man to face the dangerous and frightening situations neither because of ignorance nor for pleasure of passion, but because the act is noble and good. The courageous act is directed by reason and prudence, and it has been chosen for the sake of an end, and the end is right and noble, therefore the man acts in this way, although he is aware of the perils. In the same way, a brave man can stand all the misfortunes and hardships of life, without complaining or choosing to die in order to escape from severe pain that misfortunes bring about.

" But since all virtues imply choice – we have said before what this means and that it makes a man choose everything for the sake of some end, and that the end is the noble – it is clear that bravery, because it is an excellence, will make a man face what is frightening for some end, so that he does it neither through ignorance – for his virtue makes him judge correctly – nor for pleasure, but because the act is noble; since if it is not noble but frantic, he does not face the danger, for that would be disgraceful." (Aristotle, Eudemian Ethics III, 1230 a, 25-35).

Referring now to **temperance** (σωφροσύνη: sophrosyne), as we have said, is the mean between the **self-indulgence** (ακολασία: akolasia) and **insensibility** (αναισθησία: anaisthesia). Self-indulgence is defined as an excess of bodily pleasures, particularly the pleasures of **touch** and **taste**, namely the pleasures of food, drink and sexual intercourse. The deficiency as we know is very rare, and it hardly occurs, and particularly among rough and savage people, since they cannot distinguish different kinds of those pleasures. Most of the people who go wrong concerning the bodily pleasures, go in the direction of excess, namely are self-indulgent since they cannot control their appetites, because the appetitive element of their soul does not follow the reason (prudence), just like the children who are led by their insatiable appetites. And as we saw in Democritus' philosophy, the self-indulgent man who fulfils all of his appetites and pursues the sensual pleasures, he finally throws himself into doing something irremediable and illegal (Democritus fr. 191). On the other hand, the appetitive part of a temperate man is in accordance with reason, since he desires the proper and the noble. We will examine further below more the matter of temperance in relation to continence and incontinence.

" Hence the appetitive element in a temperate man should harmonize with reason; for the noble is the mark at which both aim, and the temperate man desires things that he ought, in right manner, and at right times; and this is what the reason directs." (Aristotle, Nicomachean Ethics III, 1119 b, 15-20).

178

After temperance, we can refer to the **good temper** (*πραότης*: praotes) with respect to **anger** (*οργή*: orge), as a "mean" between **irascibility** (*οργιλότης*: orgelotes), which is the excess, and **lack of feelings** or inirascibility, which is deficiency. The excess can be manifested in all the points, for example one can be angry with the wrong persons, at the wrong things, more than is right, too quickly, or too long. The aim of anger is to retaliate upon the others, since the revenge relieves the angry people of the pain due to their anger, as it produces in them pleasure instead of pain when inflicting vengeance or punishment upon the others. The deficiency of anger is when a man does not feel the pain of being insulted, therefore it is related to the lack of feelings, but when one feels insulted and does not react angrily, then this attitude is related more to servility, which means lack of dignity.

The "mean" between these two is the good-tempered man, who is not led by the passion of anger, tends to be unperturbed and he is angry at the right things, with the right people, in right manner, when he ought and as long as he ought, which means as the reason (prudence) dictates. Therefore he is not revengeful, and he rather tends to forgive.

" **For the good-tempered man tends to be unperturbed and not to be led by passion, but to be angry in the manner, at the things, and for the length of time that reason dictates..**" **(Aristotle, Nicomachean Ethics IV 1126 a 1).**

Referring now to the matter of continence and incontinence, we can say that **continence** (*εγκράτεια*: engrateia) is considered to be a **virtue**, but **incontinence** (*ακρασία*: akrasia) is a **vice**. For the incontinent man although he knows that what he does is bad, he does it as a result of passion, since he cannot resist the temptation of passion. On the other hand, the continent man does not follow those appetites which he knows that they are bad, because of his reason.

" **And the incontinent man, knowing that what he does is bad, does it as a result of passion, while the continent man, knowing that his appetites are bad, does not follow**

them because of reason." (Aristotle, Nicomachean Ethics VII, 1145 b, 11-15).

On this subject, as we have said, Socrates had the view that a man because of his ignorance goes astray and follows his passions. The incontinent man as he has **opinion** (*δόξα*: doxa) and not **knowledge** (*επιστήμη*: episteme) concerning pleasures, he can be easily convinced and mastered by his passions. Aristotle argues that there are different kinds of incontinence with regard to the object. Some people are incontinent with respect to bodily enjoyments, and some with respect to anger. As well as the self-indulgent is different from the incontinent man with regard to bodily pleasures. The incontinent man concerned with anger listens to reason and regrets after his anger is over, but not in a fit of anger, due to the warmth and hastiness of its nature. The incontinent man with respect to appetites does not follow the reason, but is subject to regrets. Therefore the incontinent man concerned with both anger and appetite is not like the irascible or self-indulgent man, since he regrets that he acted badly, so he is curable and his badness is intermittent. Incontinence then, cannot be considered vice in a strict sense, since it does not involve choice and the incontinent man can become better as he is subject to regrets. However self-indulgence and anger are vices and incurable. The difference between **continent** and **incontinent** man is that they both have an **opinion** (*δόξα*), but the continent without being strong-headed abides by his opinion, while the incontinent abandons his opinion.

" Therefore in a sense the one (continent man) abides by, and the other (incontinent) abandons, any and every opinion; but without qualification, the <u>true opinion</u>." (Aristotle, Nicomachean Ethics VII, 1151 b, 3-5).

Referring now to the difference between the continent man on the one hand, and the temperate and good-tempered man on the other hand, is that the continent man has an opinion concerning pleasures and anger, which he follows, while both the **temperate** and **good-tempered** have **knowledge** (*επιστήμη*) of the excess and deficiency, and of the "mean" as well, through **prudenc**e, and therefore they are also called

prudent (*φρόνιμοι*: fronimoi). Furthermore, the prudent man acts rightly, since he finds the right means in order to pursue the right aim, concerning pleasure and anger.

" **Nor can the same man have prudence and be incontinent; for it has been shown that a man is at the same time practically wise, and good in respect of character. Further, a man has <u>prudence</u> not by <u>knowing</u> only but by <u>acting</u>.**" **(Aristotle, Nicomachean Ethics VII, 1152 a 6-9).**

Furthermore to **liberality** (*ελευθεριότης*: eleutheriotes), which is considered to be the "mean" between the prodigality (*ασωτία*: asotia) as excess, and the meanness (*ανελευθερία*: aneleutheria) as a deficiency with regard to wealth, both extremes are thought to err with regard to giving and taking money. The prodigal man as he gives money to everybody, he finally ruins himself, since he wastes his substance. Usually the prodigal is also self-indulgent, therefore he wastes his substance in order to satisfy his bodily appetites. On the other hand, the meanness consists either in deficiency in giving (unwillingness to give anything, e.g. miserly or stingy people) or in excess in respect of taking (by taking anything and from any source, e.g. profiteer), as well as the combination of these two. In the latter class (mean and profiteer) we can rank all the sordid traders, pimps, money-lenders at high interest, robbers, gamesters and in generally all those who make gain from improper sources, since they all submit to disgrace, namely all the frauds.

The liberal as he acts in accordance with virtue, he will give for the sake of the noble, which means to the right people, the right amount, at the right time and according to his substance, otherwise if he exceeds will be a prodigal. Through prudence then, the liberal will act as occasion demands, with regard to giving of wealth to the right people. The prodigal is considered better than a mean man, as he tends to benefit others and he is curable, therefore through right education he can move towards the middle state, while the mean man is incurable, according to Aristotle.

" Now virtuous actions are noble and done for the sake of the noble. Therefore the liberal man will give for the sake of the noble, and rightly; for he will give to the right people, the right amounts, and at the right time, with all the other qualifications that accompany right giving." (Aristotle, Nicomachean Ethics IV, 1120 a, 22-26).

Friendship

Friendship and justice are considered to be very significant virtues by Aristotle, therefore he dedicates a lot of his ethical works to these. **Friendship** (*φιλία*: philea) at first, is based upon the feeling of love for a person, which we consider to be good and lovable. And since good is what it seems to be for each man, - namely it is subjective, as we have seen in Protagoras' saying - therefore each man has different friends from the other. According to Aristotle, there are three motives of friendship; one for the sake of what is **useful** (*χρήσιμον*: chresimon) to the people, one for the sake of **pleasure** (*ηδονή*: hedone), and the third one for the sake of **virtue** (*αρετή*: arete). In the first two kinds of friendship, the friends do not love each other for their character, but for their utility or pleasure, namely the loved person is loved because provides some goods or pleasure to the other. As a matter of fact, these kinds of friendship are incidental and not permanent, since the friendship is dissolved when the one party is no longer useful or pleasant to the other.

" Therefore those who love for the sake of <u>utility</u> love for the sake of what is good for themselves, and those who love for the sake of <u>pleasure</u> do so for the sake of what is pleasant to themselves, and in so far as the other is a person loved but in so far as he is useful or pleasant. And thus these friendships are only incidental, since the object is not beloved in that he is the man he is, but in that he furnishes advantage or pleasure. Such friendships then, are easily dissolved, if the parties do not remain alike; for if the one party is no longer pleasant or useful the other ceases to love him." (Aristotle, Nicomachean Ethics VIII, 1156 a, 15-21).

182

The friendship based upon the motive of **pleasure** is mainly formed among young people, since they live under the guidance of emotion, therefore they always pursue the pleasant and as a result their friendships are based upon that. According to Aristotle, the **amorous friendship** (erotic love) is of this kind, because it depends on emotions and aims at pleasure. Therefore the young people form and dissolve their friendship rapidly, since it aims at pleasure and when the one stops being pleasant to the other, the friendship is dissolved.

" **On the other hand the friendship of young people seems to aim at pleasure; for they live under the guidance of emotion, and pursue above all what is pleasant to themselves and what is immediately before them; but with increasing age their pleasures become different.**" **(Aristotle, Nicomachean Ethics VIII, 1156 a, 30-35).**

The friendship based upon the motive of **utility**, usually involves inequality or superiority of the one party to the other, with regard to power, wealth, social status, knowledge, health etc. So the other party which is inferior, tries to get its own interest from the superior party, and the latter usually aims at its pleasure. However, sometimes, since there is mutual interest among the different parties, people form friendship of association, which is based upon equality, e.g. political, commercial, colleagues etc.

The third kind of friendship is mainly between men who are good and alike in **virtue**. In this kind of friendship, there is mutual love and communication, and each one wish the best to the other, since they are both good in themselves and they do not aim at pleasure or utility. This kind of friendship is based upon equality and is permanent, as these people are virtuous, and virtue is an enduring thing. Aristotle regards it as a **perfect friendship** (τελεία φιλία: teleia philea), since the two friends love one another for the character, and not for the sake of utility or pleasure. Each one wishes the best to the other, and makes an equal return in goodwill and pleasantness.

On the other hand, if there is a great distance in respect of virtue or vice or wealth or anything else between the parties, then there is no possibility of friendship between them. On the contrary, when both friends get the same things from each other, and delight in each other in the same things, this relationship is more like friendship, although it is for the sake of pleasure, just as the young people do. For friendship for the sake of utility is for base persons.

" **Perfect friendship** is the friendship of men who are **good** and alike in **virtue**, for these wish alike to each other qua good, and they are good in themselves. Now those who wish well to their friends for their sake are most truly friends; for they do this by reason of their own nature and not incidentally. Therefore their friendship lasts as long as they are good, and virtue is an enduring thing." (Aristotle, Nicomachean Ethics VIII, 1156 b, 5-12).

" **Now equality and likeness, and especially the likeness of those who are like in virtue; for being steadfast in themselves they hold fast to each other, and neither ask nor give base services, but (one may say) even prevent them; for it is characteristic of good men neither to go wrong nor to let their friends to do so.**" (Aristotle, Nicomachean Ethics VIII, 1159 b, 2-8).

Wicked men usually become friends to each other for the sake of pleasure or utility, their friendship is for a short time, and as long as they delight in each other's wickedness, and in the end they become enemies to each other. Most of the people wish to be loved rather than to love due to ambition, since to be loved is similar to be honoured. Therefore, most of the people love flattery and they cannot distinguish friends from flatterers. On the other hand, a flatterer as being in inferior position pretends to be such and to love more than he is loved, in order to achieve through this friendship his aim with regard to his personal advantage. As it has been said, **friendliness** is then a virtue of the "mean" between **flattery** and **enmity**, since the noble man loves and takes care of his friend, (for virtue is active), in the same way he does to himself, as being conscious of the good in itself, and of the means to achieve it.

" **And if life is desirable, and particularly so for the good men, because to them existence is good and pleasant**

(for they are pleased at the consciousness of what is in itself good); and if as the virtuous man is to himself, he is to his friend also (for his friend is another self); - then as his own existence is desirable for each man, so or almost so, is that of his friend." (Aristotle, Nicomachean Ethics IX, 1170 b, 4-8).

Justice

The last of the virtues we are going to analyze is **justice** (*δικαιοσύνη*: dikaiosyne), since according to Aristotle is complete and **perfect virtue** (*τελεία αρετή*: teleia arete), as the one who possesses it, can exercise not merely for his own affairs, but towards the others too. Therefore, Aristotle like Plato regards justice not a part of virtue but virtue entire. In order to be able to act justly, one must be good-tempered so as e.g. not to strike the other or not to speak evil, must be temperate in order not to commit adultery or outrage, must not be mean and profiteer so as not to commit fraud and so on. Therefore, in order to be able to exercise justice towards the others, one must exercise all the virtues (temperance, good-temper, liberality, bravery etc.). Concerning justice towards oneself, this refers to the state of mind lying in the mean between excess and deficiency, namely virtue or justice itself.

" **And it is complete virtue (justice) in its fullest sense because it is the actual exercise of complete virtue. It is completed (*τελεία*) because he who possesses it can exercise his virtue towards others too and not merely by himself." (Aristotle, Nicomachean Ethics V, 1129 b, 30-34).**

" **Justice in this sense then, is not a part of virtue but virtue entire, nor is the contrary injustice a part of vice but vice entire. What is the difference between <u>virtue</u> and <u>justice</u> in this sense is plain from what we have said; they are the same but being them is not the same; what as a <u>relation to others</u> it is justice, as a certain kind of <u>state</u> without qualification it is virtue." (Aristotle, Nicomachean Ethics V, 1130 a, 9-14).**

Aristotle begins his inquiry about justice and injustice from the definition of the just and unjust man, for he always follows the inductive method (from the parts to the whole), as we have seen. **Unjust man** is considered a man who is **lawless, unequal** and **grasping** concerned with goods, since he always chooses the greater part from the things that are good for him and the less from the bad ones, in other words he is the friend of inequality. On the other hand, **just man** is the **lawful** and the **friend of equality**.

" **Both the lawless man and the grasping and unequal man are thought to be unjust, so that evidently both the law-abiding and the equal man will be just. The just then, is the lawful and the equal, the unjust the unlawful and the unequal.**" **(Aristotle, Nicomachean Ethics V, 1129 a, 31-35).**

As we can realize, significant for Aristotle is, apart from the equal, the lawful as well, since the laws of a community ensure its normal function and also the well-being of its members. Therefore, the law bids the members of community to respect and obey it, and this is only possible when the people act according to virtuous acts. In other words, abiding by the law contributes to the education of the people in accordance with certain virtues, which are considered to be essential to normal function and preservation of the certain community. Concerning the cases, which are not covered by the law and the necessity of its correction, Aristotle adds the term of the "equitable", as we are going to see.

According to Aristotle there are two kinds of justice, the **justice** in the wide sense (**co-extensive**) and the **particular** justice. The first one is referring to the virtue entire or justice itself (justice towards oneself, as we previously mentioned), since in order to be able to be a just man, one must possess all the virtues (temperance, courage, good-temper, self-sufficiency, liberality, friendliness, greatness of spirit etc., in other words to be prudent). This state is concerned with the noble man, who possesses prudence and can act always justly, and not for the fear of punishment by the law, as he is just both towards himself and the others. However, most of the people since they are not virtuous, are commanded by the law to act justly, therefore Aristotle analyzes the question of particular justice, which is related to the implementation of the law. This particular justice is concerned with matters of honour, money, safety, or anything else that the members of a society are unfairly dealt with one another, due to the motive of pleasure, which arises from personal gain, namely all the matters concerned with the science of Law.

" **Evidently therefore, there is apart from <u>injustice</u> in the <u>wide sense</u>, another <u>particular</u> injustice which shares the name and nature of the first, because its definition falls within the same genus; for the force of both lies in a relation to others but the one is concerned with <u>honour</u> or <u>money</u> or <u>safety</u> – or that which includes all these, if we had a single name for it – and its motive is the pleasure that arises from gain; while the other is concerned with all the object with which the <u>good man</u> is concerned."** (Aristotle, Nicomachean Ethics V, 1130 b, 1-5).

Particular justice is a part of the justice in the wide sense, just as a particular virtue is a part of the virtue entire, namely justice. Public education, on the one hand, teaches citizens how to act in accordance with the virtue of justice (true opinion), and on the other hand, particular justice is prescribed by the law and forbid the citizens to practice any vice, namely injustice concerning deals with their fellow-citizens. Of **particular justice** there are two kinds, the one is concerned with **distribution** and the other with **corrective justice** in all transactions. The first one is manifested in distributions of honour, wealth or anything else that is to be shared among the members of the social community, and the latter is concerned with all the transactions among the citizens, which are corresponding to the civil and criminal code of today. As we can see, Aristotle, apart from Plato's justice itself, raises the question of practical and applicable justice, which aims at the normal function of the social community. According to him, justice itself is concerned with the wise man as it is the quality of the virtuous, good and wise man, but on the other hand particular justice is concerned with each citizen, who is obliged to respect and observe it for the common good.

" Now of the <u>particular justice</u>, and the just involved in it, one kind is that which is concerned in the <u>distributions</u> of honour or wealth or the other things which are to be shared among the members of the community (for in these it is possible for one man to have a share either unequal or equal to that of the other), and another kind is that which is <u>corrective</u> in various transactions." (Aristotle, Nicomachean Ethics V, 1130 b, 30-35).

Referring to the **distributive justice**, which is concerned with the distributions of goods, its criterion is the **merit** of the persons involved in it. And each political system specifies a different sort of merit, for example democracy identifies it with freedom, oligarchy with wealth and aristocracy with virtue. Whatever the criterion is, we can say that the merit is proportional to the goods which are to be shared as follows: If we assume two persons of merit **A** and **B** respectively before the distribution, and the shares in distribution of the goods have value **C** and **D,** which receive the persons **A** and **B** respectively, then must always effect geometrical proportion among these four terms. In other words the just in distribution is the following proportion: $A/B = C/D$ or else $A/C = B/D$, as well as $(A+C)/C = (B+D)/D$. So to say then, the ratio of the persons' merit must be equal to the ratio of the corresponding distributed goods' value. In this way the merit of the persons before and after the distribution (contribution plus profit) remains the same, therefore it is considered to be just, since the just is intermediate and the proportional is intermediate.

" For there is a similar distinction between the persons and between the goods. As the term A then, is to B, so will C be to D, and therefore alternado as A is to C, B will be to D."

" Mathematicians call this kind of proportion geometrical; for it is in geometrical proportion that it follows that the whole is to the whole as either part is to the corresponding part."

" This is then what the just is – the proportional; the unjust is what violates the proportion." (Aristotle, Nicomachean Ethics V, 1131 b, 5-17).

188

Referring to the **corrective justice**, which is concerned with transactions between men, it aims at correcting the injury, which has been caused by the one who was in the wrong to the other who was being wronged. The difference between distributive and corrective justice is that, in the corrective one the law tries to restore equality after the injury, and not to preserve the same proportion like in the distributive justice. Because it makes no difference whether a good or a bad man has done the injury, but the law treats the two parties as equal, and therefore tries to restore the equality, by taking from the one who did the injury and giving to the one who suffered the injury, namely taking from the gain of the assailant. Since the just is the "mean", then it must be the mean between loss and gain, or else the mean between the greater and the lesser according to arithmetical proportion. To be more specific, if for example the gain that a person **B** profited from a person **A** is worth **5**, and the loss is of value **2** which **A** lost from **B** in their mutual transaction, then the **arithmetical middle term** of gain and loss is $(5+2)/2 = 3,5$. This value then must be added to the person A who suffered the injury and taken away from B who did the injury. Then in the end and after the appliance of corrective justice, each party will have the equal: $(B+5)-3,5 = \underline{B+1,5}$ and $(A-2)+3,5 = \underline{A+1,5}$. As we can see then, the corrective justice is the mean between gain and loss.

" **The law looks only to the distinctive character of the injury, and treats the parties as equal, if one is in the wrong and the other is being wronged, and if one inflicted injury and the other has received it. Therefore this kind of injustice being an inequality, the judge tries to <u>equalize</u> it.**"

" **Therefore <u>corrective justice</u> will be the intermediate between loss and gain.**"

" **The equal is the intermediate between the greater and the lesser according to <u>arithmetical proportion</u>.**" **(Aristotle, Nicomachean Ethics V, 1132 a, 3-7, 18-19, 32-33).**

Referring to the voluntary and involuntary actions in transactions between men, Aristotle regards **voluntary** acts to be both **unjust** and **acts of injustice**, but on the other hand, **involuntary** acts to be only **unjust** but **not acts of injustice**. Because when a man acts voluntarily, this means that he inflicts injury by knowing the person suffered the injury, the means and the end of it, and of course the act is being done neither incidentally nor under compulsion.

" **For when it is voluntary it is blamed, and at the same time is an act of injustice; so that will be things that are unjust but not yet acts of injustice, if voluntariness be not present as well. By voluntary I mean, as has been said before, any of the things in a man's own power which he does with knowledge, i.e. not in ignorance either of the person acted on or of the instrument used or the end will be attained (e.g. whom he is striking, with what and to what end), each such act being done not incidentally nor under compulsion.**" (Aristotle, Nicomachean Ethics V, 1135 a, 19-27).

On **voluntary** acts there is also a graduation concerning the injustice, according to deliberation. The voluntary acts in transactions done by choice and **after deliberation,** which result in injury, are considered to be serious acts of injustice and the doers are unjust, wicked and **vicious men.** However, if the voluntary injust act is **without previous deliberation** e.g. due to anger or other passion, is considered to be an **act of injustice** but not of the same gravity like the previous one, since the act does not imply vice and unjust man, but it is rather a **mistake** due to the man's ignorance.

" **On voluntary acts we do some by choice, others not by choice; by choice those we do after deliberation, not by choice those which we do without previous deliberation.**"

" **When he acts with knowledge but not after deliberation, it is an act of injustice – e.g. the acts due to anger or to other passions necessary or natural to man; for when men do such harmful and mistaken act they act unjustly, and the acts are acts of injustice, but this does not imply that the doers are unjust or wicked; for the injury is not due to vice. But when a man acts from choice,** he is an <u>unjust man</u> and a <u>vicious man</u>." (Aristotle, Nicomachean Ethics V, 1135 b, 9-12, 19-25).

Referring now to the **equitable** (*επιεικές*: epieikes), as we said at the beginning of this chapter, it is concerned with the correction of legal justice, if the law is defective in this case. At first, the equitable is in accordance with law's end, and it merely corrects the omission which the legislator himself could not foresee, due to over-simplicity and universality of the law's statement. And if he were present, he would have agreed with this settlement through the equitable. So the equitable is just and better than this defective kind of justice, but not better than the absolute justice.

"Hence the equitable is just, and better than one kind of justice, not better than absolute justice, but better than the error that arises from the absoluteness of the statement. And this is the nature of the equitable, a correction of law where it is defective owing to its universality." (Aristotle, Nicomachean Ethics V, 1137 b, 24-27).

To sum up with justice, to be just and to act justly is not incidental, but it is a matter of state of mind and choice after deliberation, just like with all virtues. Usually, most of the people think that acting justly is easy, for example not to steal or to wound someone, but to be just as a result of a certain state of mind, and to exercise the virtue of justice under all circumstances, and in one's lifetime, it is very difficult. Therefore, the majority of the people when they do not act unjustly, it is because of the circumstances, namely incidentally, since the same men who are considered themselves just, under different circumstances would have acted unjustly. Just as in that case of Hector of Troy, who although had always been a lawful man, threw away his shield and turned to flight, when he saw armed Achilles approaching him. However, the virtuous and noble man, since he is just man due to the state of his mind, he never acts unjustly, for he possesses the virtue of justice which is the virtue entire.

" Men think that acting unjustly is in their power, and therefore that being just is easy. But it is not; to lie with one's neighbour's wife, to wound another, to deliver a

bribe is easy and in our power, but to do these things as a result of a certain <u>state of mind</u> is neither easy nor in our power."

" They forget that these are not <u>just</u> acts, except incidentally; to be just the actions must be done and distributed in a certain manner; and this is more difficult task than knowing what is good for the health." (Aristotle, Nicomachean Ethics V, 1137 a, 5-14).

In conclusion we could say that **justice** is concerned with good things that the people participate in, and in all those there can be an **excess** of justice, probably among the **gods** or **deficiency** of it among the **incurable bad men**, while the "**mean**" is essentially **human**.

" For some beings, presumably the gods, cannot have too much of them (goods), and to others who are incurable bad, not even the smallest share in them is beneficial but all such goods are harmful, while to others they are beneficial up to a point; therefore justice is essentially something human." (Aristotle, Nicomachean Ethics V, 1137 a, 25-30).

E. Epicurus (341 – 270 BC)

The philosopher whose name has been related to '**pleasure**' (ηδονή: hedone), as Epicurus based his philosophy upon the impulsive tendency of the human being to pursue pleasure and avoid pain. Epicurus was born on the island of Samos and at a very young age was taught Plato's philosophy by Pamphilus and Aristotle's as well by Praxiphanes. Afterwards, he turned to the studying of Democritus' atomism for ten years under Nausiphanes of Teos.

Since 311 BC he started to develop his own philosophy, first in Lesbos and then in Lampsacus, in Asia Minor, where he fled, after having been chased by the political establishment of the Aristotelian and Platonist philosophers. In the year 306, since the political conjuncture allowed him, he settled in Athens, where he founded his own philosophical

School, which was called 'Garden' (*Κῆπος*: kepos), as its meetings were hold in the kitchen-garden. Epicurus' liberal attitude toward women and slaves (since the 'Garden' was the only philosophical School, that allowed them to participate in its meetings) aroused resistance in Plato's Academy and Aristotle's Lyceum, with the result of slander and libel.

According to him, the aim of philosophy is to heal the human soul of its passions, just like medicine heals the human body of disease.

" **Vain is the word of a philosopher, by which no mortal suffering is healed. Just as medicine confers no benefit if it does not drive away bodily disease, so is philosophy useless if it does not drive away the suffering of the mind (soul)" (Epicurus, Fragments 54).**

The end of philosophical reflection, should be the one which leads to 'happiness' (*ευδαιμονία*: eudaimonia), since the pursuit of happiness is the driving force that guides the human being in all of its actions.

" **We must, therefore, pursue the things that make for happiness, seeing that when happiness is present, we have everything, but when is absent, we do everything to possess it." (Epicurus' Letter to Menoeceus 122).**

The achievement of happiness, according to him, can only come through the state of **tranquillity** (*αταραξία*: ataraxia, **absence of disturbance** or **peace of mind**), and this is not possible without the understanding of pains, fears and desires. Therefore, the need of this knowledge inevitably leads us to the study of nature, as the natural laws are in direct contact with the human nature.

" **If apprehensions about the heaven and our fear lest death concern us, as well as our failure to realize the limits of pains and desires, did not bother us, we would have no need of natural sciences."**

" **It is impossible for anyone to dispel his fear over the most important matters, if he does not know what is the nature of the universe, but instead suspects something that happens in myth. Therefore it is impossible to obtain** unmitigated pleasure without natural science." (Epicurus, Principal Doctrines 11, 12).

Gnoseology – Method of Canon

According to Epicurus, the basic means of achieving knowledge and criteria of truth are the 'sensations' (*αίσθησις*: aesthesis), 'preconceptions' (*πρόληψις*: prolepsis), 'emotions' (*πάθη*: pathe) and the 'focusing of thought into an impression' (*φανταστικές επιβολές της διανοίας*: phantastikes epiboles tes dianoias). Dialectic, on the contrary, can lead us to draw wrong conclusions.

" **Epicureans reject dialectic as disorientated** (*παρέλκουσα:* **parelkousa). Because, for the physical philosophers is sufficient to use the right words which refer to the concepts of the world. Epicurus then, in his work <The Canon>, says that the criteria of truth are the senses, the preconceptions and the feelings. Epicureans add to these the focusing of thought into an impression. He himself is referring to those in his <Epitome> to Herodotus and in <Principal Doctrines>.**" (Diogenes Laertius, Epicurus' life 31).

The 'senses' are the first criterion of truth, since they create the first impressions and testify the existence of the external world. Sensory input is neither subjective nor deceitful, but the misunderstanding comes, when the mind adds to or subtracts something from these images, which have been printed in the form of impressions to our mind. Therefore, not the senses are the ones which lead us to falsehood, but the judgements and the opinions that stem from the sense impressions. The senses are the basis upon which we have to rely, in order to proceed to the understanding the phenomena.

" **And whatever image we receive by direct apprehension of our mind or our sense organs, whether of shape or of essential properties, that is the true shape of the solid object, since it is created by the constant repetition of the image or the impression it has left behind. There is always falsehood and error involved in importing into a judgement an element additional to sense** impressions, either to confirm or deny." (Epicurus, Letter to Herodotus 50).

" Epicurus said that all the tangible things are real and each impression comes from existing objects and is determined by the object that moves the sense." (Sextus Empiricus, To Rationals 8.63).

" Therefore all the impressions are real, while the opinions are not real and are susceptible of changes." (Sext.Empiricus, To Rationals 7.206-45).

" If you battle with all your sensations, you will be unable to form a standard for judging even which of them you judge to be false." (Epicurus, Principal Doctrines 23).

The 'preconceptions' (προλήψεις) are the concepts – terms concerning each thing, which have been formed in the mind, according to the sensory input, for example the terms 'man', 'warm', 'sweet', etc. These preconceptions are directly related to memory and can be recalled at any time, only by the use of the respective word. Epicurus also calls them 'the meanings that underlie the words' (υποτεταγμένα τοις φθόγγοις: ipotetagmena tois fthogois, semantic substance of the words) in his letter to Herodotus.

The 'feelings' or 'emotions' (πάθη: pathe) are related to the senses and the preconceptions. They are the inner impulses that make us feel like or dislike about certain external objects, which we perceive through the senses, and are associated with the preconceptions that are recalled.

" In this moment that the word <man> is spoken, immediately due to the preconception, an image is projected in the mind, which is related to the sense data." (Diogenes Laertius, Epicurus' life 33).

" First of all Herodotus, we must comprehend the meanings that underlie the words, so that, by referring to them, we may be able to reach judgements concerning opinions, matters of inquiry, or problems and leave everything undecided as we argue endlessly or use words that have no sense." (Epicurus, Letter to Herodotus 37).

Apart from these there is the 'assumption' (υπόληψις: hepolepsis), which is either the hypothesis or the opinion about something (matter or action), and can be right or wrong. The assumptions are created by the association of senses, preconceptions and emotions. Since they are produced mechanically and automatically without any rational analysis and verification of whether are correct or not, they need to be confirmed (*επιμαρτύρησις*: epimarteresis, **confirmation**), a process which must follow each assumption.

" **For the opinion they (the Epicureans) use the word <hepolepsis>, which they claim can be right or wrong.**" **(Diogenes Laertius, Epicurus' life 34).**

Referring to the '**focusing of thought into an impression**' or else '**intuitive apprehensions of the mind**', they are the printed images made on the mind that come from our sensations, preconceptions and emotions, and form the basis of the assumptions and beliefs. They refer to the images and impressions that appear in the mind, on the occasion of the external events, and are associated with the respective preconceptions and feelings. All this unity (**sense – preconception – emotion – focusing of thought into an impression**) leads to the formation of a certain assumption or belief (**hepolepsis**).

After Aristotle, as we saw previously with the use of impressions by the desirable part and the intellect, Epicurus is referring to the same subject again, namely to the impressions in the form of images, which are projected on the mind. An element that the Stoics also adopted later, as we are going to see, with the 'correct use of impressions'.

So the capability of knowledge presupposes all the above-mentioned functions, for our perception of the external world is created by all those factors in the course that we have already mentioned. As for the assumptions and opinions, comes into question their '**confirmation**', which finally proves if the opinions are either correct or incorrect. This verification and confirmation (*επιμαρτύρησις*: epimarteresis) can only be done by means of the '**evident reason**' (*ενάργεια*: henargeia), which means what is self-evident and obvious through our sensory input.

We can give an example for better understanding of the whole function. When we see somebody, who is approaching us, first through the <u>sense</u> of eyesight, we perceive that an object is coming closer to us, then through the <u>preconception</u> we realize that it is a human being, afterwards through the <u>assumption</u> we suppose that he is our acquaintance e.g. Theaetetus. This assumption is associated with pleasant and unpleasant <u>emotions</u>, accompanied by the respective mental images and impressions (<u>focusing of thought into an impression</u>), which are related to our feelings towards each other. When he gets close to us, it can be confirmed (<u>confirmation</u>) that he is Socrates and not Theaetetus through the quiet <u>evident</u> fact of eyesight. Therefore, the same procedure must be followed in order to understand everything, even things, which are not observable and obvious (*ἄδηλα*: adela, imperceptible), that is to say, the confirmation through the evident reason (*ενάργεια*). In the same way we have to **reduce** each **assumption** and **belief** to something that can be proved through the self-evident reason (empirically verified). **Verification theory** and **reductionism** have been adopted, as we know, by the modern philosophy of science. In this way, one can get rid of the false assumptions and beliefs and finally settle on the real ones (confirmed).

" **Consequently the confirmation and no dispute is the criterion of truth of one thing, while non confirmation and dispute is the criterion of the falsehood. Basis and foundation of everything is the quiet obvious and the self-evident.**" (Sextus Empiricus, To Rationals 7.211-6).

All the above mentioned criteria of knowledge form the basic principles of the **method**, that Epicurus has followed in order to find the truth, which he called '**On the Canon**' or '**On the Criteria**'. Certainly the method of the opinions' confirmation we found previously both in Heraclitus' philosophy (fragment 47.) and in the other Presocratic philosophers.

" **If you reject any sensation and you do not distinguish between the opinion based on what awaits confirmation and evidence already available based on the senses, the** feelings and every intuitive faculty of the mind, you will send the remaining sensations into a turmoil with your foolish opinions, thus driving out every standard for judging. And if among the perceptions based on opinion, you affirm both, that which awaits confirmation and that which does not, you will fail to escape from error, since you will have retained every ground for dispute in judgement concerning the right and wrong." (Epicurus, Principal Doctrines 24).

Physical science

Referring to the physical science, Epicurus has adopted the views of the Atomists' theory, Leucippus and Democritus, concerning the **atoms** and **void**. Certainly there are some differences referring to the motion and the properties of atoms, as we are going to see afterwards. Particularly, in order to confirm the existence of the atoms and void, he uses the same method, which we have previously mentioned, namely 'on the Canon'.

" **Furthermore, the universe consists of bodies and void, that bodies exist, perception itself in all men bears witness. It is through the senses that we by necessity form a judgement about the imperceptible ($\check{\alpha}\delta\eta\lambda\alpha$: adela), by means of reason, just as I argued above. But if that, which we call void and place and impalpable substance did not exist, bodies would have no place to be nor anything through which to move, as they are clearly seen to be moving.**" (Epicurus, Letter to Herodotus 39-40).

As we can realize from the above mentioned text, for the 'imperceptible' matter of the void's existence (assumption), Epicurus uses as a 'confirmation' the 'obvious' fact of bodies' motion, which is perceived through the 'senses' ($\varepsilon\nu\acute{\alpha}\rho\gamma\varepsilon\iota\alpha$).

Referring now to the 'bodies', there are two types of them. The bodies which are compounds by themselves and those from which the compounds have been formed (atoms: $\acute{\alpha}\tau o\mu\alpha$). The atoms are indivisible and unchangeable and retain their qualities, even when they participate in the formation of the compounds. If the atoms could be divided to infinity, then they would have been reduced from existent (being) into nonexistent (not-being), something that is 'evidently' wrong. The properties of the atoms are completely different from the ones of the compounds, which they form. Their only properties are mass, shape, size and whatever is related to shape.

" **And of the bodies some are compounds and others are those from which the compounds have been formed. These latter are indivisible and unchangeable if everything is not about to be reduced to nonexistence, but some strong elements remains in the breakup of the compounds, one that is solid by nature and incapable of being dissolved. As a result, the first beginnings must be indivisible (ἄτομοι) bodily substances. (Epicurus, Letter to Herodotus 40-41).**

" **And furthermore, we must consider that atoms exhibit none of the qualities belonging to the visible things except shape, mass and size and whatever is necessarily related to shape. For every quality changes, but the atoms do not change, since, in the dissolution of compound substances, there must remain something solid and indestructible, which causes changes not into the nonexistent, nor from the nonexistent, but as a result of the transpositions of some particles and the approach or departure of others. Therefore, it is necessary that these shifting particles be everlasting and not share in the nature of what is changeable, but rather possess their mass and configurations. For they must needs remain permanent."** (Epicurus, Letter to Herodotus 54).**

The velocity of the atoms while moving through the void is equal, which means that they move at the same velocity regardless of their shape and weight. While they are moving through the void in several directions, they collide with one another. However, those which participate in the formation of the compounds substances, apart from their motion in all directions at the equal velocity - as the entire compound which they have been formed, also moves in several directions - they follow the motion of the compound as well, and as a result they turn out to do a complex motion. Due to this complex motion, some of them move more swiftly than anothers. As the compound substance is moving in one direction they collide with other ones and as a result they decelerate (αντικόπτονται: antikoptontai), and that deceleration eventually can be perceived through the senses themselves, since the whole motion appears as a unity which is moving in one direction.

" **Furthermore the atoms must possess equal velocity, whenever they move through the void, with nothing coming into collision with them. For neither will heavy bodies move more swiftly than the small and light, when nothing encounters them; nor do the small bodies move more quickly, since they maintain uniform course, provided nothing collides with them. Nor is the motion upwards or sideways owing to collision faster, nor the motion downwards owing to its weight...**

Furthermore, in compound substances one atom will be said to be swifter than another, although the atoms are of equal velocity, because even in the least period of continuous time, the atoms are moving in clusters towards one place. However, in a passage of time perceptible only to the mind, they move not in one direction, but are constantly colliding with one another until the <u>**constancy**</u> <u>**of their motion**</u> **comes under scrutiny of the senses."** (Epicurus, Letter to Herodotus 61, 62).

Up to this point, as we can realize, there are not significant differences with the Atomists' theory. But at this point, Epicurus disagrees with Democritus' theory concerning the matter, in other words, whether the atoms' motion is determined by 'necessity' (ειμαρμένη: hemarmene) or not. Epicurus argues that all the atoms possess their own and free motion, which one he called '**deviating**' or '**random swerve**' (παρεγκλιτική: parengleteki). This tendency of the atoms to deviate from their ordinary course is an inherent quality of that least quantity of the matter, as for example the gravity, and it is not due to the necessity of the motions, which means that every motion is produced by a previous one (cause and effect). On this particular view, Epicurus based his principle of free will and action, throughout one can change his own character and as a matter of fact his own destiny.

" **Because, if one adopts the view of Democritus, which says that the atoms have no choice of free motion, and as a result everything is determined by the necessity, we shall say to him : < Whoever you are, you do not know that the atoms have free motion, which Democritus was not able to see, but Epicurus brought it to light. A deviating motion, as he has proved on the basis of phenomena>. And the most important is, if we believe in necessity, each blame and praise will lose its meaning." (Diogenes Oenandeas fr. 54. 2,3).**

" **Who, do you think is better than the man who keeps a reverent opinion about gods... Who laughs at fate, which is painted by some as mistress over all things?.. Some things happen by necessity, others as a result of chance; other things are subject to our control. Because necessity is not accountable to anyone, he sees that chance is unstable, but what lies in our control is subject to no master; it naturally follows, then, that blame or praise attend our decisions." (Epicurus, Letter to Menoeceus 133).**

From this last fragment, we can realize that Epicurus disagrees with Democritus' **'necessity'** ($ειμαρμένη$) and raises the question of **free will** and action, as the free action is the only one that can be blamed or praised. Therefore, according to him, each one of us has the capability to follow his own personal way, diverted from any laws of necessity and destiny.

Referring to the creation and existence of the Universe, Epicurus like Democritus, adopts the views of Anaximander on the infinite, unlimited and everlasting Universe. Furthermore he adopts Democritus' view for the creation of the Universe by the coherence of the atoms, when they come together. Let us see, how Epicurus himself proves the existence of the infinite Universe, by using the same method of 'Canon'.

" **Having made this distinction, we must now consider what is not evidence to our senses; first of all that nothing** is created from what does not exist. For everything would be born from everything without the need for seed. And if that which is destroyed were dissolved into what does not exist, everything would be destroyed, since that into which they were dissolved does not exist. Moreover, the universe was and always will be the same as it is now. For there is nothing into which it changes. Beyond the universe there is nothing which, entering into it, could accomplish the change." (Epicurus, Letter to Herodotus 38-39).

" Furthermore the universe is without limit. For that which is limited has an outermost edge; the outermost edge will be seen against something else. As a result, the universe having no outermost edge has no limit; having no limit it would be boundless and unlimited. Also, the universe is boundless both in the number of the bodies and the magnitude of the void. If the void were limitless and the bodies limited, the bodies would not remain anywhere, but be borne and scattered into the limitless void, having nothing to support them and check them by colliding with them. But if the void were limited, there would not be enough room in it for a limitless number of bodies." (Epicurus, Letter to Herodotus 41-42).

" Moreover, there are infinite worlds, both like and unlike this one. For the atoms being endless, as has just been demonstrated, are borne over a great distance. For these atoms out of which a world might be, and by which it might be made, have not been used up for the creation either for a single world or for a limited number, nor of however many worlds are alike or however many are different from these. Therefore, there is no impediment to the infinitude of worlds." (Epicurus, Letter to Herodotus 45).

Concerning the **time**, Epicurus points out that the time does not exist by itself and detached from the motion. Time is a relative dimension, which the people have introduced, always in relation to the motion or rest of the objects. Therefore, none of us can perceive the time detached from the events.

" Moreover we are to firmly grasp this additional point as well. We must not search for time as we do for the other things that we look for in an object, referring to the images we have in our minds, but must draw from direct experience, according to which we speak of ' a long time' or ' short time', applying our intuitions (*προλήψεις*) to this as we do to other things...

For this stands in need not of demonstration but only of reflection on the fact that we associate time with days and nights and portions of them, just as we do with feelings and lack of feeling, motion and rest, recognizing time as a particular sort of accident of these things, by virtue of which we call in time." (Epicurus, Letter to Herodotus 72-73).

Soul

With regard now to the soul, the mind and the body, as well as their mutual relation, Epicurus considers that the soul is bound together with the body, and the capacity of thought is one of the functions of the soul. One part of the soul is the cause of sensation of the body, besides with the capacity of its motion (i.e. what is nowadays called nervous system). A second part of the soul also exists, which consists of more subtle components and is related to the functions of thought, feelings and all the faculties of the mind.

These two parts of the soul are bound up with the body and when the body is destroyed, the soul disperses and no longer possesses the faculty of sensation in the dead body. Because if we assume that the soul is 'incorporeal', then it should be identified with void, since it does not consist of atoms. However the void, neither can 'act' (*ποιείν*: poien) nor to 'be acted' (*πάσχειν*: paschen) upon. On the other hand, the soul has both these qualities, as we can realize from the 'obvious' fact - which we can perceive through our senses - that we have sensation of the body, feelings and faculties of the mind. Therefore, the soul is not 'incorporeal', consists of atoms, which are within the body, is associated with the functions of the body, and is created and dispersed simultaneously with the creation and the destruction of the body respectively. Therefore, he criticizes Empedocles' view about reincarnation, arguing that if the souls could survive without the assistance of the body, there would have been no need for them to go from one body to another.

" Next you must, referring to the perceptions and the feelings – for in these there will lie the most reliable certainty – consider that the soul is a body with fine particles dispersed throughout the entire organism and most resembling a wind that contains a certain mixture of heat, in some ways resembling this (the wind) and in others this (the heat). And there is a part of the soul that is very different even from these in subtlety of composition, and is therefore more interactive, or more in sympathy, with the rest of the organism. All this is made evident by the power of the mind, its feelings, its mobility, and those faculties of which we deprive when we die." (Epicurus, Letter to Herodotus 63).

" Moreover, if the entire body is destroyed, the soul disperses and no longer possesses the same faculties, nor does it move, so that as a result it does not possess sensation.

It is not possible to imagine the soul existing and having sensation without the body, and experiencing these movements, when no longer exists that which encloses and surrounds the soul, in which now exists and has these movements.

We must in addition, note that the word 'incorporeal' is most commonly applied to what may be thought of as existing by itself. It is impossible to imagine incorporeal as an independent existence except as the void. The void can neither act nor be acted upon, but only furnishes to body motions through it... But as the case stands, both these occurrences are clearly distinguished (εναργώς) in connection with the soul. (Epicurus, Letter to Herodotus 65-67).

" Empedocles, if the souls could exist without the body, without the need of putting them into a living creature,

204

and in the interests of which you transform them, what do you need this transition for?" (Epicurus fr.42, Diogenes Oenandeas).

Pleasure – Peace of mind

According to Epicurus, the purpose of the human being must be the achievement of the state of **'peace'** or **'tranquility of mind'** (*αταραξία*), which can only come, when one becomes the master of his state of mind, for the only things that one can control is the inner self and his desires. Therefore, things that make for happiness (*ευδαιμονία*: eudaimonia) are not riches, power and authority, but rather the freedom from pain (*αλυπία*: alepea), the gentleness of feeling (*πραότης*: praotes) and the state of mind in accordance with nature.

" **The tranquil man is not troublesome to himself or to another.**" (Epicurus, Vatican Sayings 79).

" **Happiness and blessedness do not belong to abundance of riches or exalted position or offices or power, but to freedom from pain and gentleness of feeling and a state of mind that sets limits that are in accordance with nature.**" (Epicurus, Fragments 85).

" **Live your life without attracting attention.**" (Epicurus, Fragments 86).

" **The great importance for happiness has the state of mind, of which we are the masters ourselves.**"(Diogenes Oenandeas, fr. 112-113).

In order to be able to become the masters of our state of mind, we have to begin with our nature and reflect on the main motive of all of our actions. According to Epicurus, this main motive of all of our choices and actions in life is the pursuit of '**pleasure**' (*ηδονή*: hedone) and the avoidance of '**pain**' (*πόνος*: ponos). This aim underlies each one of our desires. When our desires of pleasure are fulfilled, then we consider ourselves happy, on the contrary when they are not gratified, we consider ourselves unfortunate. This precise tendency, of pleasure's pursuit we must take advantage of, in order to get to the peace of mind (*αταραξία*), through the 'sober reasoning of pleasures', which means the reflection on our choices and avoidances.

" We must, therefore, pursue the things that make for happiness, seeing that when happiness is present, we have everything, but when it is absent, we do everything to possess it." (Epicurus, Letter to Menoeceus 122).

" Therefore, we declare that pleasure is the beginning and the goal of a happy life. For we recognize pleasure as the first good and as inborn; it is from this that we begin every choice and every avoidance. It is to pleasure that we recourse, using the feeling as our standard for judging every good." (Epicurus, Letter to Menoeceus 128-129).

The 'sober reasoning of the pleasures' starts with the analysis of the pleasure's desires in relation to the nature of the human being and its needs. Therefore, Epicurus classifies the **desires** in three categories: **a.Natural and necessary, b. Natural and unnecessary and c. Neither natural nor necessary.**

" Of the desires some are natural and necessary while others are natural but unnecessary. And there are desires that are neither natural nor necessary but arise from idle opinions." (Epicurus, Principal Doctrines 29).

The criterion to classify our desire as necessary is the following: when our desire is not fulfilled and we do not feel any pain and our body is free from disturbance, then the certain desire is not necessary. Since our natural tendency is the avoidance of pain and the physical well-being, and when due to the absence of a certain pleasure, we do not feel pain, in that case we do not have the need of the certain pleasure. Because we have no longer trouble in our soul, so as to go in search of the body's and soul's well-being.

" Everything we do is for the sake of this, namely, to avoid the pain and fear. Once this is achieved, all the soul's trouble is dispelled, as the living being does not have to go in search of something missing or to seek something else, by which the good of the soul and the body will be fulfilled. <u>For we have the need of pleasure at the time when we feel pain, owing to the absence of pleasure.</u>

When we do not feel pain, it is because we no longer have need of this pleasure." (Epicurus, Letter to Menoeceus 128).

Therefore, according to this criterion, we could classify in the **first category** of pleasures (natural and necessary), whatever contributes to the body's and the soul's well-being and to survival in general. Here then we can classify the pleasures related to nutrition, accommodation, clothes and the body's care, so as to be healthy and alive. Apart from those, natural and necessary, Epicurus classifies the '**peace of mind**' (*αταραξία*) and the '**freedom from bodily pain**' (*απονία*: aponea), which he calls them '**static**' (*καταστηματικαί*: katastematikai) pleasures. On the other hand joy and gladness are regarded as '**active**' and '**changeable**' pleasures (*κινητικαί*: kinetic). The most important pleasures, in Epicurus' view, are the static, for they contribute to the invariable state of body and soul's well-being. As for the virtues, they are the means to achieve the state of peace of mind and freedom from bodily pain. However, this does not mean that he underestimates the importance of the 'kinetic' pleasures, as we are going to see below.

" **Peace of mind and freedom from bodily pain are static pleasures; joy and gladness, however, are regarded as active emotions, in accordance with their mobility.**" (Diogenes Laertius X 135, Epicurus fragment 1).

The natural and unnecessary desires, which fall into **second category**, it is true they are based on our natural needs, but on these we add luxury. Here we can refer to luxurious residences, tables, expensive tastes etc. However, as we ought to be in harmony with our nature, we must realize the limits that the nature puts. Therefore, '**self-sufficiency**' (*αυτάρκεια*: autarkeia) and not luxury is in accordance with our nature. So the desires of the second category can be reduced, when we live in accordance with our nature, for nature can teach us the self-sufficiency and not the luxury. Apart from that, frugal life and self-sufficiency can arm us with decisiveness, self-discipline and courage, virtues which are essential to cope with the difficulties of life.

" Natural wealth is limited and easily obtained; the riches of idle fancies go on forever." (Epicurus, Principal Doctrines 15).

" We must not spoil our present estate by longing for what is absent but realize, that this too, was one of the things we hoped for." (Epicurus, Vatican Sayings 35).

" Becoming accustomed therefore, to simple and not luxurious fare, is productive of health and makes humankind resolved to perform the necessary business of life. When we approach luxury after long intervals, it makes us better disposed toward them and renders us fearless of fortune." (Epicurus, Letter to Menoeceus 131).

" Self-sufficiency is the greatest of all wealth." (Epicurus, Fragments 70).

" The greatest fruit of self-sufficiency is freedom." (Epicurus, Vatican Sayings 77).

As for the **third category** of desires (neither natural nor necessary), are those which refer to the possession of riches, winning of fame and coming to power. Epicurus opposes against them, except the self-sufficiency that we have already mentioned, the obvious fact that in order to achieve all those, one must become a slave of the crowd, public opinion and authority.

" The possession of the great riches does not resolve the agitation of the soul or give birth to remarkable joy – nor does the honor and admiration of the crowd, nor any other of those things arising from unlimited desires." (Epicurus, Vatican Sayings 81).

" The mean soul is puffed up by successes, but brought down by adversity." (Epicurus, Fragments 76).

" A life of freedom cannot acquire many possessions since to accomplish this requires servility to the rabble or to kings.." (Epicurus, Vatican Sayings 67).

Further to the 'sober reasoning' of pleasures, we could say that the criterion to accomplish a certain desire and enjoy the pleasure that arise from this desire, is to reflect on the outcome of the desire's accomplishment. If with its non-accomplishment we suffer pain, then we have to fulfill this desire. However, if we are not suffering, then it is not necessary to accomplish it.

" **The following method of enquiry must be applied to every desire: What will happen to me if what I long for is accomplished? What will happen if it is not accomplished?**" (Epicurus, Vatican Sayings 71).

" **We have need of pleasure when we suffer pain because of pleasure's absence. But when we are not suffering this pain although in a state of sensation, there is no need for pleasure. For it is not natural pleasure that sets wrong-doing into action, but rather the striving after idle fancies.**" (Epicurus, Fragments 60).

Apart from that, we have to reflect on the consequences of the certain enjoyment of that pleasure. In other words, when the fulfillment of that desire brings us greater pain and troubles to the others, then it would be better not to gratify the certain desire.

" **Since pleasure is the first good and natural to us, it is for this reason also that we do not choose every pleasure; instead there are times when we pass over many pleasures, whenever greater difficulty follows from them.**" (Epicurus, Letter to Menoeceus 129).

" **No pleasure is evil in itself; but the means of obtaining some pleasures bring in their wake troubles many times greater than the pleasures.**" (Epicurus, Principal Doctrines 8).

The reflection on the pleasures is the 'sober reasoning' (*νήφων λογισμός*: nefon logismos), which examines the roots of every choice and avoidance. By virtue of it we can come to the understanding of our real, natural needs of our body and soul, and distinguish them from the 'artificial' needs, which have been arisen from our false beliefs (*υπολήψεις*), and agitate our soul. This reasoning examination of the pleasures can lead us to the highest point of spiritual pleasure, which comes through peace of mind and tranquillity of the soul, when there is no longer agitation in the soul about the fulfillment of any desire, which is not natural and necessary. In this way we can get rid of the wrong opinions (*υπολήψεις*) about the pleasures' satisfaction, and also of the feeling of insecurity concerning the means of obtaining pleasures.

Furthermore, Epicurus dissociates sensual pleasures from the pleasure, which arises from peace of mind, as a response to his fault-finders, since some people misinterpreted his philosophy, whereas some others distorted it intentionally in order to present that the only goal of his philosophy is the pursuit of pleasure.

" When we say that pleasure is the goal, we are not talking about the pleasure of the profligates or that which lies in sensuality, as some ignorant persons think, or else those who do not agree with us or have followed our argument badly; rather it is freedom from bodily pain and mental anguish. For it is not continuous drinking and revels, nor the enjoyment of women and young boys, nor of fish and other viands that a luxurious table holds, which make for a pleasant life, but sober reasoning which examines the motives for every choice and avoidance, and which drives away, those opinions resulting in the greatest disturbance to the soul." (Epicurus, Letter to Menoeceus 131-132).

" The pleasure in the flesh will not be increased when a pain resulting from want is taken away, but only varied. The limit of understanding as regards pleasure is obtained by a reflection on these same pleasures and the sensations akin to them, which used to furnish the mind with its greatest fears." (Epicurus, Principal Doctrines 18).

At this point we can see how Epicurus by using the same method of 'Canon', draws a conclusion about the need of desires through the 'evident reason' (ἐναργές) of the absence of pain. In other words, our desires arise from 'preconceptions' (προλήψεις), which lead us to be of the 'opinion' (ὑπολήψεις), that they should be fulfilled in order to obtain the pleasure. In the process of 'confirmation' (ἐπιμαρτύρησις), which follows, he analyzes each desire, in order to find out which one must be fulfilled, by using as 'evident' (ἐναργές) criterion the presence or absence of pain. Those desires, which when are not fulfilled do not lead to pain, they are not necessary. So the process of 'verification' of the 'assumption' is carried out through the 'obvious' and 'evident' pain. Of course, everything on condition that as long as the pleasure lasts there can be no pain, which means the presence of the one excludes the presence of the other.

" **The limit of the extent of pleasure is the removal of pain. Wherever pleasure is present, for however long a time, there can be no pain or grief, or both at once.**" (**Epicurus, Principal Doctrines 3**).

The same method is applied in the matter of happiness, which as being an '**assumption**' can be proved wrong or right (**confirmed**) through the '**evident**' feeling of pleasure or pain. Therefore, Epicurus defines happiness as a permanent state of pleasure and absence of pain, namely peace of mind or else tranquillity, which can be achieved by the sober reasoning of the pleasures. Each one of us while feeling an instant pleasure - which he perceives through the '**senses**' with the absence of pain - he regards this feeling as instant happiness (**preconception**), therefore assumes that he must pursue this feeling always (**assumption**), that is to say the fulfillment of all desires. At this very moment, must intervene the reasoning in order to examine which one of the '**assumptions**' is wrong or right through the process of '**confirmation**'. The confirmation must be accomplished by means of '**sober reasoning of the pleasures**', which means, by analyzing one by one each desire, feeling and impression (focusing of thought into an impression) that are associated, in order to find out which one must be fulfilled, by using as '**evident**' criterion the following: 'which one of these pleasures when is not accomplished does not make us suffer pain' (**evident reason**). We can realize now, from the previous analysis, the consistency of Epicurus' thinking with his method of Canon, which one he follows faithfully from the analysis of the Universe to the analysis of human nature.

As he goes on with his analysis by the same criterion, he refers to the so-called '**virtues**' (*αρεταί:* aretai), which he regards as means for happiness and not as an end in itself. The virtue of 'prudence' is the means of the sober reasoning of pleasures, as we referred previously in the matter of appreciation of desires. Therefore he names 'prudence' (φρόνησις: phronesis) greatest good, from which all the other virtues derive, since prudence help us to realize which ones of our desires are natural and necessary, and which are not.

" **The beginning and the greatest good of all these is prudence. For this reason prudence is more valuable even than philosophy: from it derive all the virtues.**" (Epicurus, Letter to Menoeceus 132).

Apart from the appreciation of desires, **prudence** can help us to get rid of the fears that accompany the desires, even of the very **fear of death**, which makes things very hard for us and prevent us from enjoying the life. Since death is the loss of bodily sensation, when we die stops any sensation, which means that we stop feeling anything afterwards. Therefore, there is no reason for anxiety, for we are never to meet death (our sensation), since when death comes the sensation is absent, and when sensation is present death is absent. Furthermore, prudence can relieve us of the desire of immortality, since what has been dispersed has no sensation. In this way, we can get rid of the false 'assumption' (υπόληψις) of the fear of death, by objecting against that, the 'evident reason' that sensation and death can never meet each other. For this reason, if we realize that we shall never come to existence again, we shall not delay our happiness, and as a result wisdom, since prudence, beauty, justice and pleasant life they can not be separated.

" **Death, therefore – the most dreadful of evils – is nothing to us, since while we exist, death is not present, and whenever death is present, we do not exist.**" (Epicurus, Letter to Menoeceus 125).

" **Death is nothing to us. For what has been dispersed has no sensation. And what has no sensation is nothing to us.**" (Epicurus, Principal Doctrines 2).

" **We are born once and cannot be born twice, but we must be no more for all the time. Not being the master of tomorrow you nonetheless delay your happiness. Life is consumed by procrastination, and each of us dies without**

212

providing leisure for himself." (Epicurus, Vatican Sayings 14).

" Sweet becomes the life when the fear of death is absent." (Diogenes Oenandeas, Epicurus new Fragment 130).

" It is impossible to live pleasantly without living prudently, well and justly, nor it is possible to live prudently, well and justly without living pleasantly. The man for whom this latter condition is impossible cannot live prudently, well and justly; he for whom the former is impossible cannot live pleasantly." (Epicurus, Principal Doctrines 5).

Virtues

From this last fragment we can realize that, when Epicurus is referring to the 'virtues' of Ancient Greek philosophy, he regards them as means for happiness and not as an end in itself. For this reason he regards **prudence** as the greatest virtue, since is the means for the appreciation of desires and fears that agitate our soul. With the help of prudence, we can possess happiness after having reached to the state of tranquillity and peace of mind. On our way to tranquillity, the virtues compose the means to achieve our end, otherwise, without virtues it is impossible to achieve the freedom of bodily pain and peace of mind.

Let us examine in detail all the main virtues of Greek Antiquity in order to realize how can they contribute to the achievement of tranquillity. As for **prudence**, we have seen that it can help us to valuate our desires and also to relieve us of the fear of death. Through prudence we can become **abstemious** so as not to be guided to the excess of the sensual pleasures, which destroy our body and create great disturbance to our soul, due to the desire for their unlimited repetition (profligacy).

" The flesh considers the limits of pleasure to be boundless, and only infinite time makes it possible. But the mind, having gained reasonable understanding of the end and limit of flesh, and having expelled fears about eternity, furnishes the complete life, and we no longer have any need for time without end. But the mind does not flee from pleasure nor, when circumstances bring about the departure from life, does it takes its leave as though falling short somehow of the best life." (Epicurus, Principal Doctrines 20).

Referring to **justice**, as a matter of fact, the one who does not harm the others does not feel remorse, fear of revenge or fear of punishment, therefore his soul has no disturbance. He understands reasonably, through prudence, the needs and the rights of his fellow-men and does not infringe upon them.

" **The just man is most free of perturbation, while the unjust man is full of the greatest disturbance."** (Epicurus, Principal Doctrines 17).

Justice, of course, presupposes abstinence and **self-sufficiency**, as we have seen previously. Referring to **bravery**, one can possess it through prudence, after having expelled the fear of death and by giving a real meaning to his life. Apart from that, prudence is the one that helps a man to become brave, since it enables him to stand the difficulties of life with courage, as well as not to be indolent in prosperity.

" **The mean soul is puffed up by successes but brought down by adversity."** (Epicurus, Fragments 76).

Furthermore, **friendship** is considered to be very significant virtue, by Epicurus, which although begins with utility, can become a real virtue, that the wise man possesses and helps his fellow men to live peacefully and happily.

" **All friendship is desirable for itself, but it begins with need."** (Epicurus, Vatican Sayings 23).

" **The noble man is most concerned with wisdom and friendship. Of these one is a mortal good, the other immortal."** (Epicurus, Vatican Sayings 78).

" **Friendship dances around the world proclaiming to all us to rouse ourselves to give thanks."** (Epicurus, Vatican Sayings 52).

In order to possess the above-mentioned virtues, it requires a **reasonable understanding** of the desires, knowledge of oneself and his nature altogether, which can only come through prudence.

From all the above-mentioned arguments, it is evident that Epicurus does not agree with the philosophy of Plato and Socrates, concerning the existence of the "**Good in itself**" and the virtues that spring from the knowledge of the 'Good', and lead to happiness. According to him, all the virtues are the means that help us to achieve the tranquillity, which is the state of continuous pleasure and absence of pain, in other words happiness (*ευδαιμονία*). Neither believes he in eternal and objective values (**Ideas**), - just like 'Justice in itself', ' Beauty in itself', 'Love in itself', etc. - nor in eternity, which (desire of eternity) he regards, as a tendency of the flesh and instincts to get unlimited pleasure (Principal Doctrines 20), and not as a faculty of the mind.

" **There is no such thing as 'justice in itself', it is rather always a certain compact made during men's dealings with one another in different places, not to do harm or to be harmed." (Epicurus, Principal Doctrines 33).**

He also disagrees with Aristotle's notion that considers the virtue to be the 'good in itself', since as we have seen, virtue for Epicurus is the means and not the purpose of our life. For him the nature of 'good' is the 'static' pleasure of peace of mind and the absence of bodily pain. In the next fragment we can see how Epicurus is criticizing ironically Aristotle and his Peripatetic (walking) School about the nature of the 'good'.

" **That which creates unsurpassable joy is the removal of a great evil. And this is the nature of good if one grasps it correctly and then holds steadily to it, without walking about (*περιπατεί*: peripate) uttering vain rubbish about the good." (Epicurus, Fragments 61).**

In other words, in his opinion, the nature of good is inseparable from pleasure, since the obtaining of pleasure is the significant motive of the human behaviour, and on this impulsive inclination we must base our philosophical research into the achievement of happiness. Otherwise, without pleasure, there is no motive for the human being to go in search of 'virtues' and the 'good'. Therefore, prudence and wisdom can guide us to happiness, which is the permanent pleasure after tranquillity.

" Let beauty and virtue and suchlike be honored, if they provide pleasure; if they do not provide pleasure, let them go." (Epicurus, Fragments 12).

" For my part I do not know how I shall conceive the good, if I take away the pleasures of taste, if I take away sexual pleasure, if I take away the pleasure of hearing and if I take away the sweet emotions that are caused by the sight of a beautiful form." (Epicurus, Fragments 10).

Furthermore, Epicurus criticizes the philosophy of the Stoics and makes his meaning clear, that the virtues are the means and not the end of happiness, since the goal of one's life is the pleasure of tranquillity.

" Because, as I say, the problem is not what makes for happiness, but what does happiness mean and what at heart our nature desires; I claim that this is pleasure, and to all, Greek and barbarians, now and ever, I shout loudly that this is the purpose of well being. As for the virtues – that those people (Stoics), tire out them in vain, since from means they transform them into aim – in no way they form the aim. The virtues are the conditions on which one can reach the aim." (Epicurus, Diogenes Oenandeas, fr.32).

In order to dissociate himself from the **hypocrisy** and aimless **moralizing** of his times, he declares that he would not find fault with the dissolutes, if they could fill themselves with pleasure and dispel the pain and the fear about death.

" If the things that beget pleasure in dissolute individuals could dispel their minds' fears about the heavens, death and pain and could still teach them the limits of desires, we would have no grounds for finding fault with the dissolute, since they would be filling themselves with pleasures from every source and in no way suffering from pain or grief, which are evil." (Epicurus, Principal Doctrines 10).

Referring to the matter of 'necessity' (εμαρμένη: hemarmene) of Democritus and 'chance' (τύχη: tyche), as we saw in Letter to Menoeceus 133, Epicurus initiates the matter of free will, since those things that depend on us and have been decided by us, are the most significant. Because if we base our happiness upon chance, we shall fail, as chance is unstable. On the other hand, those events which are coming to be by necessity, are not accountable to anyone, therefore we cannot change them. However, the deeds that depend exclusively on us, those are significant, since they can help us to possess prudence, and are the only ones that can be praised or blamed and lead us to happiness.

" **Because necessity is not accountable to anyone, he sees that chance is unstable, but what lies in our control is subject to no master (παρ' ημίν αδέσποτον: par' emin adespoton); it naturally follows then, that blame or praise attend our decisions.."**

" **He thinks that is preferable to remain prudent and suffer ill fortune than to enjoy good luck while acting foolishly." (Epicurus, Letter to Menoeceus 133, 135).**

" **The one who is beaten in philosophical discussion gains more the more he learns." (Epicurus, Vatican Sayings 74).**

When Epicurus is referring to collective consciousness, says that the people are just for the fear of punishment by the law. Even those who believe in gods or God can turn to injustice, therefore he is referring to Egyptians or Judeans, who although are the most god-fearing of his times, are the most infamous.

" **All without exception, somehow are injust, others for pleasure others for fear. The ordinary people are just due to the laws – as long as they are just – and because of punishment which overhangs their heads. Although some conscientious are among them, because of piety, they are only a few..."**

" **Clear proof that piety cannot dissuade one from being injust, is the nations of Egyptians and Judeans. Although they are the most god-fearing from all the people, they are the most profane. Neither because of the existing gods** people are just, nor because of the Platonic and Socratic Judges of Hades." (Epicurus, Diogenes Oenandeas fr. 126).

On the other hand, if all the people could understand the common good, they would have avoided the harmful actions and chosen the good for all, and as a result, they would not have a need of the Laws. However, this presupposes prudence and wisdom, which cannot be accomplished by the great majority of the people, since they do not possess it. As we can realize, Epicurus associates prudence with social consciousness and justice.

" However, if all the people could realize equally their interest, without forgetting it, there would not have been the need of laws. By their own preference, they would have avoided the forbidden and chosen the proper ones..."

" The threat of punishment is addressed to those who do not provide for the common good.." (Ermarchus, Porphyrius 1. 7. 1 – 9. 4).

" We cannot spread wisdom everywhere, for the reason that not all the people are ready to accept it. If we assume that this was possible, then the life of gods would pass to the humans. Then, everything would have been full of justice and altruism and we would not have need of walls or laws or anything else that we make up one for the other."(Epicurus, Diogenes Oenandeas 56).

" I never desired to please the rabble. What pleased them I did not learn; and what I knew was far removed from their understanding." (Epicurus, Fragments 43).

From the last fragment we can realize, that Epicurus dissociates himself from the crowd, the majority of the people, the public opinion and the reasoning of the herd, which we saw in the other philosophers' notions as well. Because, if the wise man tries to please the majority in order to achieve fame, he will become inevitably slave of the public opinion and common sense, and as a result he will lose the capability of unbiased judgement and deep thought, since he has to conform his philosophy to the social establishment of his times, so as to be praised by the majority of the public opinion and become famous.

" **Speaking frankly, I would prefer, when discoursing on nature, to utter useful things, like oracles to humankind, even if no one should understand them, than to agree with the popular opinion and enjoy the constant accolades offered by the crowd." (Epicurus, Vatican Sayings 29).**

Furthermore, he criticizes the hypocrisy of his contemporary philosophers who adduce that they have found the way to happiness, whereas their philosophy leads its followers to unhappiness. However, in his opinion, as we have seen, philosophy and pleasure are inseparable.

" **We must not pretend to be philosophers, but be philosophers in truth. For we do not stand in need of the appearance of health, but of true health." (Epicurus, Vatican Sayings 54).**

" **In other occupations, the reward comes with difficulty after their competition, but in philosophy delight coincides with knowledge. For enjoyment does not come after learning, but learning and enjoyment comes together."** (Epicurus, Vatican Sayings 27).

In conclusion, we can refer to 'tetrapharmacus' (τετραφάρμακος: quadruplicate remedy, four-part cure) of Epicurus, which we consider to be the quintessence of his philosophy, since it shows us the way of dealing with everything that troubles our soul and make us feel pain.

" **God is not fearful, death does not cause anxiety, good is easily achieved, evil is resistable." (Philodemus to Sophists IV 7-14).**

F. Stoicism

Stoicism formed a significant philosophical tide, which started from the 4th century BC and lasted until the 5th century AD, when emperor Iustinianus with a legislative decree closed down all the existed philosophical Schools, so to say Platonic, Epicurean and Stoic. This event signified the official sealing of the dominance of Christianity, since all the philosophical teachings, apart from Christianity, were forbidden. After the burning down of the Bibliotheque of Alexandria by fanatic Christians, on 4th century AD, where all the official documents of Ancient Greek philosophy were destroyed, followed the closure of all the philosophical Schools and signified the end of Ancient Greek philosophy.

Founder of the Stoic philosophical School is considered to be **Zeno of Citteus (336 – 264 BC)**, whom succeeded as Head of Stoic School **Kleanthes (331 – 232 BC)** and then **Chrysippus (281 – 208 BC)**. These three philosophers belong to the '**Old Stoa**'. Then followed the '**Middle period**' of Stoicism with its main representatives **Panaetius** from Rhodes **(180 – 110 BC)** and **Poseidonius** from Appamea **(135 – 51 BC)**. The '**Later period**' of the Stoics is represented mainly by **Seneca (4 BC – 65 AD)**, **Epictetus (55 – 135 AD)** and **Marcus Aurelius (121 – 180 AD)**. Some basic principles of Stoicism we can also find later in the philosophy of **Spinoza** and **Hegel**.

The main purpose of the human being, according to Stoicism, must be the states of mind, characterized as "**apathea**" (*απάθεια*: absence of passion, peace of mind) – a state similar to Epicurus' "ataraxia" (*αταραξία*) – and "**euroia**" (*εύροια*: serenity), two states of mind which can lead us to "**happiness**" (*ευδαιμονία*: eudaimonia). The means by which we can achieve these states of mind is "**virtue**" (*αρετή*: arete).

" **Now if virtue promises happiness, peace of mind and serenity, then progress towards virtue is certainly progress towards each of these.**" (Arrian's, Epictetus' Discourses <Diatribai> A, 4 On Progress 3).

'Up to us' and 'indifferents'

The human being consists of two elements, one is the body which is in common with the animals, and the other is the **reasoning faculty** (*λόγος*: logos) and the **intelligence** (*γνώμη*: gnome) in common with the gods. Therefore, a man should not be satisfied by fulfilling only his bodily needs, but in order to live in accordance with his nature, he must develop this divine part, which is the only element of merit within him.

" It is sufficient, therefore, for them (animals) to eat and drink and rest and breed, and perform other such functions as belong to each of them; but for us, to whom god has granted in addition the faculty of understanding, these functions are no longer sufficient. For if we do not act in a proper and orderly manner, and each of us in accordance with his nature and constitution, we shall no longer attain our end. For where the constitution of beings is different, their offices and ends are different likewise." (Arrian's, Epictetus' Discourses A, 6 On Providence 14-16).

The faculty of reasoning and judgement, which the Stoics call "**right use of impressions**" (*ορθή χρήσις των φαντασιών*: orthe chrisis ton phantasion), is what distinguishes us from the animals, therefore it is in accordance with our real nature, and upon this faculty we must base in order to attain happiness, since each being is happy, when lives in accordance with its nature.

" **The <u>reasoning faculty</u>; for that alone of the faculties that we have received comprehends both itself – what it is, what is capable of, and with what valuable powers it has come to us – and all the other faculties likewise. For what else is it that tell us gold is beautiful? For the gold itself does not tell us. Evidently the <u>faculty that can deal with impressions</u>.**" (Arrian's, Epictetus' Discourses A, 1 On What Is In Our Power, And What Is Not 4-5)

Therefore, whatever we do in our life, we should first ask ourselves which things are **up to us** or else **in our power** and in accordance with our nature (*εφ' ημίν*: eph' hemin), and which are **not in our power** (*ούκ εφ' ημίν*: ouk eph' hemin), and therefore must be **indifferent** (*αδιάφορα*: adiaphora) to us.

Those things which are not in accordance with our nature (indifferents), are those that do not depend on ourselves and are determined by other, different factors. "Indifferents" are according to the Stoics, body, property, fame, political situations, health, disease, life, death and in short, all the **external material things** (*εκτός*: ektos). All the above mentioned do not depend on us, as there are unlimited factors that determine their outcome, therefore we should not bother about them. We have to let them work out in accordance with their nature, which means as the divine law determines them.

" **In our power are choice, and all actions dependent on choice; not in our power, the body, the parts of the body, property, parents, brothers, children, country, and in short, all with whom we associate.**" (Arrian's, Epictetus' Discourses A, 22 On Preconceptions 10).

" **What then, is to be done? To make the best of what is in our power, and the rest as it naturally happens. And how is that? As god pleases.**" (Arrian's Epictetus' Discourses A, 1 On what is in our Power ... 17).

The external things, as we can realize, do not depend on us, since the '**divine providence**' ($\theta\varepsilon\acute{\iota}\alpha\ \pi\rho\acute{o}voi\alpha$: theia pronoia) takes care of them and decides on their progress. Therefore, they are not in our power and must be indifferent to us, since the divine law ($\varepsilon\iota\mu\alpha\rho\mu\acute{e}v\eta$: hemarmene) determines what has to be created and destructed.

" **Well then, each of the animals is constituted by god for a purpose, one to be eaten, another for husbandry, or for the production of the cheese, and the rest of them for some other comparable use;**

But god has introduced man into the world as a spectator of himself and of his works; and not only as a spectator, but an interpreter of them." (Arrian's, Epictetus' Discourses A, 6 On Providence 18-19).

" **So a wise and good man, after examining all these things, submits his mind to him who administers the universe, as good citizens submit to the laws of the state.**"(Arrian's, Epictetus' Discourses A, 12 On Contentment 7)

Since God has constituted everything in the universe for a special purpose, he surveys everything and protects those creatures he wants to keep alive. Therefore he has assigned to each man a '**guardian angel**' ($\alpha\gamma\alpha\theta\acute{o}\varsigma\ \delta\alpha\acute{\iota}\mu\omega\nu$: agathos daimon), who helps and protects him every moment.

222

" If you are capable of all this, is not god capable of surveying all things, and being present with all, and having a certain communication with all?"

" No, but nevertheless he has assigned to each man a director, his own personal daemon, and committed him to his guardianship; a director whose vigilance no slumbers interrupt and whom no false reasonings can deceive." (Arrian's, Epictetus Discourses A, 14 That The Deity Watches Over Us All 9, 12).

As we have seen the Stoics believe in God, who has constituted all things in the universe, surveys them every moment, and takes care of all the creatures and decides on their progress. Therefore, they conclude that all the 'external material things' must be 'indifferent' to us.

Certainly, this does not mean, that we have to be careless about the daily events and not to carry out our **duties** (*καθήκοντα*: katheconta). On the contrary, we should display our skill with regard to them – (*ἐπιμέλεια*: epimeleia), **careful behaviour**: a significant virtue for the Stoics - without however, accepting them for their own sake, and as a result, neglecting those that are in accordance with our nature.

" .. Likewise, life is indifferent; but the use of it not indifferent. When you are told, therefore, that these things are indifferent, do not, on that account, ever be careless; nor, when somebody urges you to be careful, be abject or in awe of the materials of action." (Arrian's, Epictetus' Discourses B, 6 On What Is Indifferent 1-2).

Referring now, to those things which are 'up to us' or 'in our power', according to Stoicism, are the '**capacity for choice**' (*προαίρεσις*: prohairesis) and the '**right use of impressions**', which means the choice and the attending only to certain rational impressions, among all the **impressions** (*φαντασίαι*: phantasiai) that appear to the mind, in other words the faculty of judgement.

" – Tell me then, what things are indifferent.
- Things outside the sphere of choice.
- Tell me also what follows.

- Things outside the sphere of choice are nothing to me.
- Tell me too what you considered to be the good things.
- A right choice and a right use of impressions." (Arrian's, Epictetus' Discourses A, 30 What We Have At Hand In Difficult Circumstances 3).

Logos – Controlling part (Hegemonikon)

This 'capacity for choice' (*προαίρεσις*) is a part of universal "**Logos**" (*Λόγος*), which means the universal constitution that determines all things. When we do not submit to the external material things, namely we consider them as indifferent to us, then we can live in accordance with our nature, since we comply with this part of mundane Logos, which is within us. This part of Logos which is in us, is autonomous and provides us with the capacity for choice. Due to the way we react to the external material things, we can either comply with Logos, or live our life in sensational pleasure. There lies the capacity for choice.

This part of the soul, which is of divine origin, since, is part of the eternal and universal Logos, the Stoics call it "**Controlling or governing part**" (*Ηγεμονικόν*). It pervades the human body, is identified with reason and intellect (capacity for choice), and provides the virtuous and wise man with the capability of permanent commune with divine providence and law. In order the wise man to get at this level, he must be able to reject the external irritants that come from the external events. In other words, while he is perceiving through the senses the external events, he deals with the impressions (**right use of impressions**), which arise from the senses, in order to transform the emotions, that accompany the impressions, into conscious will to his moral perfection, and as a consequence the achievement of the state of "**apathea**" and "**peace of mind**". In this way he can reach the state of permanent "**serenity**" (*εύροια βίου*). The wise man, as long as is in this permanent state, is complied with the eternal and divine law (Logos), incarnates his real nature, and achieves happiness (*ευδαιμονία* or *vita beata* of Seneca).

" **For, if god had created that portion of his own being which he has separated from himself and given to us such that it was capable of being restrained or compelled, either by himself or by any other he would not have been good, nor have taken care of us in the way he ought.**" (Arrian's, Epictetus' Discourses A, 17 The Logic Is Indispensable 27).

" **For what purpose then, have we received reason (Logos) from nature? To make proper use of impressions. And what is reason itself? Something compounded from impressions of a certain kind; and thus by nature becomes contemplative of itself too.**"

" **Therefore the first and the greatest task of a philosopher is to put impressions to the test and distinguish between them, and not admit any that has not been tested.**" (Arrian's, Epictetus Discourses A, 20 On How Reason Is Able To Contemplate Itself 5, 7).

" **Rather it says, 'in every circumstance I will preserve the <u>controlling part</u>** (*ηγεμονικόν*) **in accord with nature'. Whose governing part? His in whom I exist.**" (Arrian's, Epictetus' Discourses A, 15 What Does Philosophy Promise? 4).

" **You have only to turn your thoughts to these matters some day, and bestow even a little time on your own <u>controlling part</u>. Consider what is this that you possess, and where it has come from, this faculty that uses all other things, that puts them to the test, and chooses, and rejects.**" (Arrian's, Epictetus' Discourses D, 7 On Freedom From Fear 40).

As each human being, has part of Logos within, has the capability of feeling the unity of the human community and the universe in general. A man, neither feels detached from his fellow men nor from the nature and universe, but rather he feels like being "**a citizen of the world**", a part from the whole, a part of the "**universal city**". On this principle is based the Stoics' doctrine of "**cosmic sympathy**" (*κοσμική* σνμπάθεια), according to which, every change that happens in one part of the universe affects and pulls down the neighboring parts. So all the human beings are intimately bound to each other and their souls are interacted, and as being parts of the whole (Logos), each one affects and feels the other.

" But if the plants and our bodies are so intimately bound to the universe and affected by its influences, must our souls not be much so?" (Arrian's Epictetus' Discourses A, 14 That The Deity Watches Over Us All 5).

" For what is a man? A part of a city first, of that made up by gods and men; and next, of that to which you immediately belong, which is a miniature of the universal city." (Arrian's, Epictetus' Discourses B, 5 How Is Greatness Of Mind Compatible With Careful Behaviour 26).

Philosophical Training – Apatheia

According to Stoicism, good - evil and problems of daily life, exist in order to train the human beings for the capacity of transforming the impressions of the externals, and the possession of virtues. Therefore, we should not complain about the difficulties of everyday life, since these circumstances are our best chances to train ourselves for the rejection of the externals (αδιάφορα) and the achievement of the state of apatheia (απάθεια).

" What would have been the use of those arms of his (Heracles) and his strength overall; of his endurance, and greatness of mind, if such circumstances and opportunities had not stirred him to action and exercised him?" (Arrian's, Epictetus' Discourses A, 6 On Providence 34).

" Why then, are we angry? Because we admire those things which such people take from us. Do not admire your clothes, and you will not be angry with the man who steals them. Do not admire the beauty of your wife, and you will not be angry with the adulterer. Know that a thief and an adulterer have no place among the things that are properly your own, but only among the things that belong to the others, and which are not in your power. If you give up these things, and look upon them as nothing, with whom will you still be angry? But as long as you admire them, be angry with yourself rather than with others." (Arrian's, Epictetus Discourses A, 18 That We Should Not Be Angry With Those Who Fall Into Error 11-12).

Therefore, the purpose of philosophy is to teach the man which things are 'up to him', and in accordance with his nature, as well as to educate him properly in order to be able to use the impressions in a right way, so as to attain by himself the state of peace of mind and serenity.

" What then, is to be properly educated? To learn how to apply natural preconceptions (προλήψεις: prolepsis) to particular cases, in accordance with nature; and for the future, to distinguish that some things are in our own power (εφ' ημιν), others not (ουκ εφ' ημιν)." (Arrian's, Epictetus' Discourses A, 22 On Preconceptions 9).

The motive for the acquirement of **prudence**, as we have seen also in the previous philosophers, is when one fails in his desires and falls into what he wants to avoid. Then he realizes that the desires for the externals are idle, since they neither are up to us nor in our power. On the other hand, those who are within the sphere of choice and in accordance with our nature, can lead us to attain **serenity** (εύροια), **peace of mind** (απάθεια) and real **freedom** (ελευθερία: eleftheria). Therefore, prudence is a significant virtue, since it helps us to improve morally ourselves, by "applying the preconceptions" and distinguishing among them, which are in accordance with our nature, and which are not.

" Do we then, find any bad man who is free from sorrow and fear, and does not fail in his desires and falls into what he wants to avoid? – None. So we find that none is free." (Arrian's, Epictetus' Discourses D, 1 On Freedom 5).

Other significant virtue is the "**courage**" (θάρρος: tharros), that one must have to be able to cope with the difficult circumstances, and "**caution**" (σύνεσις: synesis), which comes from prudence. We must transfer caution to things that are in our power, otherwise, if we transfer it to those that are not in our power - for example to avoid difficulties - then we turn out to be full of fear and perturbation. Since we are always trying to find a way to avoid difficult situations, that will inevitably lead us to a permanent state of anxiety.

On the contrary, if we use caution to analyze and confront the fear of pain or death, and courage towards circumstances which cause pain, then we shall be able to live without fear, sorrow and anxiety, and enjoy real freedom.

" **In the things that lie outside the sphere of choice, be confident; in the things that lie within it, be cautious.**"

" **For if the person should transfer his caution to the sphere of choice and the actions of choice, then along with the will to be cautious, he will at the same time have it in his power to avoid what he wishes to avoid; but if he transfers it to things that are not in our power and lie outside the sphere of choice, by fixing his aversion on what is not in our own power, but dependent on others, he will necessarily be subject of fear, inconstancy and perturbation. For it is not death or pain to be feared, but the fear of pain or death.**" (Arrian's, Epictetus' Discourses B, 1 That There Is No Conflict Between Confidence And Caution 5, 12, 13).

The philosophical training is very significant, specially for the weak persons, because when they are taught the capacity of argument and persuasive reasoning without the real reasoning faculty, they turn out to become vain, since they are not really interested in solving philosophical problems and improving themselves morally, but rather in flaunting their persuasive reasoning.

" **For in general every faculty is dangerous to weak and uninstructed persons, as being apt to render them presumptuous and vain.**" (Arrian's, Epictetus' Discourses A, 8 That For The Uneducated Our Reasoning Capacities Are Not Free Of Danger 8).

Through the philosophical education, one can possess real virtues and regain the lost dignity of his own human nature, as he stops depending on the 'externals'. He can possess strong will, so as not to yield to difficulties that he meets with on his way to moral perfection. He can distinguish himself from the simple-minded people and the reasoning of crowd or herd, since the one who wants to be admired by the multitude (μαινόμενοι: mainomenoi, madmen), teaches what the crowd wants to hear, and not what the few people who desire the great and exceptional things. Because, although all of us have the capability for the "great" and "exceptional" achievements of the soul, only a few of us can manage to distinguish ourselves from the crowd and attain "apatheia" and "serenity".

" But I want to be the purple, that small and shining band, which gives lustre and beauty to all the rest. Why do you bid me resemble the multitude then? In that case, how shall I still be the purple?"

" Only consider at what price you sell your own will and choice, man; if for nothing else, that you may not sell it cheap. But what is great and exceptional perhaps belongs to others, to Socrates and those who resemble him.

Why then, if we are born to this, do not all or many of us become like him? Why, do all horses become swift? Are all dogs keen at the scent?" (Arrian's, Epictetus' Discourses A, 2 How Is One To preserve One's True Character In Everything 18, 33, 34).

" What I want is that all who meet me should admire me, and as they follow after me cry out, What a great philosopher!

- Who are these people, by whom you wish to be admired? Are they not the very people whom you have been in the habit of describing as mad? What then, do you want to be admired by madmen?" (Arrian's, Epictetus' Discourses A, 21 To Those Who Wish To Be Admired 3, 4).

The philosophical training, according to the Stoics, is a long-lasting procedure, and consists of reasoning test of all our preconceptions, in order to distinguish between them the true from the false ones, by using the data of the senses. Because none can deny these data, as our daily life is based upon them. None of us when he wants to go to the public baths, goes to the mill, as he uses these data to reach his destination. At this point we should also refer to the retrospective practice of self-analysis of the Pythagoreans, which the Stoics exercised daily, in order to find out their faults and weaknesses, and as a matter of fact the false preconceptions, that prompted them to the wrong actions.

By the means of "**right use of impressions**", all preconceptions must be tested, by the faculty of reasoning, in order to establish the true and reject the false that lead one to the wrong actions. Furthermore, referring to any **equivocal** (*μεταπίπτοντες*: metapiptontes) or **hypothetical** (*υποθετικοί*: hypothetikoi) **syllogisms** (*συλλογισμοί*: premises), one must grant each premise to the end, and if the conclusion that follows is false, he must then abandon the concession of the premise, and reconsider the initial hypothesis. The same method, as we have seen, has been applied by Plato (**dialectic**). In this way, one can gradually examine all the **preconceptions** and settle only on the **true ones** (*εναργείς*: enargeis), which he can use for the transformation of the impressions, so as not to be misled by the "externals".

At this point we can see some similarities between the method of the Stoics for the ascertainment of truth through the use of impressions, and the method of " Canon" of Epicurus. In other words, the preconceptions which arise from the senses, must be examined through the reasoning faculty, in order to find out which are false and which are true. After this examination remain only those that can be certified (*εναργείς*), and those are the true ones. Therefore, it is similar to the Canon's procedure: senses – preconceptions – focusing of thought into an impression – assumption – confirmation.

" **But when it comes to our poor miserable controlling part (*ηγεμονικόν*), we yawn and slumber and accept every impression that offers, for here the damage that we suffer does not strike us.**

" **When, therefore, you wish to know how careless you are about good and evil, and how eager about things indifferent, consider what your attitude is to blindness on the one hand and delusion of the mind on the other, and** you will find that you are far from feeling as you ought, in relation to good and evil.

But this demands a long preparation, and much effort and study. What of it? Do you expect that the greatest of arts (philosophy) can be acquired with little study?" (Arrian's, Epictetus Discourses A, 20 On How Reason Is Able To Contemplate Itself 11, 12, 13).

" It escapes most people, that the study of arguments which have equivocal or hypothetical premises, and those which are developed by questioning, and in a word, all such arguments, has a connection with how should we behave (καθῆκον) in our lives."

" For what is required in reasoning? To establish what is true, to reject what is false, and to suspend judgement in doubtful cases"

" But if the premises do not remain as they were when they were granted, it is equally necessary for us to abandon our concessions of the premises, and no longer accept what is inconsistent with the premises." (Arrian's, Epictetus' Discourses A, 7 On The Use Of Arguments Resting On Equivocations, And Hypothetical Arguments, And The Like 1, 5, 18).

" Impressions come to us in four ways. Things are, and appear so to us; or they are not, and do not appear to be; or they are, and do not appear to be; or they are not, and yet appear to be.

Thus is the task of the educated man, to form a right judgement in all these cases." (Arrian's, Epictetus' Discourses A, 27 In How Many Ways Do Impressions Arise .. 1, 2).

The way that one can deal with the impressions, is based upon the Stoics' doctrine, that everything can be conquered only by itself. The person's own judgement and capacity of choice cannot be overcome by another, but by itself, e.g. passion can overcome passion, habit can overpower habit etc. One cannot conquer the other's personal judgement by the application of fear. We must oppose to the false preconception of fear of death, the natural and evidential preconception (*εναργής πρόληψις*) that death is not evil, since it is a necessity and cannot be avoided, and that no one has escaped death so far, therefore it is not dependent on us, so it belongs to the "indifferents". The sorrow and the fear of death arises from the origin of **passion** (*πάθος*) itself, which means that we usually wish for something, which can never come about. Because all our passions are unreasonable, since we expect that everything in life will come in accordance with our desires, in order to feel the pleasure of satisfaction (**pleasure:** *ηδονή*), and when this does not occur, we feel sorrow and disappointment (**pain:** *λύπη*).

" **You fail to see that it was a person's own judgement that conquered itself, it was not conquered by another. Nothing else can overcome the power of choice but that itself.**" (Arrian's, Epictetus' Discourses A, 29 On Steadfastness 12).

" **Well, is it any otherwise with regard to impulse and desire? What can overpower one impulse but another impulse? What can overpower desire and aversion but another desire and aversion?**" (Arrian's, Epictetus' Discourses A, 17 That Logic Is Indispensable 24).

" **What aid then, is it possible to discover against habit? The contrary habit.**"

" **Oppose to one habit the contrary habit; to sophistic arguments, the art of reasoning, and the frequent use and exercise of it. Against specious appearances we must have clear preconceptions, polished and ready for use.**"

" **When death appears an evil, we ought immediately to remember that evils may be avoided, but death is a necessity.**"

" **Must I die trembling and lamenting? For the origin of passion is wishing for something that does not come about.**" (Arrian's, Epictetus Discourses A, 27 In How Many Ways Do Impressions Arise And What Should We Have At Hand To Help Us In Dealing With Them 4, 6, 7, 10).

All the "**passions**" (*πάθη*), according to the Stoics, that are within us, arise from the "externals" which create those desires and emotions, and prompt us to fulfill them. Therefore, we cannot be released from the external world, since our "controlling part" (*ηγεμονικόν*) gives its approval (**assent**: *συγκατάθεσις*, synkatathesis) to passion, and we end up in wrong judgement. The term "**assent**" is referring to the energy of the 'controlling part', which can transform our emotions into will-power, after a reasoning faculty. Therefore, under the influence of passion our assent and judgement are wrong, and not in accordance with our nature.

For this reason, the people under the influence of passion, go astray in matters good and evil, and their judgement is wrong. The only way to help those people, is to show them their error and not to get angry with them, and have pity on them, since everybody has nothing higher than his personal opinion to rely on. If one is convinced that his actions are wrong, then due to his self-respect and personal dignity he will amend his errors and change his behaviour.

On the other hand, the man who realizes that the 'externals' do not concern him, as are not up to him (indifferents), he starts living in accordance with his nature, and as a result his "assents" and judgements are becoming in accordance with Logos and released from passion.

" **If what the philosophers be true, that all men's actions proceed from one source, namely passion, such that in the case of assent, it is the passion that something is so, and of dissent, the passion that is not so, and by Zeus, in the case of suspended judgement, the passion that is uncertain. So also, in the case of impulse towards a thing, the feeling that it conduces to my advantage, and that is impossible to judge one thing advantageous and desire another, and to judge one thing appropriate and be impelled by another – if all this is in fact true, why should we still be angry at the multitude? < They are thieves and robbers>. What do you mean by thieves and robbers? They have gone astray in matters of good and evil. Ought we then, be angry with them or to pity them? Do but show them their error, and you will see how they will amend their errors; but if they do not see it, they have nothing higher than their personal** opinion to rely on." (Arrian's, Epictetus' Discourses A, 18 That We Should Not Be Angry With Those Who Fall Into Error 1-4).

" Whoever, therefore, dully remembers that a person's impressions are the standards of his every action – these impressions may be either right or wrong, and if right, he is without fault, if wrong, he himself pays the penalty, for it cannot be that one person should be the one who has gone astray, and another person the one who suffers – whoever then, remembers this, will never be angry with anyone, will never be harsh towards anyone will never revile, or reproach, or hate, or be offended by anyone." (Arrian's, Epictetus' Discourses A, 28 That We Should Not Be Angry With Others .. 10).

" I for my part am content if my desires and aversions are in accordance with nature, and if I exercise my impulse, to act and not to act, as I was born to do, and likewise my purpose, design and assent." (Arrian's, Epictetus' Discourses A, 21 To Those Who Wish To Be Admired 2).

Particularly, the philosophical training of the Stoics includes three stages. On the <u>first stage,</u> the disciple must be able to apply the "**preconceptions**" and distinguish among them, those which are "**in our power**" or else in accordance with our nature, and those which are "**indifferent**". On the <u>second stage</u>, he must be able to act in accordance with his moral duty (*καθήκον*), so as to be able to possess the virtues. On this stage it is essential that the disciple can deal with the sense-impressions (**right use of impressions**), in order to be able to choose his actions and to act rightly, according to his purpose of moral perfection, firmly in his principles, and unaffected by the 'externals'. On the <u>third stage,</u> his very feelings are in harmony with his nature and his purpose of the achievement 'peace of mind' (*απάθεια*). In other words, his 'assents' are in accordance with 'Logos', therefore he possesses a real will-power, since his faculty of reasoning and his sentiments are harmonically bound together for the purpose of his moral perfection, and always in accordance with nature.

" Let us for the present leave aside the <u>second area of study</u>, concerning our impulses and the appropriate regulation of them; let us leave aside the <u>third</u> too, concerning assent. I make you a present of all these. Let us insist on the <u>first</u>, which affords an almost sensible proof that you do not apply your preconceptions rightly." (Arrian's, Epictetus' Discourses B, 17 How Should We Apply Our Preconceptions To Particular Instances 15, 16).

To sum up with philosophical training, the disciple begins by applying the preconceptions, in order to distinguish between them, what is 'up to him' ($\varepsilon\varphi$' $\eta\mu\iota\nu$) and what is 'not up to him' ($o\upsilon\kappa$ $\varepsilon\varphi$' $\eta\mu\iota\nu$). Then, he goes on gradually with the '**right use of impressions**', so as to be able to transform the wrong preconceptions into the right ones, as well as the sense-impressions for the purpose of right action and peace of mind ($\alpha\pi\alpha\theta\varepsilon\iota\alpha$). This continuous alertness and wrestling with the impressions of the 'externals' acquires the will-power, that one must possess in order to be able to bear hardships, and possess always the state of tranquillity and under all circumstances, just like an invincible athlete.

" Who then is the invincible man? He whom nothing outside the sphere of choice can disconcert. So I go on to consider him in each specific circumstance as one does in the case of an athlete...

What if you throw a bit of silver in his way? He will despise it. What, if a girl? What then, if it is in the dark? What if he be tested by a touch of fame, or calumny, praise, death? He is able to overcome all these things. What then, if it is burning hot, that is to say, if he is drunk, or depressed, or asleep? Now that is what I mean by an <u>invincible athlete</u>." (Arrian's, Epictetus' Discourses A, 18 That We Should Not Be Angry.. 21-23).

From all the above mentioned, we can realize that the purpose of life, according to the Stoics, is firstly, the release from the '**externals**' ($\alpha\delta\iota\alpha\varphi\rho\rho\alpha$), even from the very fear of death and under all circumstances. Apart from that, one must rely only on the '**capacity for choice**' and the '**right use of impressions**', since are the only ones, that one has authority over them, and can get him to the '**peace of mind**' (*απάθεια*), '**serenity**' (*εύροια βίου*), and as a result to '**happiness**' (*ευδαιμονία*).

" **If these things are true, and we are not stupid or acting a part, when we say that good or ill for man lies in choice, and that all else is nothing to us, why are we still troubled? Why are we still afraid?** No one else has authority over the things that seriously concern us; and the things over which others have authority are of no concern to us. **What is left for us to worry about?**

Your good faith is your own; your sense of shame is your own. Who then, can deprive you of these?

When you concern yourself with what is not your own, you lose what is your own." (Arrian's, Epictetus' Discourses A, 25 On The Same Subject 1, 2, 4).

" **That you may know that those things are not false, on which serenity and peace of mind depend, take my books and you will see, how true and in harmony with nature are the things which give me peace of mind**" (Chrysippus).

As a conclusion, we quote a fragment which, in our opinion, includes all the virtues of Stoicism, and also the means to the achievement of peace of mind and serenity.

" **Of such a nature will I show myself to you: faithful, modest, brave, unperturbed. What, and immortal too, and exempt from age and disease? No, but as one who dies like a god, who bears illness like a god. This is in my power; this I can do. The other is not in my power, nor can I do it. I will show you the sinews of a philosopher. What sinews are those?**

Desire that never fails in its achievement; aversion that never meets with what it would avoid; appropriate impulse; carefully considered purpose; and assent that is never precipitate. **That is what you shall see.**" (Arrian's, Epictetus' Discourses B, 8 What Is The True Nature Of The Good 27-29).

III.   CONCLUSION – EPILOGUE

After having presented the main principles of Ancient Greek philosophy, we can return to our initial speculations concerning the human nature itself and its imprudent and instinctive disposition.

As we have seen, the matter of a man's imprudent attitude has been closely examined by all the Greek philosophers, who emphasized the importance of release from this disposition. Therefore, they qualified the people without prudence as "sleepers", "mortals", "many", "fools", "ignorant", "mad" etc.

This common ascertainment of the philosophers about the human attitude, was attributed to the instinctive tendency of a man to **pursue the pleasure** and **avoid the pain**. The pursuit of pleasure consists in the enjoyment of the sensual pleasures (food, drink, sex, luxury etc.), as well as in pursuing the means of the achievement of these pleasures, namely wealth, power, fame etc. The emotions which accompany this double impulse, when one succeeds in pursuing the pleasure, are delight, joy, superiority, enthusiasm etc. However, when one fails in this pursuit, he feels sorrow, disappointment, anger, hatred, aversion etc.

With regard to the human soul, we have seen that it is multiform and is divided mainly in three parts. The first one is referring to the **instincts** and **appetites** (appetitive, vegetative, nutritive or else irrational part), the second one to the **emotions** and the **will** (spirited or deliberative part), and the third one to the **rational** part (intellective, which possesses reason). The first two parts have in common both animals and men, but the third one is characteristic of men only.

This impulse then of pursuing the pleasure and avoiding the pain, arises from the irrational part, and is the one which provides the animals with elementary knowledge so as to be able to survive. Therefore, this impulse is instinctive, irrational and mechanical (animals instinctively repeat what gives them pleasure and avoid what gives them pain). However, when a man fails in his desires or falls into what he wants to avoid, he really starts thinking and reflecting, therefore, as we have seen, it is not good for men's education all their desires to be fulfilled (Heraclitus fr. 176, Democritus Fr. 178, virtues of self-sufficiency, continence and moderation in Plato, Aristotle, Epicurus and Stoics).

The **rational** part is considered the one which could help the man to realize his needs and "potentialities", so as to be able to get away from his instinctive impulses. Therefore, all the Greek philosophers regard it as the most significant part of the soul, since it is the one that takes care of the body, the fulfillment of the right desires, and in general it takes care of a man's harmony and equanimity.

As main virtue of the rational part, as we have seen, was considered **prudence** (*φρόνησις*: phronesis), which enables a man to realize his true needs with regard to his instinctive impulses. Apart from that, it allows him to realize in advance the consequences of his actions (**foresight**), and to act in accordance with the right decision. Finally, through prudence one can get rid of the wrong "preconceptions", opinions and fears, which arise from ignorance. All these factors contribute to the fact that, all the Ancient Greek philosophers concluded that prudence is the greatest virtue.

In addition, since a man as a social being co-exists with his fellow-men, and in order to live in harmony with them, he ought to respect their needs and rights, the same as he respects his needs. Therefore, taking into account this factor in his dealings with them, he should be just, as long as he understands that. For this reason, as we have seen, **justice** (*δικαιοσύνη*: dikaiosyne) is a main and significant virtue as well. This double nature of a man, namely as a **rational** and **social being**, means that he should be interested in developing both these qualities. Moreover, the virtues which contribute to this aim are prudence and justice, since the right social attitude presupposes a sense of justice.

238

This virtue of justice of course, as it has been confirmed, is concerned with what is inside us and not only with external attitudes. It is a result of continuous exercising of a certain state of the soul (aethos, habit), since each one of us due to his upbringing and education has adopted some false and subjective principles or attitudes. Furthermore, in order to be able to be just, one must not be greedy or incontinent or mean or irascible etc. Therefore, as virtues of Greek Antiquity are mainly regarded **moderation**, **bravery**, **continence** and **self-sufficiency**. Certainly all these virtues require knowledge of oneself and understanding, which can be acquired through **prudence**, and therefore it is considered the greatest virtue.

With regard to the matter of **happiness** (*ευδαιμονία*: eudaimonia), as we have realized, it is distinguished from pleasure and joy, and is rather a stable and inner state of the soul. For the external events as they are interchanged, sometimes give us **pleasure** (*ηδονή*: hedone) - when we achieve what we desire - and sometimes they incur displeasure and disappointment (**pain:** *λύπη*, lype), when we fall into what we want to avoid. Therefore, we should not search for happiness in pursuing the pleasure and avoiding the pain, which arise from the external events, because as the externals are interchanged, it is impossible that always happen to us pleasant events.

Furthermore, as the man is a rational being, he cannot be content only with sensual pleasures, since his main part, the rational one cannot be satisfied with the bodily pleasures but with the development of his intellect and culture. For each being can be happy when it lives in accordance with its nature, and since the main part of a man's nature is the intellect, then he must search for his happiness in developing his intellect.

The conclusion then of the Ancient Greek philosophers was that happiness is an inner state of the soul, and can be achieved through the serenity or harmony of the parts of the soul, peace of mind, moderation, state of the "mean", liberation of the mind from wrong preconceptions, liberation from the desires of bodily pleasures, and liberation from the fear of death (wisdom, good spirits, mean, justice, peace of mind). For the state of the soul is the only one that is our own, we can control it and keep in balance, regardless of the external events. Therefore, the one who possesses prudence can achieve this state of mind.

Of the same importance for happiness was considered by the philosophers for the development of the intellect, the searching out the "primary principles" and the unity of the constitution, which governs the universe (**Logos, Being, Nous, Good**). This state of mind (wisdom) enables a man to get away from the state of the "irrational" being and elevates him to the "divine" level. Since the man who possesses the knowledge and comprehension of the unity of the universal constitution, complies with it, and as a consequence he can have higher and noble sentiments (spirited part), which can be transformed into conscious will. In this way he can shake off his miserable emotions of pettiness and self-interest, and achieve the peace of mind.

The searching for the "**primary principles**" (*αρχαί*: archai) of the universe and the method of approaching it, as we have seen, followed many paths and contributed to the development of the analyzing and composing methods of thought. The philosophers started with the **inductive** by interpreting the sense-impressions, in order to find out the first laws which govern the phenomena. Afterwards, through the **deductive** they proceeded to the first conclusions and the formulations of premises and **syllogisms**. After having applied these principles and doctrines to everyday life (**confirmation**), they concluded that some of those principles were wrong, and that confirmation led them to reconsider the initial principles, and invent new ones on the basis of the new facts (trial and error).

Furthermore, they considered all these principles as hypotheses, and proceeded through **dialectic** to find out one common principle which includes all the previous principles. This one was called by them the "**primary principle**" which governs all things in the universe.

240

Afterwards the "first principle" was applied to everyday life and established the moral values and ethics of the philosophers.

The method of reasoning that we previously described and all the Ancient Greek philosophers followed, was adopted by all scientists, as we know, and contributed to the development of scientific thought, and finally led to scientific discoveries throughout the history of humanity. This continuous and progressive course of knowledge has shown that knowledge is unlimited and boundless, just as it was considered by the Greek philosophers.

In addition, the belief of many scientists in the main principles of the different philosophical schools of the Greek Antiquity, as well as their belief in the existence of some invariant principles which remain indestructible (**attributes of the being**), led them to their scientific discoveries (heliocentric system, gravity, atomic theory, electromagnetic radiation, theory of relativity, quantum mechanics, uncertainty principle, genetic code, etc.).

In our opinion, Ancient Greek thought has established methods and systems of reasoning, which helped the mankind to search for answers to the questions, that has preyed upon a man's mind since thousands of years, and helped him to go beyond himself (transcendence), where he succeeded in.

We hope, the present essay has helped you to find some answers to your questions concerning the human nature and its moral values, or at least this presentation and interpretation of the Ancient Greek philosophical concepts will spark off a further searching for true moral values of your own, further self-knowledge and more inward liberation.

BIBLIOGRAPHY

PRESOCRATICS

- Texts and numbering of the original Fragments of Presocratics are in accordance with the work "**Die fragmente der Vorsocratiker**" by Diels H. and Kranz, W. Berlin 1951-2.
- Allen E. Reginald "**Greek Philosophy-Thales to Aristotle**", The Free Press 1966.
- Barnes J. **"The Presocratic Philosophers"**, Routledge Revised Edition October 1982.
- Burnet J. **"Early Greek Philosophy"**, Kessinger Publishing, February 2003.
- Guthrie W. K. "**A History of Geek Philosophy - Earlier Presocratics and the Pythagoreans**", Cambridge University Press, February 1979.
- Guthrie W. K. "**A History of Greek Philosophy – The Presocratic tradition from Parmenides to Democritus**", Cambridge University Press, February 1979.
- Kirk G. S., Raven J. E. and Schofield M. "**The Presocratic Philosophers**", Cambridge University Press, Second edition 1983.
- Mourelatos A. P. D. "**The Pre-Socratics**", Garden City N.Y. 1974.
- Reclam Universal Bibliothek "**Die Vorsocratiker I, II**", Volumes two Stuttgart 2000.
- Wright M. R. "**The Presocratics-The main Fragments**" Duckwork Publishing June 1985.
- Hierocles "**Golden Verses of Pythagoras**" Concord Grove Pr. December 1983.
- Firth M. Florence "**The Golden Verses of Pythagoras**", Kessinger Publishing, November 1904.

- Iamblichus' **"Life of Pythagoras"**, Kessinger Publishing, July 2003.
- Axelos Kostas **"Heraclitus and the Philosophy"** Exantas Publishing, Athens 1974-1976.
- Kahn H. Charles **"Pythagoras and the Pythagoreans: A Brief History"**, Hackett Publishing Company, September 2001.
- Kahn H. Charles **"The Art and Thought of Heraclitus"**, Cambridge University Press, September 1981.
- Robinson T. M. **"Heraclitus-Fragments"**, University of Toronto Press, June 1991.
- Gallop David **"Parmenides of Elea - Fragments"** University of Toronto Press, July 1991.
- Inwood Brad **"The Poem of Empedocles"**, University of Toronto Press April 2001.
- Bailey C. **"The Greek Atomists and Epicurus"** Oxford 1928.

PLATO

- Ackrill J. L. **"Essays on Plato and Aristotle"** Oxford University Press, USA; New edition September 27, 2001.
- Agora Publications **"Plato's Republic"** July 2001.
- Barnes & Noble Publishing **"Republic"**, June 2004.
- Bloom Allan **"The Republic of Plato"** Basic Books, Second Edition Sept. 1991.
- Bury C. **"Timaeus, Critias, Cleitophon, Menexenus, Epistles"** (Loeb Classical Library), Harvard University Press, March 1960.
- Cooper M. John **"Plato Complete Works"**, Hackett Publishing Company 1997.
- Gill C. **"The Symposium"** Penguin Books. May 2003.
- Guthrie W. K. C. **"Protagoras"**, Penguin Books, June 1957.

- Harvard University Press "**Euthyphro, Apology, Crito, Phaedo, Phaedrus**", 1999.
- Jowett B. "**Plato Republic**", Dover Thrift Editions April 2000.
- Kalkavage P. "**Plato Timaeus**", Focus Publishing/R. Pullings & Co, June 2001.
- Kraut Richard "**The Cambridge Companion to Plato**", Cambridge University Press, October 30, 1992).
- Patzer Andreas "**Antisthenes der Sokratiker**", Diss, Heidelberg 1970.
- Taylor Thomas "**Republic of Plato**", Kessinger Publishing, March 1997.
- Tredennick H., Tarrant H. "**The Last Days of Socrates, Euthryptho, Apology, Crito, Phaedo**", Penguin Books February 1995.
- Vlastos Gregory "**Platonic Studies**", Princeton University Press; 2nd edition December 1, 1973.
- Vlastos Gregory "**Studies in Greek Philosophy**" Princeton University Press December 23, 1996.

ARISTOTLE

- Ackrill J. L. "**A New Aristotle Reader**", Princeton University Press, January 1, 1988.
- Barnes J. "**The Cambridge Companion to Aristotle**", Cambridge University Press January 27, 1995.
- Barnes J. "**The Complete Work of Aristotle**", Revised Oxford Translation, two volumes, Princeton University Press 1998.
- Barnes J. Thomson J. A. K. "**The Nicomachean Ethics**" Penguin Books March 2004.
- Frans De Haas, Jaap Mansfeld "**On Generation and Corruption**", Oxford University Press 2004.
- Harvard University Press, "**Metaphysics, Books I-IX**", Loeb Classical Library, June 1979.

- Lawson-Tancred Hugh **"The Metaphysics"** Penguin Classics; New edition June 1, 1999.
- Harvard University Press, **"On the Soul, Parva Naturalia, On breath"**, Loeb Classical library Nr. 288, June 1975.
- Hughes G. **"Aristotle on Ethics"**, Routledge June 2001.
- Kaufman W. **"Nicomachean Ehics"**, Dover Thrift Editions, 1998.
- Lawson H. – Tangred **"De Anima, On the Soul"**, Penguin Books, June 1987.
- Nuvision Publications **"On Generation and Corruption"**, January 2004.
- Oxford University Press **"The Nicomachean Ethics"**, June 1998.
- Peripatetic Pr. **"On the soul"** December 1981.
- Rackham H. **"The Nicomachean Ethics"**, Harvard University Press, June 1982.
- Ross W. D. **"Aristotle's Physics"** Oxford 1936.
- Ross W. D. **"Aristotle"** Routledge; 6th edition July 1, 1995.

EPICURUS

- Digireads.com **"The Works of Epicurus"**, January 2004.
- Eugene O' Connor **"The Essential Epicurus"**, Prometheus Books, New York 1993.
- Edelstein **"Epicureanism, Two Collections of Fragments and Studies"** Garland Publ. March 1987.
- Hackett Publishing Co **"The Epicurus Reader"**, March 1994.
- Prometheus Books **"Epicurus Fragments"** August 1992.
- Russel M. Geer **"Letters, Principal Doctrines, Vatican Sayings"**, Bobbs-Merrill Co, January 1964.

- Reclam Universal Bibliothek "**Epikur**" Stuttgart 2001.

STOICISM

- Brennan T. Brittain C. "**Epictetus, Discourses and Other Writings**", Cambridge University Press, April 2004.
- Harvard University Press "**Epictetus Discourses Books 1 and 2**", Loeb Classical Library Nr. 131, June 1925.
- Harvard University Press "**Epictetus Discourses Books 3 and 4**", Loeb Classical Library Nr. 218, June 1928.
- Gill C. "**Epictetus, The Discourses**" Everyman 1995.
- Hicks D., Hicks C. S. "**The Emperor's Handbook: A New Translation of The Meditations**" by Marcus Aurelius, Scribner November 5, 2002.
- Long A. A. "**Hellenistic Philosophy: Stoics, Epicureans, Sceptics**", University of California Press; 2nd edition September 1986.
- Long George "**Enchiridion**" by Epictetus, Prometheus Books, Reprint Edition, January 1955.
- Long George "**Discourses of Epictetus**" Kessinger Publishing, January 2004.
- Oates Whitney Jenning "**The Stoic and Epicurean philosophers, The Complete Extant Writings of Erpicurus, Epictetus, Lucretius and Marcus Aurelius**", Random House, 9th printing 1940.
- Reclam Universal Bibliothek "**Die Philosophie der Stoa**", Stuttgart 2001.
- "**Stoic Philosophy of Seneca Essays and Letters'** W. W. Norton & Company September 1, 1968.

Lightning Source UK Ltd.
Milton Keynes UK
UKOW051801171111

182250UK00001B/20/A